WHAT IS FACT AND WHAT IS FICTION ABOUT THE CHOSEN PEOPLE?

What do Christians owe to Jews?

How can those who believe in Jesus communicate with His people?

This remarkable book by a New York City clergyman presents a seldom seen side of Jewish-Christian relationships. It is a sensitive, insightful bridge over ancient waters, presenting the facts and fallacies, the legends and the fascinating truth about a people who have been maligned and misunderstood throughout the centuries.

From God's covenant with Abraham to ritual life and laws and the miracle of contemporary Israel, here is an exceptional journey of discovery by an evangelical minister who returned to the Jewish roots to touch true Christian love and fellowship . . . an odyssey he urges all Christians to take.

Paul Carlson, author and former award-winning reporter, is pastor of the Glen Morris Presbyterian Church in New York City. This book has grown from his personal acquaintance with and his deep love for Israel, Judaism, and the Jewish people.

O CHRIS-TIAN! O JEW!

Paul R. Carlson

David C. Cook Publishing Co.
850 NORTH GROVE AVENUE • ELGIN, IL 60120
In Canada: David C. Cook Publishing (Canada) Ltd., Weston, Ontario M9L 1T4

David C. Cook Publishing Co., Elgin, IL 60120

Printed in the United States of America
Library of Congress Catalog Number: 74-78937

ISBN: 0-912692-39-1

This book is lovingly dedicated to my mother, Betty Robins Carlson, who deepened my understanding of my **Akeida** with Israel, and to my father of blessed memory, Rudolph Frederick Carlson, a Lover of Zion, who has now found rest in God's own **Shabbat Shalom.**

CONTENTS

Preface

RABBI Lewis Browne tells the engaging story that, when he began work on his own popular history of the Jewish people, he gathered together paper, pens, and ink and repaired to his study for the next seven hours.

It was long after midnight when he finally wrote across the top of a blank sheet of paper:

Stranger Than Fiction:
A Short History of the Jews

by Lewis Browne

— o —

Chapter I

"And," he adds, "no more."

As my own imperfect labor of love has come to an end, I am also reminded that Bernard J. Bamberger revealed that he experienced similar literary frustrations as he arrived at the conviction that "the attempt to write a comprehensive yet popular history of Judaism was both quixotic and presumptuous."

If this was true for a Jewish author, it is doubly so for a Christian. Yet as I finish my own work, I admit to the same bias as Solomon Grayzel, who has furnished us with another, excellent history of the Jews. "I believe in Judaism," he declared. "And I have faith in the Jewish people."

While this may sound strange coming from an evangelical minister, I believe the time is long overdue for Christians to investigate the rich spiritual heritage of Israel and to identify with the Jewish people in their struggle for survival.

However, it has not been an easy task for me to write on a subject of such intense personal love and interest. For example, it had been my hope to follow the course of Jewish history down through the centuries of the post-Biblical period. For this is a story which, as Lewis Browne suggests, reads "stranger than fiction." But time and space would not allow such a luxury.

I had also hoped to write more about the relationship of Jesus of Nazareth to His own people. But, alas, this fascinating story will have to come in another book.

Indeed, there is no chapter in this book on which volumes could not be written. To suggest, for example, that the modern Zionist movement is the product of the nineteenth century is misleading. But again, only certain highlights could be presented in so brief a study.

Therefore, as the reader takes note of all the imperfections of this book, I can only hope that he will remember that the author worked under two cruel and oppressive taskmasters, Joseph Bayly and Charles Van Ness, those literary pharaohs who would have authors write without the straw of time. (The reader should know that Editor Bayly writes a national column entitled "Out of

My Mind.")

However, on a more serious note, I hope that the Christian reader will be led to appreciate the just demand of his Jewish brethren that they be permitted to interpret their own great faith and tradition free from the embellishments of Christian theology. And I would also hope that my Jewish friends will be compassionate in their criticism of a Christian author who has not forgotten Jerusalem above his chief joy.

It must be noted that this book might never have been written had it not been for the friendships established over the years with a host of Jewish friends.

The author recalls with deep affection Rabbi Yehudah E. Perkins, who taught him his first words in Hebrew. He also thinks of Dr. and Mrs. Isaac Wilchesky, who ministered to his needs and those of his family in an hour of deep personal crisis. Then, too, there are the enduring friendships which he has found with Rabbis Irving and Allen Block, Rabbi and Mrs. Richard I. Schacket, and Samuel and Helen Leifer.

I would also like to acknowledge the gracious gifts of time and understanding given to me by many Christian friends—including my distinguished professor, Dr. Lee A. Belford of New York University, whose *Introduction to Judaism* remains a model of clarity and simplicity, and Dr. Bernhard E. Olson of the National Conference of Christians and Jews.

To all of these friends, the author can only say, *Shalom Aleichem!*

1

When Israel Was a Child

POOR FATHER ABRAHAM wasn't lucky enough to have a good Jewish mother!

The father of the Jewish people began life among the *goyim*,[1] the son of Terah the idol-maker and a citizen of the great pagan city of Ur of the Chaldees.

Yet, if the *Midrash Rabba* is correct, Abraham quickly demonstrated the qualities of a good *yeshiva bucher,* exercising a sharp mind and an independent spirit even though he was denied a rich diet of lox and bagels.

A favorite Jewish folk tale from *Rabba* has it that Terah one day left Abraham to mind the store while he shlepped off to see about some other business. While he was gone, in walked a man to buy an idol.

"How old are you?" asked Abraham.

"Fifty years old," replied the prospective customer.

"And you, who are fifty years old," said Abraham caustically, "would bow down to a thing of clay which we made only yesterday!"

---

1. A glossary of Hebrew and Yiddish terms is found at the end of the book.

9

Abraham was still thinking about the lost sale when in came an old woman to buy an idol.

"But," asked Abraham, "what happened to the large idol you bought last week?"

"Thieves stole it," the old woman admitted sheepishly.

"And you would pray and entrust yourself to an idol," asked Abraham, "that cannot even save itself from thieves?"

The old woman had no sooner left the store empty-handed than Abraham locked up for alterations. He took an axe and cut off the feet of the smallest idol. Then he chopped off the hands of the next and put out the eyes of a third. Finally, he placed the axe in the hands of the last and only remaining idol left in the shop.

Terah was blinded by rage when he returned to the mess. *"Gevalt!"* he screamed. "Who did this?"

Abraham didn't bat an eyelash. "The largest idol took the axe and slew all the others," he replied blandly. "See! He still has the axe in his hands.

"And if you don't believe me," said Abraham innocently, "ask him."

While such *aggadic* tales hardly bear the weight of Torah, they have delighted Jewish children for centuries. Yet none of the folklore of Abraham's seed is more fascinating than the story of the Jews themselves. For it is stranger than fiction!

The world's debt to the Jews

Max I. Dimont has pointed out that, although the Jews represent less than one half of one per cent of the three billion people on the Great Planet Earth, fully 12 per cent of all Nobel prizes in physics, chemistry, and medicine have gone to Jews. Their contributions in the fields of religion, philosophy, science, literature, music, and finance are nothing less than staggering.

It is because of the priceless heritage of Israel that

Christians around the world have come to know the Gospel of Jesus Christ, a Jew among Jews and an Israelite steeped in the traditions of His own people. To a pagan world, Paul declared: "Wherefore remember, that ye being in time past Gentiles in the flesh . . . were without Christ, being aliens from the commonwealth of Israel, and strangers from the covenants of promise, having no hope, and without God in the world" (Ephesians 2: 11, 12). In a word, had there not been an ancient covenant people to whom the "oracles of God" had been committed, there would have been no "Light to lighten the Gentiles," and a pagan world would have remained in spiritual darkness (Romans 3: 2; Luke 2: 32).

But Christendom's 850 million adherents are not the only ones who owe a spiritual debt to the Jews. For this ancient people also provided the Islamic world with an unwavering belief in monotheism; and today 400 million Muslims claim direct descent from Abraham and Ishmael.

Meanwhile, more than one billion other inhabitants of our Global Village now venerate the name of a Jew known as Karl Marx, whose book *Das Kapital* is regarded as the secular gospel of the Communist world. Countless others have found a kind of this-worldly redemption from mental and emotional ills through the labors of a Jewish psychoanalyst, Sigmund Freud, who proclaimed the evangel: "Where id was, there let ego be."

Moreover, it was a Jewish mathematician, Albert Einstein, whose theoretical physics paved the way for the atomic age and opened up the pathway to the moon. If some have suffered nightmares because of Einstein's calculations, it must be remembered that millions of parents sleep easier these nights because of the endeavors of yet another Jew, Jonas Salk, whose vaccine has brought about the almost total eradication of crippling poliomyelitis in children.

11

Ironically, these offspring of Abraham have managed to leave this indelible imprint upon mankind even though a hostile Gentile world, more often than not, only willed their total extinction. At times, many Jews themselves conspired with their oppressors—by seeking assimilation into cultures which would not let them forget their Jewishness and at length turned upon them with a vengeance. Still the Jew survived!

This strange people moved among the Babylonians, Persians, Greeks, and Romans as outcasts from their own land. Yet now the fabled glories which once belonged to Babylon, Persia, Greece, and Rome are part of forgotten lore. But the Jew remains.

These same people were hunted and hounded from country to country for 2,000 years. They were the innocent and mute victims of the *pogroms* and the Holocaust, somehow surviving the *ghettos,* the *shtetl,* and the Pale of Settlement, even as their tired and wounded hearts burned with the messianic vision, *L'shanah habaah bi Yerushalayim!* Next year in Jerusalem!

That vision, the vision of a homeland, finally turned into reality in 1948.

An evangelist with a greater flair for the dramatic than for good taste once described the Jew as a sociological miracle. "He has somehow managed to survive," said the evangelist, "even though Pharaoh tried to slay him, Nebuchadnezzar tried to burn him, the great fish tried to digest him, Antiochus and Titus tried to slaughter him, assorted rulers tried to deport him, Hitler tried to exterminate him, and Nasser tried to push him into the sea."

The story is told that a cynical Frederick the Great once asked a court chaplain to tell him in one word why he believed in God. His reply was almost instantaneous: "The Jew!"

Abraham of Ur

The genesis of this ancient people occurred, according to the Bible, the day the Lord appeared before Abraham and declared:

> Get thee out of thy country, and from thy kindred, and from thy father's house, unto a land that I will shew thee: And I will make of thee a great nation, and I will bless thee, and make thy name great; and thou shalt be a blessing: And I will bless them that bless thee, and curse him that curseth thee: and in thee shall all families of the earth be blessed (Genesis 12: 1-3).

Max Dimont has suggested that God's revelation to Abraham might be explained in terms of what psychoanalysts refer to as *projection*. That is to say, explains Dimont, that "Abraham himself (may have) conceived the idea of a covenant with an Almighty Father figure, represented as Jehovah, and projected onto this father figure his own wish to safeguard his children and his children's children for future generations."

However, as Dimont himself concedes, "the fact remains that after 4,000 years the idea of a covenant between the Jews and Jehovah is still alive and mentioned daily in prayers in synagogues throughout the world. Though many aspects of Jews and Judaism have been changed or modified during their subsequent 4,000-year history, this idea of a covenant with God has remained constant."

John Bright, the distinguished Old Testament scholar, fully agrees. "We can find no period in her history when Israel did not believe that she was the chosen people of [God]," he writes. "And this choosing had taken place in history."

Indeed, says the equally distinguished Bernhard W. Anderson, "Israel's greatness would lie, not in herself, but in the God who was active in her history to overcome the confusion, disharmony, and sin sketched in lurid colors in the primeval history."

While it may stretch the modern mind to conceive of a God who acts in history, the strange story of this strange people is utterly incomprehensible without a concession to this possibility—which eludes both rational and empirical categories.

Yet Abraham's experience, as well as those of Moses and the prophets after him, seems to indicate that human discovery is often the other side of divine revelation. "The initiative is always divine," says Sherwood Eddy. "The slow and halting response is human."

In Abraham's case, the decision to abandon the comforts and security of Ur involved the divine commingling of the spirit, mind, and will of man with those of his Maker.

Samson Raphael Hirsch, whose memory is held in awe and gratitude by Jews around the world, has hinted that the Children of Israel would have perished like their pagan contemporaries had they not "received from Abraham the courage to be a minority."

"While everybody in the whole world was making every effort to establish [himself]," he writes, "[Abraham] was to give up his homeland and his rights as a citizen, of his own freewill to make himself a refugee, to throw a protest in the face of the gods worshiped by all the nations.

"This demands courage and the conviction of the truth of the inner feeling, and consciousness of God," Rabbi Hirsch observes. "This demands the Jewish conception of God and Jewish confidence and boldness. And that was the first thing Abraham had to do to justify his appointment.

"With the call to isolation which Abraham obeyed," says Hirsch, "the salvation of the world through Judaism was decided."

Americans on credit cards might share the opinion of one disgruntled tourist to 20th Century Ur. "No wonder Abraham left," he wrote in the register of the mud hotel. "Even Job would have!"

But the Ur of Abraham's day bore no resemblance to the plot of baked desert which is Ur today. Then it was a cultured city with an extensive library, a city of split-level, air-conditioned homes, a city of educational institutions in which children were taught square root and logarithms.

This cosmopolitan city of as many as half a million souls also boasted an elaborate postal system and was famous for its textiles and factories. Its quays thronged with shipping, even as its citizens lived the proverbial good life in homes adorned with rich oriental furniture and beautiful rugs and carpets.

"So when God called Abraham out of Ur," says Howard Hendricks, "He called him to leave the scene. He called him to leave the center of civilization, family, home, friends, business, religion, everything that a man regards as security."

All of this means that skeptics can no longer claim, as they did 50 years ago, that Abraham (if he existed at all) was an uncultured, aimless wanderer who knew nothing of urban life, the use of metal, or the art of writing.

The archaeologist's spade has rather demonstrated that the Jewish historian Josephus may not have been too wide of the mark when he suggested that Abraham himself brought arithmetic from Chaldea to Egypt. In fact, says Will Durant, "it is not impossible that this and other arts came to Egypt from 'Ur of the Chaldees.'"

Yet for all of its worldly sophistication and splendor, Ur was a city devoted to the worship of the moon-god Nanna and to some 5,000 other, lesser deities. The devotion given to some of these gods involved a crude system of temple prostitution.

"In Abraham's time in Ur," says Sherwood Eddy, "each prosperous family had its own family chapel and each citizen placed himself under the protection of a special deity. Worship was conducted by the head of the family and the Sumerian father was the priest as well as master of his household."

Sir Leonard Woolley has made the interesting observation that the local equivalent of Nanna is Terah in the North Syrian texts. If Abraham's father was called Terah-Nanna, it meant that this progenitor of the monotheistic Israelites was himself under the special protection of the moon-god and bore his name.

But then a strange people began to elbow their way into history as Abraham, the son of a man lost in idolatry, came to the then novel conclusion that there was only One God and that he had been called by the Eternal to venture forth in faith to a land known as Canaan. God promised to give this land flowing with milk and honey to Abraham and his seed after him as an *eternal possession,* if only he would venture forth in faith, believing (Genesis 17: 6-8).

The stories concerning Abraham's short-lived career as an idol salesman might lead one to believe that here we have an instance in which revelation and reason went hand in hand. For these particular *midrashim* would seem to imply that the great patriarch accepted the call of God only after he made the empirical observation that a pantheon of immoral and competing deities was intellectually untenable.

But there is another beautiful *aggadic* tale which would indicate that Abraham's apprehension of the true God came solely through revelation when he was but a small child.

Abraham's father, so the story goes, was an official in the court of Nimrod when the king received word from his seers that Terah's wife was about to give birth to a son who would rule many nations. Accordingly, the frightened Nimrod offered to buy the infant so that he might slay him. But Terah and his wife were able to spirit their baby safely away to the desert, where the child spent his first years in a cave.

It was there that the Angel Gabriel ministered to Abraham's every need. It was also there in the wilderness that he came face to face with *Melech Ham'lochim*—the King of Kings. And, when at last Abraham was reunited with his mother, he introduced her to a knowledge of this God who alone made Heaven and earth.

But this is only a pious legend lacking the weight of *Torah*. It is to that sacred source that we must ultimately turn to find the God who reveals Himself in history and prods His chosen ones to take the step of faith.

"All our revelations of God emanate from God to man," says Rabbi Hirsch. "God speaks to the prophet, not in him. The Hand of God comes *onto* the prophet not *out* of him.

"In all the Hebrew expressions for the revelation of God," says this beloved *Gaon*, "man is, in every case, only the receiver, never the active producer. And all these expressions are the most definite denial of all those views which deny actual revelation, but nevertheless try to gloss over their denials by classing them together as products of human imagination and ecstasy.

"*How* God spoke to us human beings can remain an eternal mystery," says Hirsch. ". . . It suffices for us that He did speak and made Himself visible in some way to them."

However, there are hints in both the Jewish and Christian traditions that Abraham might have balked a bit about the vision set before him. For example, *Bereshit Rabba* has it that the patriarch expressed his concern for

17

his father if he were to suddenly pack up and venture forth into the unknown. God's response was that He could look after old Terah.

When we turn to Christian Scripture, we find Luke recording an address in which Stephen suggests that God's call to Abraham came not only in Haran but in Ur as well.

"Men, brethren, and fathers, hearken," said Stephen. "The God of glory appeared unto our father Abraham, when he was in Mesopotamia, *before* he dwelt in Haran, And said unto him, Get thee out of thy country, and from thy kindred, and come into the land which I shall shew thee" (Acts 7: 2, 3).

"There may have been two calls," suggests William Sanford LaSor. "An earlier one that was the means whereby God got Abraham out of Ur and as far as Haran, and then the second call whereby God got Abraham 'out of the rut' into which he had settled in Haran, and moved him down into Canaan, where God wanted him in the first place."

How typically human this would be! "Haran was the only other important town of Mesopotamia to have the moon-god for its special patron," says Woolley. "From the one city of Nanna, Terah goes to the other." The life of faith is so often just like that: We are willing to go so far and no further.

Whatever may be the case, Abraham continued his journey to the Promised Land. With him went his wife Sarah and Lot his brother's son, "and all their substance that they had gathered, and the souls that they had gotten in Haran" (Genesis 12: 5).

It was as a family that they marched off to Zion!

No one can dispute the greatness of this good man. "Even looked at quite superficially," says Hirsch, "it is already evident that Abraham was to receive back from

God everything that he had given up—and, indeed, in a considerably enhanced measure.

"He gave up his nationality," observes the *Gaon*. "But instead of having to attach himself to another one, God says that he himself is to be the founder of a new one. By giving up his birthplace, he is not to miss the civic rights which are the natural source of prosperity, for in God will he gain the right to prosper on earth.

"And," says Hirsch, "inasmuch as he forsakes his family, and thereby gives up the respect and honor given to well-known old families, in him a new name is to grow to great renown."

This is a case in which faith and works went hand-in-hand. For Abraham not only believed God; he also obeyed Him. It was for this reason alone that he was accounted "the Friend of God" (II Chronicles 20: 7; James 2: 23), and was to become "a father of many nations" (Genesis 17: 5).

Yet could it be, as some have suggested, that Abraham was only the product of a pious imagination? Surely this was the view of no less a Biblical scholar than Julius Wellhausen, whose research influenced generations of both Christian and Jewish religious leaders. "We attain to no historical knowledge of the patriarchs," said Wellhausen flatly, "but only of the time when the stories about them arose in the Israelite people."

However, modern scholarship knows better. "The Hebrew patriarchs are not mythological figures, not gods nor semigods," says the distinguished Nahum Sarna, "but intensely human beings who appeared fairly late on the scene of history and whose biographies are well rooted in a cultural, social, religious and legal background that ought to be verifiable. . . .

"Irrespective of the dating applied to the Pentateuchal documents," says Sarna, "one thing has emerged crystal

19

clear. The traditions of the Book of Genesis are now acknowledged to be an authentic reflection of the age with which they claim to deal."

While some scholars believe that Abraham and his kinsmen represented an element in Mesopotamian society known as the *Habiru,* others are not quite so sure. However, none other than William Foxwell Albright, onetime dean of archaeologists, concedes that such a possibility "would square extraordinarily well with Hebrew traditional history and would clear up many details which seem otherwise inexplicable."

James Kelso, an equally distinguished archaeologist, has suggested that the term Hebrew may come from a word which meant caravaneer. For him, Abraham was a merchant prince who established a sales route which extended all the way from Haran to Egypt!

But perhaps the explanation best in keeping with the Biblical story is that the term Hebrew originally referred to a group of wanderers who passed from place to place.

"For the first 800 years of their existence," says Dimont, "they wandered in and out of the great civilizations surrounding them. They had no buildings, no cities, no armies. . . . All they carried with them were their ideas, which eventually conquered the world without making them its masters.

"By the act of crossing the River Euphrates," writes Dimont, "Terah and his family group become the first people in the Bible identified as *Ivriim,* of which the English version is 'Hebrews,' the people 'who crossed over,' the people 'from the other side of the river.' "

Whatever may be the case, the Biblical portrait of Abraham is that of a man whose consciousness of the Eternal was so great that he forsook the comforts and security of civilization to set out on a pilgrimage that was to lead him out of a dying paganism and into the

20

Promised Land. In a word, Abraham dared to be different![2]

While Christian Scripture describes the patriarch as a man who "looked for a city . . . whose builder and maker is God" (Hebrews 11: 10), the day was to come in Israel's own spiritual odyssey when Joshua was to remind his people of this towering figure out of their past who had the vision to cross over "from the other side of the river."

> And Joshua said unto all the people, Thus saith the Lord God of Israel, Your fathers dwelt on the other side of the flood in old time, even Terah, the father of Abraham, and the father of Nachor: and they served other gods. And I took your father Abraham from the other side of the flood, and led him throughout all the land of Canaan, and multiplied his seed, and gave him Isaac. And I gave unto Isaac Jacob and Esau: and I gave unto Esau mount Seir, to possess it; but Jacob and his children went down into Egypt (Joshua 24: 2-4).

Between the lines of that noble address, an address that marked Joshua's valedictory as a leader of Israel, one can find the story of a people whose history showed signs of both strength and weakness, victory and defeat,

---

2. There remains an aura of mystery even within scholarly circles concerning this people. The designation *Habiru* is first found in the Cappadocian texts (19th Century, B.C.E., later in the famous Mari Letters (18th Century, B.C.E.) and in the still later Nuzian, Hittite, Amarna, and Ugaritic texts (15th and 14th Century, B.C.E.). If we remember that Abraham himself did not begin life as a Jew, it is interesting to note that all uses of Hebrew in Genesis are used to describe non-Israelites (14: 13; 39: 14, 17; 40: 15; 41: 12; 43: 32). However, Merrill Unger notes that Shem and Eber represent the line of which the people of the Old Testament formed a part. But, he says, "the Hebrews' ancestor Eber (Genesis 11: 16f) included more than the Abrahamic line. Some of Eber's posterity remained in Babylonia when Terah left, and some in Haran when Abram migrated to Canaan."

faith and doubt. The genius of the Bible is that it demonstrates an inner integrity by dealing realistically with the so-called human condition and portraying even the lives of God's elect with warts and all!

God establishes His covenant

One blemish on the record of Abraham and Sarah erupted when they lost faith that God would honor His pledge and bless them with a son, one who was to be an heir to the promises made by God to the patriarch.

In an all-too-human story, the Bible relates that the barren and aging Sarah decided to take matters into her own hands. If she could not present Abraham with a son, she reasoned, then perhaps an heir could be conceived by Hagar, her Egyptian maid.

When Hagar did in fact conceive and bear Ishmael, the results of Sarah's own faithlessness were disastrous. Not only did she and her Egyptian servant begin to squabble, but she also accused Abraham of causing Hagar to lose respect for her.

The poor patriarch, hardly an innocent bystander, was forced to stand idly by as Sarah pointedly made life utterly miserable for the used and abused Egyptian slave. Finally, unable to tolerate the situation any longer, Hagar fled into the desert, where the Angel of God found her by the well on the road to Shur.

This episode in the lives of Abraham and Sarah brought heartache not only to themselves but also to their wretched servant girl. And all of it could have been avoided if only they had not become impatient and had rather trusted God to keep His promises.

So it is that the story of the conception and birth of Ishmael represents not so much a lack of morality as a crisis of faith. It is possible to explain Abraham's relationship with Hagar in terms of prevailing customs; but his corresponding loss of confidence in God is less justified in light of his earlier relationship to the Eternal.[3]

However, what follows is the story of a God whose steadfast love is all-embracing. This divine love touches Hagar and her yet unborn son as much as it does Abraham and Sarah, and their seed after them.

For the God of the Bible is not the God of the Jews alone. He is rather the God of the nations. He may determine to manifest His glory through Israel; but ultimately Israel's blessings shall become the inheritance of all who walk in faith.

Even in these far reaches of antiquity God was working out His own blueprint for the settlement of the Middle East crisis. In that light, the Prophet Isaiah could look forward to the dawn of an age when the Lord Himself would declare: "Blessed be Egypt my people, and Assyria the work of my hands, and Israel mine inheritance" (Isaiah 19: 25).

So it was that the Angel of God admonished the wretched Hagar to "return unto thy mistress and submit thyself under her hands." For God promised, "I will multiply thy seed exceedingly that it cannot be counted for multitude.

"Behold, thou art with child, and shalt bear a son," declared the Angel of the Lord. "And thou shalt call his name Ishmael, for *God hath heard* thy suffering."[4]

That's it! The very name of Hagar's unborn son would confirm the fact that the God of Abraham hears even the plaintive cry of those outside the covenant of promise. We are thereby confronted with the *particularity* of Is-

3. The social institution of concubinage is known to have existed in ancient Babylon. In addition, scholars now know of Nuzi contracts which actually stipulate that the barren wife must provide her husband with a slave woman so that he will not die without an heir.
4. Ishmael means "God hears."

rael's election and the *universal* dimension of the love of Israel's God!

This awesome, yet beautiful story introduces us to One who not only *hears* but *sees* the suffering of mankind. And in His compassion He does something about it!

The wretched slave girl fled into the desert to escape the wrath of her mistress. But even as she looked over her shoulder to see if anyone was pursuing her, she discovered that she could not flee from the presence of a concerned and compassionate God. Out of this experience the place of Hagar's confrontation with the Eternal was named *Beer-lahai-roi*—"Well of the Living One Who Seeth Me."

However, there was still to be fulfilled God's promise to Abraham.

Hagar gave birth to a son who would, like the later Bedouin, forsake the life of cities for the freedom and mystique of the desert. But Ishmael, as one born out of due season, was not meant to be the heir of God's covenant with Abraham. It is true that the patriarch was the father of Ishmael. But, as family-loving Jews still relate, it is not enough to be born through Abraham. One must also be raised and nourished at the breast of Sarah. For all of her human frailties, she became the epitome and model of the proverbial "good Jewish mother."

When Ishmael was 13 years old, God again appeared before Abraham, this time with the challenge to submit himself completely to the Holy One of Israel. Abraham responded by abdicating his own sense of independence, falling down in the presence of God.

As the patriarch found himself gripped by a feeling of absolute dependence, God Himself promised Abraham that he would become "a father of many nations," that "nations and kings shall come out of thee."

Far more is involved in this pledge than the promise of divine blessing upon the emerging nation of Israel.

Rather, as Rabbi Hirsch observes, Abraham is to become the lever by which all nations are to be raised "to spiritual and moral heights."

"Without Abraham's spirit," says Hirsch, "the masses of the nations are a mixed-up, swaying throng. Nobody knows from where they come; nobody knows where they are going. Their movement lacks all direction and purpose.

"They are no mass of people formed into a united group around a common central directing force for a common purpose, but a disorderly, muddled mass," he writes. "Abraham brings a centralizing spirit to them, [and] becomes thereby their spiritual father."

This universal nature of Abraham's destiny is matched by the particularity of Israel's election and mission. For God makes it clear that the patriarch himself will become the father of "the model nation," or, as Hirsch describes it, "a plurality [of] several nations."

It will consist of tribes, each one of which is to show its own special natural character (soldiers, sailors, teachers, students, husbandmen, merchants, priests, confectioners, etc.) and thus demonstrate factually that the covenant of God, the godly calling of mankind, is not attached to any special profession and not hindered by any.

Not lion-hearted courage, not business acumen, not the urge to study, form the condition for, nor are they any hindrance to, the mission of Abraham to mankind. A military nation like Judah, a nation of mercantile marine like Zebulun, a nation of scholarship like Issachar, of agriculture like Asher, all are called upon to make the common calling which Judaism teaches, a reality in the activities of their different lives. No church, but a nation was what God wished to found with Abraham, a nation for the whole multitude of nations.

To this end, God promised to establish His covenant with Abraham and his descendants after him forever. "And I will give unto thee and unto thy descendants after thee the land wherein thou art a stranger," said the Lord, *"all the land of Canaan for an everlasting possession, and I will be a God unto them."*

There had been that dramatic experience earlier in the patriarch's pilgrimage when the Holy One of Israel promised that the day would dawn when Abraham's heirs would enjoy all of the land of the "Kenites, and the Kenizzites, and the Kadmonites, and the Hittites, and the Perizzites, and the Rephaims, and the Amorites, and the Canaanites, and the Girgashites, and the Jebusites."

The promised kingdom was to extend all the way from Egypt to Mesopotamia—a vast area which, as scholars point out, was never attained even in the most flourishing days of David and Solomon.[5] But God has not yet finished the final chapter of Israel's story.

Surely the Biblical vision of Israel's boundaries far exceeds the niggardly limits imposed by the United Nations. Even the dramatic expansion experienced in the aftermath of the Six Day War failed to do justice to God's inviolable covenant with Abraham.

In one of the most solemn episodes recorded in Scripture, God commanded His chosen agent of blessing to ritually slaughter certain animals and to divide the pieces into two rows. "And it came to pass," says the Bible, "that, when the sun went down, and it was dark, behold a smoking furnace, and a burning lamp, that passed between those pieces." It was in that solemn setting—and in a form known and practiced among the ancients—that God "cut a covenant" with Abraham.

---

5. A particularly interesting discussion of these boundaries is found in Yehezkel Kaufmann's *The Religion of Israel*, pp. 201-202. See also, *Whose Land?* by James Parkes, p. 23.

"Abraham did not participate," Nahum Sarna observes. "Only God bound Himself to a solemn obligation, the patriarch having been the passive beneficiary."

But now, as God invested Abraham and Sarah with names fit for their calling, it became clear that the "father of many nations" was to abandon that passive role for one of active participation in bringing about the goals of the covenant. That spiritual progression was, as Dr. Sarna notes, not only to be dramatized by a change in names, but also "supplemented by a physical alteration, a painful, self-inflicted act carried out in submission to the divine command."[6]

> And God said unto Abraham . . . This is my covenant, which ye shall keep, between me and you and thy seed after thee; Every man child among you shall be circumcised. . . . the flesh of your foreskin . . . a token of the covenant betwixt me and you. . . . And the uncircumcised man child whose flesh of his foreskin is not circumcised, that soul shall be cut off from his people; he hath broken my covenant (Genesis 17: 9-11, 14).

This act, traditionally performed on the eighth day after birth, was not unknown among other ancient Near Eastern peoples. However, the faithful children of Abraham practiced it for entirely unique reasons.

For Israel, far more was to be involved in the rite of circumcision than mere social custom or personal hygiene. "It is an ineradicable token of the immutability of God's unilateral promises to Israel," says Sarna, "and at the same time its operation constitutes a positive act of iden-

---

6. The record of God's command that the patriarch and his wife change their names is found in Genesis 17. Traditionally, Abraham has been interpreted to mean "the father of many nations," while Sarah has been translated as "princess." While the exact etymology is less certain, the theological meaning is quite clear: The names indicate "a transformation of destiny."

tification and dedication as a member of the covenanted community."

While the rite of circumcision has been the butt of many a crude Gentile joke, Christians would do well to remember its sacred character. There is a wholesome meaning to this act which touches the soul of Judaism.

This "first law of Judaism" testifies to the need for the godly man to submit not only his soul, but his body to the Lord. "Not annulment, abolishment, but 'limitation,' is the fundamental idea of the covenant of God," says Rabbi Hirsch. "To the Jewish covenant of God, celibacy and castration are as grievous excesses as debauchery and licentiousness.

"To be a Jew," he affirms, "means making the sensuous life, kept within the prescribed moral limits, holy to God."

Although a critic of his fathers' faith, Baruch Spinoza was also led to see yet another significance of this ancient rite. "So great importance do I attach to this sign," he remarked, "I am persuaded that it is sufficient by itself to maintain the separate existence of the nation forever."

For faithful Jews the world over, this *bris* is still performed on the eighth day by either the father or a *mohel*. In either case, the ancient prayer is offered: "Blessed are You, Lord our God, Master of the Universe (*Riboyne Shel O'lem*), who have made us holy with Your commands, and have commanded us to bring this boy into the covenant of Abraham our father."

The significance of Isaac

Two things should already be quite apparent in this intimate relationship between God and His people. There is first the enduring nature of the covenant, and there is second an eternal triangle involving God, Israel, and the land. One simply cannot fathom the soul of Judaism unless this love for *eretz Yisroel* (the land of Israel) is fully understood and appreciated.

Many an American Jew has prided himself on his spirit of skepticism, if not agnosticism, until he has made his *aliyah* to the homeland. There before the western wall of the ancient Temple, as he ponders the epic history of his people, a sense of awe and wonder sweeps his soul. It is so deeply moving an experience that it cannot even be dampened by the prosperity of Tel Aviv's Dizengoff nor by the luxury of the hotels and beaches of Herzliya!

It was one thing for God to give Abraham in perpetuity a deed to this land. But it was another matter entirely for the patriarch to have a rightful heir to such a valuable (although contested) piece of real estate. Would it not have been ironic for Abraham to have died intestate!

To leave this promised land in the hands of pagan neighbors—to watch the shadows fall on life and upon this kingdom without a crown prince—this was the cruel joke which threatened Abraham. Surely, the patriarch and his wife had done all within their own power to make certain that the divine deed would remain within the family. They had first thought of willing their property to Eliezer, the Syrian steward. Then they had entered into that scheme to see that Abraham's name would be preserved through an Egyptian slave.

It took time for the father of the Jewish nation to learn that man's extremity is God's opportunity.

"I will bless [Sarah] and give thee a son also of her," said the Lord. "Yea, I will bless her, and she shall be a mother of nations; kings of people shall be of her."[7]

"Then," says the Bible, "Abraham fell upon his face, and laughed, and said in his heart, Shall a child be born unto him that is an hundred years old? and shall Sarah, that is ninety years old, bear?"

---

7. The Hebrew of Genesis 17: 16 suggests that God had "already appointed a son unto thee from her."

The absurdity of it all was not lost upon Sarah herself, who—when the Lord returned—was sitting at the door of the tent listening to the conversation. She, too, could not contain her laughter.

"After I am already worn out," she mused, "should I have the deepest satisfaction, my lord being also an old man?"

God seems almost hurt—if not provoked—by this undercurrent of doubt. "Is anything too wonderful for God?" He asks. "At the appointed time . . . Sarah *shall* have a son."

In due season, of course, that divine optimism overshadowed all human skepticism. The aged couple called their newborn Isaac (*Yitzhak*), a play on the Hebrew word for laughter.

While the name may reflect a gentle rebuke against parental doubt, some translators interpret Sarah to exult: "God has brought me laughter. All who hear of it will rejoice with me!"

But the Biblical context would appear to support Rabbi Hirsch's contention that Sarah was anything but a proud mother. Here she was an old woman who had given birth when it was almost time to die. Little Isaac might well become an orphan at an early age.

Here was not the pride of parenthood, according to this interpretation, but the fear of ridicule and mocking taunts. "God hath made me into a laughing-stock," fumes Sarah. "All that hear will laugh at me!"

While it is so easy to understand such typically human emotions, Rabbi Hirsch makes the further observation that the strange course of Judaism from its inception has always been greeted by mocking laughter.

"The world knew the 'pretension' with which [Sarah and Abraham] dared to swim against the tide of the times," the *Gaon* notes. "Yea, [it also knew] the hopes they were bold enough to entertain of ultimately stem-

30

ming this mighty stream and turning it into another direction."

If the pagans who watched "at the cradle of the Jewish nation could not refrain from a mocking smile," he asks, what of those who today know nothing of Judaism's role in history and can only smirk at Israel's hopes and claims for the future?

Whatever may be the case, the Biblical narrative makes it quite clear that Sarah herself ultimately adjusted to the rigors of motherhood. So much so, in fact, that she became highly annoyed when the son of the Egyptian either mocked or played too rough with her own little boy. And 4,000 years have failed to end that spirit of rivalry between Isaac and Ishmael!

Equally tragic is the fact that Sarah presumed to solve the first Middle East crisis by ordering Abraham to dismiss Hagar and her son of the desert. While it was enough that such an act smacked of being callous and heartless, it was even more deplorable because it demonstrated Sarah's lack of faith that Isaac alone was the sole heir of the divine promise.

Yet the final irony was still to come. God had overshadowed Sarah at a time when she was well past childbearing age. He had proved that His word was His bond. Now He was about to ask Abraham to display a similar loyalty.

Until that crucial moment, Abraham had been a lovable example of that old rhubarb that where there are two Jews there are three arguments.[8] How he enjoyed do

---

8. The author recalls with much affection a delightful Oneg Shabbat (a Sabbath kaffee klatch) during which he listened in fascination as a delightful lady carried on two arguments *with herself* regarding the course of politics. Her behavior was so human and so Biblical! The God of the Bible is no far-off, impersonal force, but One who has feelings, can change His mind, and enter into controversies with His people (Hosea 4: 1). Far from requiring them to be rigid or dogmatic, He welcomes complaints and a wide range of thinking on any matter, a point which we'll discuss in relating some of the Yom Kippur prayers of the Sages.

bating with Deity. And it appears that God Himself was no less stimulated by such involvements!

It is hard to imagine a more intimate relationship than that illustrated by Abraham's appeal on behalf of the condemned sin cities of Sodom and Gomorrah.

"Wilt thou then also drag into ruin the righteous with the guilty?" the patriarch inquires. "Sacrilege would it be to ascribe such a thing to thee!"

Now that was a pretty good argument. Abraham continued to hammer home his plea that God should spare these cities if there were only 50 righteous among them. Well, if not 50, would God settle for 45? Maybe 40 . . . or 30 . . . or 20. Ten?

On that occasion, Abraham's persistence prevailed. Except for Lot's wife's tragic end, he and his family were also spared—thanks to the efforts of a great friend of the heavenly court.

But now Abraham was strangely submissive as God called upon him to make the ultimate sacrifice. He had pleaded for the sinners of two X-rated cities; but now he stood mute, unable to plead for the very life of his own beloved Isaac. Indeed, his only response to the divine demand was one of obedience. "Behold," he said, "here am I."

There have been those who dismiss the God of the patriarch as a deity who required the practice of "butcher-shop religion." Others have taken the opposite course and interpreted the *Akeida* of Isaac as an illustration of the fact that the Holy One of Israel did not require human sacrifice.[9] Rabbi Hirsch observes with a note of irony, "We naturally have surpassed the spirit of Abra-

9. It is true that the Biblical story condemns human sacrifice, the fire of Molech (Leviticus 18: 21), and certainly presents an ethical ideal unknown in ancient paganism, represented by the king of Moab offering his firstborn at a critical moment in battle (II Kings 3: 27).

ham and proved ourselves to be on a still higher level inasmuch as we have abolished sacrifices altogether."

Unfortunately, all efforts to reduce the trauma, or to explain away its dread reality, have ultimately failed. God had done nothing less than to command Abraham to make the three day journey to Moriah, there to sacrifice Isaac in a supreme test of obedience.

On the one hand, consider the internal torture of Abraham himself. It was not only that he loved Isaac; that boy was born out of due season to inherit the covenant pledge. It was strange, to say the least, for God now to demand that the long-awaited heir be sacrificed on the altar of blind allegiance.

On the other hand, Isaac was also put to the test. If he was a man in his thirties, as the Sages suggest, then he could not help but have an inkling of the fate which awaited him. A glimpse of that inner turmoil which may well have engulfed him is found in those poignant *midrashim* that portray father and son sharing their doubt and despair as they make their way together to the sacred mount.

The Bible itself offers the picture of a young man who, whatever his thoughts, had absolute confidence in his father. Isaac knew that Abraham loved him. He knew too that the patriarch was no pagan who would allow crude superstition to dominate his better judgment.

It was probably in a spirit of conflict *and* confidence that father and son ultimately arrived at their fateful destination. As all was being readied for the sacrifice, Isaac at length inquired: "Behold the fire and wood; but where is the lamb for the offering?"

At that point, the knife that was intended for Isaac must have pierced the heart of Abraham himself. "My son," he replied, "God will provide himself a lamb for a burnt offering."

Surely this is not the portrait of a reformer or a so-called "pathfinder" in the evolution of religion. It is rather that of a brokenhearted father, who for reasons which elude our total grasp, placed obedience and faith in God above a father's love for his son. That faith, that obedience, did not go unrewarded.

As the raised knife was about to descend, the Angel of God spoke and brought a message of life in the face of impending death. He told Abraham that his faith had been vindicated and the lad was not to be harmed. Only then was Isaac unbound and a ram offered in his place.

Deep was the imprint made by this binding and redemption of Isaac. Father and son named the site of sacrifice, as a testimony that God both sees after His own and provides for them in the hour of deepest need.[10]

Moreover, God reaffirmed His covenant with the patriarch. "By myself have I sworn," He declared, "because thou hast done this thing, and hast not withheld thy son, thine only son: That [unconditionally] I will bless thee, and [unconditionally] I will multiply thy seed as the stars of the heaven, and as the sand which is upon the sea shore; and thy seed shall possess the gate of his enemies" (Genesis 22: 16, 17).

This is the covenant under which Israel still makes claim to the land. Yet Jewish faith and determination have been matched at every point by the grim realities of history and the hatred and blind opposition of the nations of the world.

The irony of it all is more pressing because God Himself waited until the *impossible* moment to provide the patriarch with an heir. This was compounded by a command which would have killed that intended heir.

---

10. Genesis 22: 14 *(Yahweh-jireh)* is variously translated *The Lord Will Provide* (RSV), or *On the Mount of God One Is Seen* (Hirsch, cf. KJV).

Then, too, Abraham and Sarah were "strangers and sojourners" in a land inhabited and ruled by a pagan people. "Sarah died in Kirjath-arba, which is Hebron in the land of Canaan." How can we fathom Abraham's grief, as he faced not only the loss of his beloved wife but also the prospect of begging for a burial site on land granted to him by divine and eternal decree!

If ever a story debunked the notion of the "perfidious Jew" of Gentile mythology, it is the account of the avarice of Abraham's neighbors.

On the surface, it would appear that the Hittites were making a generous offer to give the patriarch a burial plot without charge. But that is to miss the reality of the situation. Abraham was forced to bargain in the typical Oriental manner and, in the end, to pay 400 silver shekels—an enormous price.[11]

Yet it was there in the cave of the field of Machpelah that Sarah entered into her Sabbath's rest. And it was also there that Abraham staked his claim for those who would come after him.[12]

Several hundred years were to elapse before the children of Israel would take possession of their inheritance. God may have granted the deed; but Abraham himself had paid a steep price. For all of those shekels could hardly compare with the bones of a woman who had shared his vision, conceived his son, and faced that sense of isolation and alienation that grips all who dare to be different.

11. Sarna, et al., have noted that the Biblical text itself reveals a rich use of legal terminology characteristic of ancient Near Eastern court records. For example, the description of the cave as being 'at the edge of the field' is a common means of property identification in extant land-sale documents. Furthermore, as Hirsch points out, the sale price in this case was so exorbitant that Ephron was ashamed to say it personally and preferred to make it through a third party.

12. Kelso notes that the price of the burial plot is quoted at 'the current market rate.' Jeremiah got a better deal. He paid only 17 silver shekels for a similar piece of real estate (Jeremiah 32: 9)!

No wonder then that E. A. Speiser has aptly remarked that, while Israel as a nation would be inconceivable without Moses, "the work of Moses would be equally unthinkable without the prior labors of the patriarchs. . . . The covenant of Mount Sinai is a natural sequel to God's covenant with Abraham. The two together become the twin cornerstones of the spiritual history of Israel, and are honored as such throughout the Bible."

Housman may have spoken for peoples and nations when he quipped: "How odd/ of God/ to choose/ the Jews." But more to the point is this response:

> *But not so odd*
> *As those who choose*
> *The Jewish God*
> *And spurn the Jews.*

2

Let My People Go

BITTERSWEET memories crossed the mind of the elderly Jew as he prepared for another Passover.

There were those earlier days in Eastern Europe when Gentiles made no bones about what they thought of their Jewish neighbors:

If they crept along the wall, they were cowardly, the old man mused. *If they stepped out of the shadows, they were impudent. If they were thrifty with their money, they were miserly. If they were generous with it, they were ostentatious. If they strove to get on, they were eaten up with ambition. If they behaved modestly, they were lacking courage . . .*

Yet, even in the midst of daily hostilities, the Jews somehow always managed to negotiate the darkest corners and bleakest streets in their fetid *ghettos* to celebrate the annual Passover.

Any other people in these circumstances would try their utmost to forget their revolution (the Exodus from Egypt, which Passover commemorates). They certainly would not want to be reminded of their former state of freedom, thereby making their present life in exile more miserable.

The Jews, however, did not lose their identity, the old man recalled soberly. *They never forgot their past joys and sorrows, their past victories and defeats, triumphs and catastrophes, hope and times of despair . . .*

Preparing now for another *Seder,* the old man thought of a bit of wisdom from the sages who wrote the Passover *Haggadah*: "In every generation, one ought to regard himself as though he personally came out of Egypt."

"Just imagine," the man remarked to his wife. "It has been more than 3000 years since the Exodus. Ancient peoples and nations passed away and new ones came into existence. The Jews were scattered all over the world, and were strangers wherever they settled. They were despised and persecuted, kept on the verge of extinction. But *this* Passover, Israel is again in her ancient land."[1]

Pesach (Passover)

The old man now began to speak of the Passovers of his childhood.

"How real to me was the story of the march of the Children of Israel toward the Promised Land! How real were the four questions—the four cups of wine and the finding of the *Aphikoman,* Elijah's full cup of wine."

The old man smiled. "When at the right moment my brother opened the door 'to let Elijah in,' I could have sworn I saw Elijah's cup quiver as if touched by an invisible hand."

Though the years had crept silently upon him, the old man felt that same childlike confidence now, as he watched his wife getting things ready for another Passover. It was to be a time of quiet joy, as children and

1. Dr. Chaim Weizmann once said, "A Jew in Israel who does not believe in miracles is not a realist."

grandchildren gathered around the *Seder* table mindful of the Biblical injunction: to witness to God's redemption from Egyptian bondage, in every generation.

"And when the Lord brings you into the land of the Canaanites, the Hittites, the Amorites, the Hivites, and the Jebusites, which he swore to your fathers to give you, a land flowing with milk and honey, you shall keep this service in this month. Seven days you shall eat unleavened bread, and on the seventh day there shall be a feast to the Lord. Unleavened bread shall be eaten for seven days; no leavened bread shall be seen with you, and no leaven shall be seen with you in all your territory. And you shall tell your son on that day, 'It is because of what the Lord did for me when I came out of Egypt.' And it shall be to you as a sign on your hand and as a memorial between your eyes, that the law of the Lord may be in your mouth; for with a strong hand the Lord has brought you out of Egypt. You shall therefore keep this ordinance at its appointed time from year to year" (Exodus 13: 5-10, RSV).

The appointed time was in the month of Nisan, the first month of the religious year and the seventh of the civil year.[2] According to tradition, Nisan is not only the month of *Pesach,* or the Passover, but also that of the creation of the world, of the births of the patriarchs, of the erection of the Tabernacle, and of Israel's redemption.

The first of the three Pilgrim Festivals of the Jewish year, Passover is a week-long observance. As a perpetual memorial to God's redemptive act, the Israelites were commanded to commemorate their great national epic each year:

2. Nisan falls between March and April.

In the fourteenth day of the first month at even is the Lord's passover. And on the fifteenth day of the same month is the feast of unleavened bread unto the Lord: seven days ye must eat unleavened bread (Leviticus 23: 5, 6).[3]

Theodor H. Gaster has observed that Passover testifies to release and achievement on three distinct planes. At each of these levels, he says, there is cooperation between God and man. He writes:

> On the seasonal plane, Passover inaugurates the reaping of the new grain; man sows the seed, but God . . . provides the rainfall and sunshine which quickens it. On the historical plane, it commemorates the birth of the Jewish nation: Israel was prepared to face the hazards of the wilderness, so God, in His providence, brought it to Sinai, gave it the Law, and concluded the Covenant. On the broad human plane, it celebrates the attainment of freedom and of the vision of God: man casts aside his idols and repudiates his ignorance and obscurantism, and in that very act God reveals His presence and imparts knowledge.

While Passover is therefore recognized in Jewish tradition as "the season of our freedom," says Gaster, it is freedom of a special kind. "In Jewish tradition," he notes, "freedom, in the modern sense, is scarcely a virtue; at best, it is an opportunity. What matters is *volitional dedication,* and it is this and this alone that forms the theme of the Passover story.

"If Israel had gone forth out of Egypt, but had not accepted the Covenant at Sinai," says Gaster, "it would have achieved liberation—that is, mere release from

---

3. Passover is observed for eight days among many Jews of the Diaspora. It is celebrated for seven days by Reform Jews and those in Israel.

bondage—but it would not have achieved *freedom,* in the Jewish sense of the term. For the only freedom, says Judaism, is the yoke of the Torah; the only true independence is the apprehension of God."

So sacred was this event in the life of ancient Israel that provision was made for a *Pesach sheni*—a second Passover—to be observed only by those who, through ritual uncleanness or unavoidable absence from Jerusalem, were unable to sacrifice the paschal lamb on the appointed date (Numbers 9: 9-25).

There is only one instance recorded in the Bible in which a Biblical figure accepted this concession to observe the *Pesach sheni* on the same day of the second month of Iyar. That man was none other than King Hezekiah, who felt obliged first to consult with the princes of the congregation (II Chronicles 30: 2).

In our own day, Jews throughout the world still prepare for the Passover celebration each year by clearing the house of all leaven on the night before the great festival. Later, as the last remaining crumb of *bedikat hametz* is burned, the sober prayer is offered in each household:

Blessed art Thou, O Lord our God,
  Ruler of the world
Who made us holy by His Commandments
  And commanded us to purify our premises of
All leavened foodstuff.

All leavened foodstuff, upon my premises,
  Whether I have seen it or not,
Whether I have removed it or not,
  Shall be declared null and void
As the dust of the earth.

While this act recalls that fateful night long ago when the Israelites were forced to flee from Egypt with "dough before it was leavened" (Exodus 12: 34), many families today involve the children in a game of hunting for the last remaining crumb of *hametz*.

For example, Rabbi Richard I. Schachet of Community Temple Beth-Ohr in Brooklyn, N.Y., loves to tell the story of the night his youngsters were awakened to search for *hametz* with candle and feather. His delightful wife Jan, a born *rebbitsin*, had already scoured the utensils and made certain that their "precincts" were free of all leaven. But then easily-detected bread crumbs were placed in spots where the children could quickly find them by candlelight.[4]

The youngsters searched and searched; but no *hametz*. So Dick laid out a few more crumbs, only to be greeted by the news that the elusive leaven was nowhere to be found.

"Finally it dawned on me," says Rabbi Schachet. "The dog had followed me around and had licked up the crumbs almost as fast as I laid them down!"

A *shlepper* that mutt was not. A *Shabbes goy, nu?*[5]

Whatever the case, this story amply illustrates the place of children in Jewish family life. Youngsters are allowed to be seen *and* heard. And they are very much a part of all that transpires within the home.

Nothing so testifies to the role of children within the Jewish family circle as the *Seder* ritual itself. Indeed, the *Seder*, the Passover order of service, is meant to help par-

---

4. Although the term is unfortunately seldom used today, the *rebbitsin*, like the minister's wife, is a mighty important person. Besides keeping the rabbi happy as wife and mistress, she is expected to participate in many synagogue functions and smooth ruffled feathers. "All rebbitsins are magicians," the saying goes. "How else can they raise a family on a rabbi's salary?" Many ministers' wives can agree.

5. Translation: This dog certainly did not drag his heels. It might be that he thought that he could help the good rabbi like the Gentile neighbor who aids a Jewish friend on a Sabbath. But it sounds better in Yiddish. *Nu?*

42

ents relate the story of the Exodus to their children according to the Biblical command.

Passover is meant to be a happy time from the moment the *Seder* table is prepared before dark by every Jewish mother. "It thrills the heart as though one heard the lilt of some sweet lullaby," said Heinrich Heine. "Even those Jews who have fallen away from the faith of their fathers in the mad pursuit of other glories are moved to the very depths of their being when by chance they hear again the old Passover melodies, once so dear to them."

Not that *Pesach* holds only pleasant memories. For stories still remain of those barbarous occasions during the Middle Ages when so-called Christians forgot all about their own simultaneous celebration of Christ's death and resurrection to strike fear in the hearts of their Jewish neighbors, as they charged them with ritual murder in the preparation of the Passover meal.

In more placid times, however, that ancient sense of joy and expectancy dominates each household as the mother lights the Passover candles before sunset. As she does so, the beautiful prayer ascends heavenward. *Baruch ato Adonoi elohenu Melech ha-olam . . .*

> Praised art Thou, O Lord our God, Ruler of the universe. Thou hast blessed us with Thy commandments and directed us to kindle the [Sabbath and] holy day light.

> Praised art Thou, O Lord our God, Ruler of the universe. Thou hast given us life, kept us safely, and brought us to this holy season.

On the *Seder* table in front of the person conducting the service are three *matzoth,* one on top of the other, each covered by a napkin or special cloth. Also before him are the shankbone and the roasted egg. In addition, bitter herbs, *charoses,* greens, and salt water are provided for all the other celebrants. In the center of the table stands The Cup of Elijah.

During the *Seder,* each participant will drink a minimum of four cups of wine. Each cup symbolizes one of the four promises God made to His people in advance of their liberation:

> I will bring you out from under the burdens of the Egyptians . . .
>
> I will rid you out of their bondage . . .
>
> I will redeem you with a stretched out arm, and with great judgments:
>
> And I will take you to me for a people, and I will be to you a God: and ye shall know that I am the Lord your God, which bringeth you out from under the burdens of the Egyptians (Exodus 6: 6, 7).

As the first cup of wine is raised, so the celebrants also rise to give praise to a redeeming God in the words of the *Kiddush*: "Behold this cup of wine! Let it be a symbol of joy today as we celebrate the festival of *Pesach*. On this day long ago our forefathers hearkened to the call of freedom . . ."[6]

As thanks was given to the Creator of the fruit of the vine, so now is praise offered to the Creator of the produce of the earth. This blessing is recited after all of the participants have taken the *karpas,* or salad greens, and dipped them in salt water. They are eaten after the blessing.

---

6. The author has attempted to follow the Passover Haggadahs from several sources, including English-Hebrew renderings of the National Jewish Welfare Board for Armed Forces Personnel, and those of Abraham Regelson and Richard I. Schachet. Several Scripture quotations come from the Pentateuch of Samson Raphael Hirsch.

It becomes immediately apparent that far more is involved here than the mere boring recitation of dust-covered history. Rather an age-old drama is being reenacted, a drama in which each participant remembers the bitter tears of his forebears and that great night when hyssop was used to sprinkle the blood of the paschal lamb on the doorpost of Hebrew homes in preparation for the Exodus. This is the lesson of the salt water and the *karpas*.

It is further evident that strict protocol is being followed as the celebrant moves toward the plate containing the three cakes of *matzoth,* popularly known as "the priest, the Levite, and the Israelite." After the middle *matzah* has been broken, one half is left on the plate; the other, called *afikomin,* is hidden to be eaten at the end of the meal.[7]

While the Seder dish containing the *matzoth* is uncovered for all to see, the celebrant begins the narrative portion of the ceremony—the *Haggadah* or the simple telling of the Exodus from Egypt.

> *See the bread of suffering which our forefathers*
> *   ate in Egypt.*
> *All you who are hungry, come eat with us!*
> *All you who are in need, come, celebrate the*
> *   Passover with us.*
> *This year we are here.*
> *May next year find us celebrating the Passover*
> *   in Israel.*
> *This year men are enslaved; may next year see*
> *   them free.*

---

7. A problem arises in transliteration from Hebrew to English. The word *afikomin,* for example, is transliterated in a variety of ways. A Jewish friend jokes about picking up greeting cards from a single display rack. Some were for Hanukkah, others for Chanukah. Other variations are Channukah and Hanuka. So with *afikoman, aphikomon.*

An interesting sidelight about the ceremony involves the fact that all participants are expected to adopt a casual, reclining position, symbolizing that of freemen at ancient banquets. "In some parts of the world, however," says Gaster, "everyone appears in hat and coat, with satchel on back and staff in hand, thus reenacting the departure from Egypt."

What is more important are the four questions, the *Mah Nishtanah,* which are now to be asked by the youngest person present: "Why is this night different from all other nights?"

... On all other nights we may eat bread or *matzoth;* why on this night only *matzoth?*

... On all other nights we may eat any kind of salad greens; why on this night must we taste bitter greens?

... On all other nights we need not dip any food in another, even once; why on this night must we dip greens twice, the salad greens in salt water and the bitter herb in *charoses?*

... On all other nights we may eat either sitting upright or at ease; why on this night are we all at ease?

Somehow the ages meet in these four questions. A small boy is linked in spirit to Moses and the Prophets. A father experiences an ever deepening affection for a son who will one day pass on this ancient tradition to his own flesh and blood. If there is any generation gap, it is only because diet colas have replaced *spritzers,* and hazel nuts have lost out to "pessedicker" candy!

"But why complain?" asks the imitable Arnold Fine. "Did they have seltzer bottles with spritzers in Moses' time? Of course not!

"First of all," says this gifted columnist, "if [Moses]

would have gone to the right instead of the left when he crossed the Red Sea, we would have had the oil wells and the Arabs' desert!

"Nu. Let's face it, who could be right all the time?"

However, on a more serious note, the four questions elicit the response that this night is different from all other nights because it recalls that night long ago when God "rescued us with a mighty hand and an outstretched arm."

But the *Seder* not only links Jewish children to an event of long ago; it also embraces them with wisdom from their great spiritual heritage. They may learn, for example, why this service is celebrated at night, as they hear the logic of Rabbi Eleazar ben Azariah:

"Think of it!" mused the Sage. "I am a man almost 70, and I was never able to prove that the Exodus story must be told at night until Ben Zoma explained it by quoting the Bible verse: 'That thou mayest remember the day of thy going forth from Egypt *all* the days of thy life.'

"By itself the words 'the days of thy life' might mean the daytime," the Sages reasoned. "But *'all* the days of thy life' includes the nights."

Other rabbis, however, were not so persuaded. For while they understood "the days of thy life" to refer to the world today, they interpreted *"all* the days of thy life" to mean all the days until the coming of the Messiah.

Whatever the case, the four questions are followed by the Section of the Four Sons. This portion of the *Haggadah* is based upon the fact that the Bible itself speaks four times of "thy son's" inquiry concerning the meaning of the Passover. On each occasion, the question is posed in different terms.[8]

8. Compare Deuteronomy 6: 20; Exodus 12: 26; 13: 14; and 13: 8.

The Sages understood this variation to typify the character of four different boys—one wise, one wicked, one simple, and the last too young to ask.

Said the father to his children:
  At the table you will dine;
You will eat your fill of *matzah;*
  You will drink four cups of wine.

Now this father had no daughters,
  But his sons, they numbered four;
One was wise, and one was wicked;
  One was simple and a bore.

And the fourth was sweet and winsome;
  He was young and He was small;
While the brothers asked the questions,
  He could scarcely speak at all.

Said the wise son to his father:
  Would you please explain the laws,
Of the customs of the *Seder*
  Would you please explain the cause?

And the father proudly answered:
  As our fathers ate in speed,
Ate the paschal lamb ere midnight,
  And from slavery were freed.

Then did sneer the son so wicked:
  What does all this mean to you?
And the father's voice was bitter,
  As his grief and anger grew:
If yourself you don't consider
  As a son of Israel,
Then for you this has no meaning,
  You could be a slave as well.

Then the simple son said simply
  What is this? And quietly the good father
Told his offspring:
  We were freed from slavery.

But the youngest son was silent;
  For he could not speak at all;
His bright eyes were bright with wonder,
  As his father told him all.

Now dear children, heed the lesson,

And remember evermore;
That the father told his children,
  Told his sons that numbered four.

That the father proudly answered:
  As our fathers ate in speed,
Ate the paschal lamb ere midnight,
  And from slavery were freed.

So we follow their example;
  And ere midnight must complete
All the *Seder,* and we should not,
  After twelve remain to eat.

If there was division among these four legendary sons, only a spirit of unity prevails in most Jewish households today as the *Seder* tempo quickens with the recitation of Israel's unique history among her ancient pagan neighbors.

The mere telling of it all should bring only gladness to those Protestant brethren who have been fed on a regular spiritual diet of three-point sermons. This one has four:

I. Israel's Origins
II. Israel's Suffering
III. Israel's Sorrows
IV. Israel's Triumph

One can almost reach out to an ancient Joshua as his words cut across the centuries to touch the hearts of faithful Jews today:

Thus saith the Lord, God of Israel: "Long ago your forefathers lived beyond the Euphrates River, until the days of Terah, father of Abraham and Nahor. And they worshiped pagan gods. Then I took your father Abraham from beyond the river and led him through all the land of Canaan. I gave him a son, Isaac. To Isaac I gave Jacob and Esau. I gave Esau Mount Seir as his inheritance, while Jacob and his sons went down to Egypt."

As the rabbis elaborate the Biblical story, the sons of Jacob followed their brother Joseph into this rich and cultured land, and there settled in the fertile area of Goshen. They were few in number, only 70 souls, when they crossed the border into Egypt. But there they became a nation great and strong. Or, as God was later to remind Israel through the prophet Ezekiel: "I made you increase like the growth of the field. And you became numerous, great in stature and in beauty, full grown and developed but without covering or ornament."[9]

But Israel's good fortune at last came to an end, when there arose in Egypt a king who knew not Joseph. It was then that "the Egyptians abused and tormented us and forced us into slave labor."

When all of this occurred is open to much scholarly debate, since, as William Sanford LaSor has noted, "it is a complex question on which the Bible itself is ambiguous."[10]

If the one set of evidences is *tentatively* accepted, it would appear that Israel's prosperity and growth occurred during the Hyksos period, when the "shepherd kings" of Semitic origin ruled on the throne of Egypt.

"It seems likely that Joseph came into the country at that time," LaSor suggests. "For that was a time when he could find those who were not too far distant in relationship from him, who could speak Semitic dialects, and whose names as we know from the Egyptian monuments were Semitic names. He would find more in common with them than he would with the Egyptians, who hated the Semites.

---

9. Compare the King James and Revised Standard versions, also The New English Bible, for Ezekiel 16: 7.

10. The mention of the city of Raamses (Exodus 1: 11) might suggest the reign of Rameses II (13th Century) rather than that of Thutmose III (15th Century) as the period of oppression and the Exodus.

"Moreover," says LaSor, "the Hyksos had located their capital in the delta region at Avaris, and that checks with the fact that when Joseph was there the capital was down in the delta region. Likewise, when his father and his brothers and their flocks came and located in the land of Goshen, they were near the capital."

All of this would suggest that Joseph and his brethren entered Egypt during the Hyksos period. If this were true, then Abraham's chronology could be squared by this set of historical indicators.

Whatever the case, there arose that new Pharaoh and a dynasty dedicated to restoring Egyptian sovereignty and glory. The shepherd kings were uprooted, and the once-favored Israelites became the objects of scorn and oppression. The new motto was "Egypt for the Egyptians."

Samson Raphael Hirsch has made the interesting observation that this first recorded case of anti-Semitism set the tone for Jew-baiting in all subsequent generations.

To find support for this, one has only to compare the policies of the new Pharaoh with those of the Middle Ages and the infamous Nuremberg Laws of the Third Reich. In each of these instances, the charges against the Jews and the suggested "Final Solution of the Jewish Question" were virtually identical:

> . . . Quite apart from any actual crimes committed by the Israelites, a scapegoat was needed to calm Egyptian public opinion in the face of crushing domestic burdens and the existence of a rigid caste system . . . . The hapless Jews were selected by [the] power elite to become the pariah upon which all of the frustrations of the Silent Majority could be unleashed.

> . . . So it was that the so-called 'International Jew' of Czarist, Marxist, and Nazi mythology [was] for Pharaoh a fictional fifth columnist who, according to official news leaks,

might aid and abet an enemy provoked by Egypt into war.

... With the stage set, Pharaoh's court appointed a special IRS unit—the *taskmasters* of the King James Version—to extort a hefty surcharge from these "foreigners who do not belong here."

... But this "emergency law" was no more successful in pushing Jews out than a similar Soviet levy later was able to keep Jews in. The complaint of the ancient Egyptians has a strangely modern ring: "If they went to the theater it was full of Jews; if they went to the circus, again all Jews" (Yalkut).

... Therefore, at the "insistence" of an aroused public, official Egypt quickly set Stage Two of the "Final Solution" into motion. Even with the grinding taxes, the Jews retained certain rights as "naturalized citizens." But now new emergency legislation turned them into slaves.

... When even forced labor failed to break Jewish morale, Stage Three of the master plan was put into effect. The hated race was to be liquidated, not by an *auto-da-fe,* nor by Zyklon B, but rather by Hebrew midwives, who were ordered to kill all male Jewish babies. What Pharaoh didn't know was that these women feared God more than men. So Israel lived!

If the descendants of Jacob were at all to blame for their unhappy condition, says Rabbi Hirsch, it was because they had become assimilated and had permitted "a lowering of the Abrahamitic spirit."

But all was not lost. Israel might have temporarily forgotten about the God of Jacob; but the God of Jacob still sought to comfort His people in the midst of their affliction.

In the valley of despair, says the *Haggadah,* "we cried unto the Lord, the God of our fathers, and God heard our voice. He saw our torment, our grief and our oppression."

Therefore, what began as a muffled cry of sorrow ended in a loud burst of triumph: "The Lord took us out of Egypt with a strong hand and outstretched arm, with awesome revelations, marvels and wonders!"

Some of the rabbis explain that the strong hand accounted for the plagues of blood and frogs; the outstretched arm for the lice and flies; the awesome revelations for the cattle disease and boils; the marvels for the hail and locusts; the wonders for the darkness and the slaying of the firstborn.[11]

Ten plagues in all. "This is the number of plagues," says the *Haggadah,* "with which the Holy One, blessed be He, struck the Egyptians."

But Israel found no satisfaction in the suffering of others. Rather, as each of the plagues is recalled, each *Seder* guest still allows a drop of wine to fall from his cup. "This is done," explains Rabbi Albert S. Goldstein, "because the pain of human beings, enemies though they be, is a loss from the wine of joy in the cup of life."

This ancient tradition may explain far better than any talk of international pressure why the Israelis felt compelled, some admittedly against their own wills, to bring food and water to 20,000 Egyptian soldiers trapped in Sinai during the Yom Kippur War.

To do otherwise would be to betray the "Litany of Wonders" which is the next highlight of every Passover *Seder*. As each wonder of the Exodus is recalled, the par-

---

11. The rabbis never seemed to tire of speculating on the actual number of plagues . . . 50 . . . 200 . . . 250. In the First Century, for example, Rabbi Jose the Galilean asked: 'How could you show that, although the Egyptians suffered 10 plagues in Egypt, there were 50 plagues at the Red Sea?' His explanation: "If one finger of God caused 10 plagues in Egypt, you can say that the whole hand of God at the Red Sea brought 50 plagues."

ticipants respond with a loud *Dayyenu*: "That alone
would have sufficed us!"

Had He brought us out of Egypt	
And not passed sentence on its people,	*Dayyenu!*
Had He passed sentence on its people	
And not upon their pagan gods,	*Dayyenu!*
Had He passed sentence on their pagan gods	
And not slain their first born sons,	*Dayyenu!*
Had He slain their first born sons	
And not given us their treasures,	*Dayyenu!*
Had He given us their treasures,	
And not split the Red Sea for us,	*Dayyenu!*
Had He split the Red Sea for us	
And not led us safely through,	*Dayyenu!*
Had He led us safely through	
And not drowned our enemies there,	*Dayyenu!*

As this awesome poem continues, the demonstrations
of God's mercy seem endless. For He not only brought
His people safely out of the house of bondage, but He fed
them manna in the wilderness, and at length gave them
the Torah at Mount Sinai. And, if all of this were not
sufficient, the God of Jacob led His children into the land
of Israel where they found a *Shabbat Shalom*—a Sabbath
rest—in the shadow of the Temple.

No wonder, then, that Rabban Gamaliel used to say,
"He who does not explain the three essentials of the
Seder has not discharged his Passover duty."

So it is that every celebrant comes to that point in the
ancient ritual when he points to the shankbone, and explains simply:[12]

> This stands for the Passover lamb which our an-
> cestors used to eat in Temple times. What is its
> meaning? It is to remind us that the Holy One,
> blessed be He, *passed over* the houses of the

12. Samaritan Jews still sacrifice a paschal lamb at their annual
Passover ceremony in Shechem (Nablus).

Children of Israel in Egypt, striking down the Egyptians and sparing our houses. Then the people bowed in worship.

Then, pointing to the top *matzah* in the ceremonial dish, the celebrant inquires: "For what reason do we eat this *matzah?*" The explanation follows:

It is to remind us that there was no time for the dough to rise when God revealed Himself to our fathers to redeem them. So they baked *matzoth* of the dough which they took with them out of Egypt. It had no chance to rise because they were rushed out of Egypt and could not wait. Besides, they had prepared no other provisions for the march.

Finally, the third "essential" of the *Seder* is displayed for all to see. As the celebrant points to the *maror,* he asks, "What is the reason for this bitter food?"[13] Then he gives the age-old answer.

It is to recall how bitter the Egyptians made the life of our fathers in Egypt. They embittered the life of our fathers with forced labor, with mortar and bricks, with every kind of field labor. In all this work they made them slave unmercifully.

Tears often begin to flow at many a *Seder* table as affluent American Jews are gripped by the sight of a loved one raising a cup of wine with a hand that will forever carry the cruel brand of a Nazi concentration camp. Others will share the pain of the ages as they survey the rapt attention of Soviet Jews who are celebrating their first *Pesach* in a free country.

It is not difficult in such a setting to imagine that one personally has been delivered out of bondage in Egypt.

---

13. Usually a piece of horseradish.

"It was not only our forefathers whom God saved," the celebrant declares. "He saved us too. For it is written: He took us out of there, so that He might bring us home, and give us the land as He had promised our fathers."

Israel is now returning home at last. Her people are borne on the wings of the world's airlines, and in the bowels of its ships, to that land bequeathed by God so long ago to the sons and daughters of Abraham, Isaac, and Jacob!

Yet even in the *galut,* or Dispersion, the sheer memory of that first Passover has been enough for Jews the world over to pause and praise the Lord, the Savior of Israel.

After the second cup of wine, the unleavened bread and the bitter herbs are blessed and mixed together with the *charoses,* a blend of apples, nuts, cinnamon, and wine, symbolic of the "mud mixed with straw" during the years of Egyptian bondage. Then, following the *Seder* meal, the *afikomin* is taken from its hiding place, broken, and distributed. No more food will be served.[14]

But the litany of prayer and praise continues as the wine is raised for the third and fourth times. With that, the door is opened for Elijah, beloved prophet of hope, and to "all who are hungry or in need."

"The custom of pouring a special cup [of wine] for Elijah . . . has its origin in a rabbinical controversy as to whether four or five cups are commanded," says Abraham Regelson. "The issue was deferred to the days of the Messiah, when Elijah will smooth out all difficulties."

While many Jews still await Elijah's coming some Passover night to herald Israel's redemption, the open door also testifies to a more sinister day when Jewry was accused of drinking Christian blood at the *Seder* feast. In

14. Youngsters who find the *afikomin* may demand a gift before it is shared by all for "dessert." But the Talmud declares that "men must not leave the paschal meal *epikomin* . . . gadding around on revels." Passover, for all of its joy, is a solemn occasion.

that terrible age, the open door was meant to allay such gross suspicions on the part of Gentile neighbors.

The tragedy of the ages has been that the virus of Christian anti-Semitism can be traced back to that fatal night when the Galilean observed the Passover with His disciples in an Upper Room overlooking the Holy City.

It was there that Jesus broke the *matzoth* and raised the cup of wine to signal the advent of a New Covenant —a covenant which, He declared, would be based upon His own sacrificial death as the Paschal Lamb. "And when they had sung an hymn," says Mark, "they went out into the mount of Olives" (Mark 14: 26).

That hymn was none other than the *Hallel* (Praise), composed of Psalms 113—118, and still sung by Jews the world over at the close of the Passover meal and at other feasts of the Jewish year.

However, Rabbi Morris N. Kertzer points to an interesting sidelight concerning the use of these great hymns during most of Passover. Only part of the *Hallel* is sung. he says, out of sympathy for Israel's fallen enemies.

"This practice goes back to an ancient legend which tells that when the Israelites crossed the Red Sea they chanted songs of praise for their deliverance," he explains. "A voice from On High spoke out: 'You must not sing songs of gladness when my creatures, the Egyptians, have drowned in the sea.'"

> *Ended the act of the Pesach night,*
> *   Each law and custom kept aright:*
> *As we've lived to do it without a stain,*
> *   God grant we do it time and again.*
> *Pure One, Dweller in height august,*
> *   Raise up the folk of countless dust!*
> *Soon lead the stem-shoots of Thy ward,*
> *   Redeemed and singing, Zionward.*

The Days of Omer

Seven weeks will now pass, the Days of the *Omer,* between Passover and Pentecost. "The *Omer* Days are observed as a kind of Lent," says Gaster. "At least during the earlier portion of them, it is not permitted to solemnize marriages, cut the hair, wear new clothes, listen to music, or attend any form of public entertainment."

However, the word *Omer* in Hebrew means "sheaf," and it harks back to the Biblical commandment (Leviticus 23: 15) that seven full weeks are to be counted from the day when the first sheaf of barley is offered to God in the sanctuary until the final celebration of the harvest-home and the presentation to Him of the two loaves of new bread.

Shavuot (Weeks)

Then comes Pentecost, the Feast of Weeks, and the second of the Pilgrim Festivals of the Jewish year. Known as *Shavuot* in Hebrew, this celebration occurs at the conclusion of the grain harvest *(hag ha-katzir),* and also commemorates God's revelation at Mount Sinai. It is therefore called "The Season of the Giving of our Torah."

Because of this association with God's revelation at Mount Sinai, an abridged Bible and *Mishnah,* known as the *Tikkun,* was developed so that Jews might review the teachings of their ancient faith at *Shavuot.*

In Reform Judaism, the festival came to be a time for youngsters to confirm their promise to obey the Ten Commandments and other articles of the Jewish religion.

Moreover, *Shavuot* is associated with the reading of the Book of Ruth in synagogue services. Some have suggested that this book was chosen because Ruth was a proselyte who accepted the *Torah.* But there is another tradition that contends that Ruth's illustrious grandson, David, was born and died on *Shavuot.*

Whatever the case, the Book of Ruth is eminently appropriate for a great harvest festival, recounting as it does a beautiful love story centering upon the wheat and barley harvests of that land flowing with milk and honey.

Meanwhile, as the synagogue is decorated with plants and greenery befitting the season, Jews thrill to the majestic words of the *Akdamot,* an 11th Century *Shavuot* prayer, which tells of God's love, of Israel's devotion to *Torah,* and of the age-long hope for Messiah's reign.

Sukkoth (Tabernacles)

However, there is yet a third pilgrim festival which is also associated with harvest. It is known as *Sukkoth,* or the Feast of Tabernacles. It has been described liturgically in terms of *zeman simhatenu,* "the time of our rejoicing."

A very joyful holiday, *Sukkoth* begins five days after *Yom Kippur* and lasts for nine days. During this period, the Jews are reminded of those long years when their forefathers followed Moses through the wilderness to the Promised Land, a time when the onward journey permitted no more than huts or booths as temporary shelters.

So it is that each Jewish family still tries to erect its own *Sukkoth* booth each year. Meals are eaten within this hut, and the family attempts to spend as much time as possible beneath the roof of leaves and branches.

As an accommodation to modern urban life, prefabricated *Sukkoth* booths are now available to city dwellers. In many instances, they will be found on the flat roofs of high rise apartment buildings. After the holiday, they can be folded and stored for another year.

Meanwhile, the booths themselves are decorated with flowers and fall fruits and vegetables as the Jewish community recalls God's ancient command: "And ye shall take you on the first day the [fruit] of goodly trees, branches of palm trees, and the boughs of [leafy] trees, and willows of the brook; and ye shall rejoice before the Lord your God seven days" (Leviticus 23: 40).

The eighth day of this thanksgiving season is marked by prayers for rain and an abundant harvest in the coming year. And, while this may all sound a bit unreal to rain-drenched denizens of the asphalt jungle, Jewish thoughts center at this time on the Old-New Land, where water is always in short supply.

"This holiday is a reminder that God is the Lord of nature and the Lord of history," says Lee A. Belford. "Ethically, it suggests that the accumulation of physical possessions is no substitute for a faith in God who provides for men according to their need."

So highly regarded was *Sukkoth* in ancient times that the Prophet Zechariah declared: "And it shall come to pass, that every one that is left of all the nations . . . shall even go up from year to year to worship the King, the Lord of hosts, and to keep the feast of tabernacles" (Zechariah 14: 16, 17).

"The prophet is referring to messianic times, when all the nations of the world will live in peace and worship one God," says Ben M. Edidin. "That he mentions *Sukkoth* as the holiday which all people of the world are to celebrate, indicates how important it was."

A further hint of its importance is demonstrated by the unusual order of sacrifices offered during the festival in Temple times. Thirteen bullocks were sacrificed on the first day, and the number was reduced by one daily, until on the seventh day only seven were offered, making a total of 70 (Numbers 29: 12-32).

Although these sacrifices had to be abandoned when the Temple was destroyed, the tradition grew that they represented the offerings made by Israel in behalf of the 70 nations which were said to inhabit the earth.

Simhat Torah

But *Sukkoth*—"the time of our rejoicing"—does not end on so somber a note. In fact, the ninth and final day is the most joyous of all—the day of *Simhat Torah,* the Torah Festival, the day when the last *sidrah* from the Pentateuch has been read and the first chapter of Genesis is begun for the coming year.

"The [annual] process of concluding the reading and beginning once again," says Dr. Belford, "suggests both the eternity of God's revelation in the *Torah* and the importance of its unceasing study."

In the Hassidic tradition, the *Torah* scrolls are carried in procession as the *hazan* advances in front, chanting:

> *Great and Mighty, O help us!*
> *Kind and Merciful, O help us!*

Upon reaching the starting point in front of the Ark, the marchers break out in singing and dancing. This routine is repeated as often as necessary to give everyone a chance to carry a scroll. The scrolls themselves are kissed as the marchers pass by.

At the morning service, one man is chosen as the *hatan Torah,* or "bridegroom of the Law," while another is selected to be the *hatan Bereshit*. The former has the coveted honor of calling upon every member of the congregation to read the last chapter of Deuteronomy, while the latter performs the same role in the reading of the first chapter of Genesis.

Nobody—not even boys under 13—is excluded from the privilege of reading from both the concluding and commencing *Torah* portions of the year. For this is a *mitzvah*, a meritorious deed, in which all can share.

"Sometimes miniature printed scrolls of paper are given to the children to commemorate the event," says Belford. "Almost invariably they are given candy or other sweets to remind them of the majesty of the *Torah* and the 'sweetness' of its study."

While most of these elements are common to all branches of *Judaism,* the *Hassidim* observe *Simhat Torah* with a particular exuberance and merriment.

After the *Hakafot* processional, everybody remains in the synagogue for dancing and a rich spread of wine, cakes, salted fish, and other refreshments. These festivities are then followed by similar ones in the homes of friends, until the whole day has been spent in joy around the *Torah.*

The High Holy Days

While *Simhat Torah* is given to joyous celebration, *Rosh Hashanah* and *Yom Kippur* are considered the High Holy Days—a time for prayer, repentance, and serious reflection.

Moreover, it must be noted that the High Holy Days differ from *Pesach, Shavuot,* and *Sukkoth* in that these three festivals are based upon both the Palestinian agricultural year and specific historical events in the life of the Covenant People.

In Biblical times, farmers would make every effort to leave their villages and make the long trek to Jerusalem to observe these pilgrim festivals. They did so in response to the divine command: "Three times in the year all thy males shall appear before the Lord God" (Exodus 23:17).

In that ancient agricultural society, Passover would come at the beginning of the barley harvest, Pentecost would come at the end of the grain harvest and the beginning of the fruit harvest, and the Feast of Tabernacles would mark the end of all harvesting and the beginning of winter.

But each of these festivals also commemorated a specific event in early Jewish history. Passover recalled the liberation of Israel from Egyptian bondage; Pentecost celebrated the giving of the Law at Sinai; and Tabernacles reminded the Jews of the booths in which their fathers sought shelter during the wilderness wanderings.

The High Holy Days, on the other hand, represent that solemn season when the Jews reflect upon the year past and look forward in hope to the year that lies ahead.

Rosh Hashanah (The New Year)

Since the Jewish calendar is based on the cycles of the moon, the new year begins in either September or October, the date varying from year to year. In Hebrew, the words *Rosh Hashanah* simply mean "beginning of the year."

However, the matter is complicated by the fact that the *Mishnah* lists four different dates as being the new year for four different and specific purposes. One of these dates acquired the significance of an annual day of judgment. "On *Rosh Hashanah*," says the *Mishnah,* "all that come into the world pass before Him like flocks of sheep."

The Biblical basis for *Rosh Hashanah* is found in Leviticus: "In the seventh month, in the first day of the month, shall ye have a [solemn rest], a memorial of blowing of trumpets, an holy convocation" (Lev. 23: 24).

"As time went on," says Edidin, "a great many important events came to be associated with this date: the creation of the world; the creation of Adam; the birth of Abraham, Isaac, Jacob, and Samuel; the day Joseph was freed from prison; and [the day] the Hebrews ceased to be slaves in Egypt.

"*Rosh Hashanah* was also to be the great day of the future," he says, "[the day] when the Jewish people would be redeemed from exile and restored to their ancient homeland."

But apart from these traditions *Rosh Hashanah* has a four-fold significance. It is the New Year, the Day of Remembrance, the Day of Judgment, and the Day of *Shofar* Blowing. And around these various aspects has grown a great body of rabbinic lore:

> Rabbi Yitzchak said, "Why do we blow the *Shofar* on *Rosh Hashanah,* once while standing and then again while seated? To confuse Satan!"

> Rabbi Abuhu said, "Why do we blow *Shofar* on the horn of a ram?" God announces, "Blow before Me on the horn of a ram so that I may remember the sacrifice of Isaac the son of Abraham and I will consider it as if you performed their deed and it was you who were sacrificed before Me."

> Rabbi Abuhu said, "The angels asked God, "Why doesn't Israel say *Hallel* [psalms of praise and joy] on *Rosh Hashanah* and *Yom Kippur?*' "God answers them: 'Here I am as a King sitting in judgment over them, with the books of life and death open before Me, and Israel should be in the mood to sing praises?' "

Actually, *Rosh Hashanah* and *Yom Kippur* are the high points of a 40-day period—which begins with the blowing of the *Shofar* after the morning service in the synagogue on the first day of the Hebrew month of Elul. The sound of the ram's horn also ushers in a ten day period of penitence—which begins with *Rosh Hashanah,* the New Year, and ends with *Yom Kippur,* the Day of Atonement. Throughout this season of repentance, the theme is that echoed in the words of Hosea: "O Israel, return unto the Lord thy God" (Hosea 14: 1).

In Jewish homes, the signal that the solemn days have arrived comes when mothers light the candles at sunset on *Erev Rosh Hashanah,* the Eve of Rosh Hashanah. These candles are meant to express the hope that the New Year will begin with light and joy.

After services in the synagogue, the family returns home for a festive meal. But not before the father bestows upon his loved ones the traditional *Rosh Hashanah* greeting, *Leshanah tovah tikatev*—"May you be inscribed for a good year!"

However, the sanctity of *Rosh Hashanah* is most felt at the synagogue service the following morning. For it is then that a sacred hush descends as everyone stands waiting for the hallowed notes of the *Shofar,* a symbol no less sacred than the *Menorah,* the eight-branched candelabrum of *Chanukah,* the Feast of Lights.

As the blasts come forth from the ram's horn, Jews are reminded of the *Akeida,* the offering of Isaac. The rich sounds also remind worshipers of the Ten Commandments which were received by Israel to the accompaniment of the *Shofar.*

Moreover, as Jews everywhere lament the destruction of the Temple, the ancient blasts symbolize the eternal hope of redemption, the day when peace and goodwill will flourish and Israel will dwell safely in the land.

Yom Kippur (Day of Atonement)

Rosh Hashanah is only the first day of the penitential season. It is said by the orthodox that all men stand before God in judgment on that day, but His judgment is withheld until *Yom Kippur,* a term some scholars trace to an ancient word for "purge" or "wipe clean."

Sometimes dubbed "instant Lent," *Yom Kippur* is the holiest day of the Jewish year. As Jews everywhere engage in fasting, prayer, and solemn meditation, they are reminded of the Biblical command: "Ye shall afflict your [selves], and do no work at all, whether it be [a native], or a stranger that sojourneth among you: For on that day shall the priest make an atonement for you, to cleanse you, that ye, may be clean from all your sins before the Lord" (Leviticus 16: 29, 30).

At the synagogue service the evening before *Yom Kippur,* the cantor and two spokesmen for the congregation stand before the invisible Judge and Tribunal. As they do so, they recite the words:

> By the authority of the Court on high, and by the authority of the Court below, by the permission of the Lord, blessed be He, and by the permission of this sacred congregation, we declare it lawful to pray with those who have transgressed.

The words are repeated three times before the cantor begins to chant the haunting hymn known as the *Kol Nidre,* which is written not in Hebrew but in Aramaic.

As the melody reminds the worshipers of the long history of violence directed against the Jews, the *Torah* scrolls are held aloft by three men, almost as a symbol that God's Law will yet prevail.

In a sense, no day of the Jewish calendar better expresses the crying need for understanding and love between Jew and Christian.

To begin with, the term *Kol Nidre* itself means "all vows," and it represents a plaintive appeal for absolution from oaths of a religious nature which the Jews, in times past, were forced to make under duress. In the Middle Ages, for example, the Jews were compelled to assume obligations contrary to their faith. And, during the Spanish Inquisition, they were given the choice of death or submission to the Christian Church.

"It is for vows such as these that the *Kol Nidre* was primarily intended," says Edidin. "Promises and responsibilities undertaken by a person under normal circumstances cannot be voided by reciting a prayer. They must be fulfilled.

"Enemies have often avowed that a Jew's promise is not worth anything, pointing to *Kol Nidre* as proof," he says. "But they are unaware of, or choose to ignore, the real intent of this prayer."

In an age that cries for redemption and reconciliation, Christians would do well to remember how the Church attempted to rape the Jewish spirit in the name of evangelism!

But *Yom Kippur* further testifies to the fact that Jews, no less than Christians, recognize that true repentance involves far more than mere lip service. Indeed, the Rabbis have been unanimous in their teaching that, while God is quick to forgive sins against Heaven, the transgressor must make direct amends to his fellowman.

So it was that Jesus was following in the train of the great Rabbis who had gone before Him, when He declared: "If thou bring thy gift to the altar, and there rememberest that thy brother hath [anything] against thee; Leave there thy gift before the altar, and go thy way; first be reconciled to thy brother, and then come and offer thy gift" (Matthew 5: 23, 24).

Finally, *Yom Kippur* demonstrates that intimate relationship which has always existed between God and His ancient people. It is an intimacy which allows the Jew to argue with his God, a relationship which also permits the Lord to engage in "a controversy with his people" (Micah 6: 2 ff).

The story is told that Rabbi Levi Yitzhak got up from his scat one *Yom Kippur* eve and began to look under each bench in the synagogue. As his congregants looked on in disbelief, Rabbi Levi Yitzhak explained: "I am looking for a drunken Jew. I have searched all over the synagogue and I have been unable to find one." Then, lifting his face heavenward, he boomingly declared:

67

Master of the Universe, behold your people Israel whom You have chosen from all people and made holy with Your *mitzvoth*. You gave us a commandment to fast on *Yom Kippur* and also one to . . . fast on the eve of *Yom Kippur*. Had you commanded the nations of the world to feast, consider what would have happened! They would have joined with gusto and drunk till their bellies were filled and their minds fogged. Would there have been many people sitting sober for prayers?

Then Rabbi Yitzhak ended his prayer with an appeal. "Your people Israel have fulfilled Your commandment and . . . there is not one person here who is drunk. What a holy people are they! And what do they ask? Only that You say a few small words: 'For a good life for all the children of the Covenant.' "

God demands of both Christian and Jew true repentance. But He also invites both into that holy, yet intimate relationship that permits the Jewish community to end its most sacred day with the *Ne'ilah* and a prayer for forgiveness:

> *Lord, though every power be Thine*
> *And every deed tremendous,*
> *Now, when Heaven's gates are closing*
> *Let Thy grace defend us.*

3

Lord, Remember David!

IF YOUR FAMILY had an English past, the chances are that you might be an Israelite!

According to Herbert W. Armstrong, that is.

Not a "perfidious Jew," mind you, but an honest-to-goodness descendant from one of the "Lost Ten Tribes of Israel."

The odds on such a possibility are best for those who take special pride in their White Anglo-Saxon Protestant background. And the point of historical certainty is reached for those whose forefathers came over on the *Mayflower*.

What happened was that God commissioned the prophet Jeremiah to carry out a strange and dangerous mission at the time of the Jewish Exile in Babylon. So devious was this divine undertaking that its significance has been lost to the most eminent Jewish and Christian Bible scholars!

But those who are privy to the mind of the Eternal (as Armstrong believes he is) know that Jeremiah began his Mission Impossible as Judah was falling under the Babylonian yoke. In the midst of the bloodshed and despair, the prophet's task was to remove the throne of David from Jerusalem and reestablish it in a new homeland.

To this end, Jeremiah escorted the daughter of the last king of Judah to Ireland, where she married the son of the Irish monarch. And, of course, they lived happily ever after.

Anglo-Israelism

But beauty was not the only booty that the prophet carried on his strange adventure. He also took with him the stone which Jacob had used as a pillow. Today that piece of ancient rock is known as the Stone of Scone and rests in regal splendor beneath the coronation throne in Westminster Abbey—so those who embrace this "Anglo-Israelite" faith insist.

If the history of the Jews is stranger than fiction, the story of the "Lost Ten Tribes" is even more so. For today, claims Armstrong, the descendants of these elusive clans make up the Anglo-Saxon people of both England and America. They alone can claim title to the hoary heritage of Ephraim and Manasseh.

Those who would doubt this "staggering turn in world events" have only to check with the Anglo-Israelites to learn that telltale signs of this amazing migration are couched within the English language itself. The word British, for example, comes from two Hebrew words, *brith* meaning covenant, and *ish* meaning man. Hence, the British are men of the ancient Davidic covenant.

So, too, with the word Saxon. This term, we are told, "is derived from the 'sons of Isaac,'" remembering that "vowels are not used in Hebrew spelling."

All of these sons of Isaac and the covenant, so the story goes, left other telltale signs of their original heritage as they meandered across Europe and at last established a new Zion in jolly Old England.

The Tribe of Dan, for example, became immortalized in history not because of its roots in Israel, but in Denmark. Not to mention its waltz along the blue Danube!

The noted "Bible scholar" Herbert W. Armstrong, founder of the Worldwide Church of God, warns his followers not to be led astray by critics who reject this fascinating fiction.

Scholars who put down his theories, says Armstrong, "have been falsely educated and deceived into closing their minds to the great causes behind world events and trends."

Moreover, he argues, "the best minds in the world are in total ignorance of the unprecedented cataclysm that is about to strike."

The key to Armageddon, he warns, lies not in the Middle East but in the United States and the British Commonwealth.

Unfortunately, at least for Armstrong, the most distinguished Jewish and Christian authorities have dismissed Anglo-Israelism as *bobbe-myseh*. That's a Yiddish phrase meaning baloney!

"Armstrong apparently has never considered the geological evidence that indicates the Stone of Scone is of Scottish origin," says William J. Petersen. "Nor the linguistic evidence that English bears no resemblance at all to Hebrew."

In fact, says the author of *Those Curious New Cults,* "there is no scientific or anthropological evidence to support Armstrong's theory of British-Israelism."

However, it is not enough that all reputable authorities have dismissed the Armstrong fantasy out-of-hand. For far more is involved in this type of cultic curiosity than mere ignorance of sound Biblical scholarship.

If liberal Christians are guilty of sacrificing Isaac on the altar of higher criticism, some conservative Christians who identify the church as the Chosen People of today have been guilty of outright anti-Semitism.

One noted Reformed theologian, for example, has gone so far as to hint of a Messianic Age purged of the Messianic people. In his diatribe against the Jews, he writes: "The continuance of this bitterly anti-Christian racial group has brought no good to themselves, and there has been strife and antagonism in practically every nation where they have gone . . . ." The veiled vision of this well-known evangelical is that of a *judenrein* utopia —a millennium without Jews.

However, there are others within the church—men and women who would condemn such anti-Semitism—who nonetheless appropriate God's blessings to themselves and assign further divine judgments to suffering Israel. Against such tendencies, James H. Brookes has written:

> These Christians appeal confidently to the fulfillment of curses against Israel . . . and triumphantly point the infidel to the punishment, captivity, and dispersion of Abraham's seed, and then coolly turn around and appropriate to themselves every promise of forgiveness and restoration and happiness given to the same scattered Israel.

"Let not a Gentile talk anymore," advises Brookes, ". . . of the meanness of a Jew!"

Of course, both Jewish and Christian claims to divine election are anathema to an unbelieving world. Yet they are firmly taught in the Scriptures.

On the Christian side are the New Testament allusions to the future blessing and glorification of the church. For example, Paul writes to the Galatians:

And the scripture, foreseeing that God would justify the heathen through faith, preached before the gospel unto Abraham, saying, In thee shall all nations be blessed. So then they which be of faith are blessed with faithful Abraham (Galatians 3: 8, 9).

The King and the kings of Israel

God's promise to Abraham was that He would give the patriarch, and his seed after him, "all the land of Canaan, for an everlasting possession" (Genesis 17: 8). Even bondage in Egypt could not nullify that pledge.

As a prelude to the Sinaitic Covenant under Moses, the Bible rather declares: "And God heard their groaning, and God remembered his covenant with Abraham, with Isaac, and with Jacob. And God looked upon the children of Israel, and God had respect unto them" (Exodus 2: 24, 25).

Whatever the course of Israel's political fortunes, says Sabatino Moscati, "Israel has its God; this God has made a pact with Israel; the working out of this pact constitutes history."

If this is true, then the God of Abraham is also the God of Moses. At the burning bush Moses was commissioned for his unique role with this divine assurance:

Thus shalt thou say unto the children of Israel, The Lord God of your fathers, the God of Abraham, the God of Isaac, and the God of Jacob, hath sent me unto you: this is my name for ever, and this is my memorial unto all generations (Exodus 3: 15).

While the revelation of the Divine Name has posed a serious problem for many scholars, William Neil has aptly observed: "This revelation to Moses . . . [is not] paving the way for the introduction of a new God to Israel, but [is] a revelation of a new understanding of the

God that Abraham and his descendants had always worshiped, in token of which God is given a new name, which from now on becomes the key to Israel's story as the people of YHWH."[1]

While liberal scholars contend that this indicates the evolution of the Hebrew concept of God, conservatives insist that the God who revealed Himself to Moses at the burning bush is the God who acts in history on behalf of His people. It is true that the Israelites were forced to undergo the rigors of serfdom in Egypt; but even these cruel circumstances were all part of the divine plan to call out "a kingdom of priests, and an holy nation" (Exodus 19: 6).

If God had allowed Israel to flourish in her own land, says Rabbi Hirsch, she would have been like all the other nations, resting in her own power and unable to understand that God alone was the effective cause for her strength and hope. What is important is the fact that the God who acts is also the God who keeps His promises:

> And the Lord said, I have surely seen the affliction of my people which are in Egypt, and I have heard their cry by reason of their taskmasters; for I know their sorrows; and I am come down to deliver them out of the hand of the Egyptians, and to bring them up out of that land unto a good land and a large, unto a land flowing with milk and honey . . .

However, the Exodus was but the first step toward Sinai. Israel's freedom was to be freedom under the Law.

> And Moses brought forth the people out of the camp to meet God; and they stood at the nether part of the mount. And Mount Sinai was altogether in smoke, because the Lord descended upon it in fire; and the smoke thereof ascended

1. And I appeared unto Abraham, unto Isaac, and unto Jacob, by the name of God Almighty [*El Shaddai*], but by my name [YHWH] was I not known to them (Exodus 6: 3).

as the smoke of a furnace, and the whole mount quaked greatly. And when the voice of the trumpet waxed louder and louder, Moses spake, and God answered him by a voice.

The Law received at this sacred mount was no secular social contract subscribed to by a loose confederation of seminomadic tribes. It was rather a Law based upon God's covenant with Abraham, as well as upon the very character of God Himself. For the word of the Lord through Moses was this: "Ye shall be holy: for I the Lord your God am holy" (Leviticus 19: 2).

Although the authority of the Law was not dependent upon human consensus, its practical administration was delegated to the twelve tribes, both during the wilderness wanderings and after the conquest of the Promised Land under Joshua.

Moreover, in time there arose in Israel a group of charismatic leaders, known as the Judges, who exercised special authority during periods of political stress and national emergency. The Book of Judges contains passages concerning these popular folk heroes, such as the celebrated *Song of Deborah*, which are of unquestioned antiquity:

> 'That warriors in Israel unbound their hair,
> that the people came forward with a will,
> for this, bless Yahweh!
> 'Listen, you kings! Give ear, you princes!
> From me, from me comes a song for Yahweh.
> I will glorify Yahweh, God of Israel.
>
> 'Yahweh, when you set out from Seir,
> as you trod the land of Edom,
> earth shook, the heavens quaked,
> the clouds dissolved into water.
> The mountains melted before Yahweh.
> Before Yahweh, the God of Israel.'
> —Judges 5: 2-5, *Jerusalem Bible*

In keeping with the democratic tradition of the tribal confederation, the authority delegated to the Judges remained modest and restricted.

However, the unfortunate hour finally dawned when so-called political exigencies led the Children of Israel to clamor for "a king to govern us like all the nations" (I Samuel 8: 5, RSV).

This demand thoroughly displeased Samuel, the last and greatest Judge of Israel who—by prayer and sacrifice alone—had prevailed with God against the powerful Philistines.

Although the aged leader warned that a central authority vested in a monarchy could erode hard-won freedoms, the Lord said unto Samuel: "Hearken unto the voice of the people in all that they say unto thee: for they have not rejected thee, but they have rejected me, that I should not reign over them" (I Samuel 8: 7).

It was on this poignant note that theocracy ended and Saul was invested as Israel's first king by none other than Samuel himself.

There are those short-lived successes during which Saul sets out to conquer the enemy and consolidate the state. But ultimately he breaks with Samuel and becomes the victim of his own paranoia, a disease graphically depicted within the Bible itself:

> And it came to pass as they came, when David returned from the slaughter of the Philistine, that the women came out of all the cities of Israel, singing and dancing to meet King Saul, with timbrels, with joy, and with instruments of music. And the women sang to one another in their play, and said,
>
> *Saul hath slain his thousands,*
> *And David his ten thousands.*

No wonder that Saul was "very wroth" at all of the attention being showered upon David. The gals certainly had not boosted his own masculine ego. Unfortunately, however, the king allowed self-pity and resentment to burst into flaming hatred against his more popular son-in-law-to-be.

> And it came to pass on the morrow, that [an] evil spirit from God came upon Saul, and he prophesied in the midst of the house: and David played with his hand, as at other times: and there was a [spear] in Saul's hand. And Saul cast the [spear]; for he said, I will smite David even to the wall with it. And David avoided out of his presence twice. And Saul was afraid of David, because the Lord was with him, and was departed from Saul (I Samuel 18: 10-12).

"The figure of the king abandoned by God, a prey to jealousy and persecution mania, stands out from the Biblical pages in all its tragedy," says Moscati. "Here Israelite historiography proves capable of depicting not only events, but characters and personalities . . . and provides a free and detached appreciation even of the kings."

When Saul dies on the battlefield, David ultimately succeeds him, and all Israel is united under his rule. The Ark of the Covenant is transferred from Shiloh, the center of tribal confederation gatherings, to the new capital in Jerusalem. State power is further enhanced by a series of successful skirmishes with pagan neighbors, and the priesthood itself is quickly attached to the court.

"David's house becomes the sacred interpreter of Israel's mission to the world," says Moscati, "and his reign goes down in Hebrew tradition as the type of the golden age, to be regretted for its passing."

But from the standpoint of Biblical faith far more is involved here than a merely unique type of ancient Near Eastern historiography. The Bible rather insists that

God's covenant with Abraham, a covenant confirmed at Sinai, will be perpetuated through His covenant with David.

> And it came to pass . . . that the word of the Lord came unto Nathan, saying, Go and tell my servant David, Thus saith the Lord. . . . [Thy seed] shall build an house for my name, and I will stablish the throne of his kingdom for ever. I will be his father, and he shall be my son. If he commit iniquity, I will chasten him with the rod of men, and with the stripes of the children of men: But my mercy shall not depart away from him, as I took it from Saul, whom I put away before thee. And thine house and thy kingdom shall be established for ever before thee: thy throne shall be established for ever (II Samuel 7: 4, 5, 13-16. Compare I Chronicles 17: 11-14; Psalm 89).

If one thing stands out crystal clear, it is the fact that ancient Israel knew nothing of "image building." Other nations might attempt to "puff" their heroes by engaging in a type of pious public relations; but such activities were completely foreign to the Biblical writers.

At the peak of political power David was a brave soldier, a skillful administrator, a shrewd statesman, a democratic monarch, and a genuinely committed servant of the Lord. But David was also a cruel victor in a cruel age; and his adulterous relationship with Bathsheba led him to conspire the murder of her husband Uriah, one of David's own most trusted and valiant warriors.

> And the Lord sent Nathan unto David. And he came unto him, and said unto him, There were two men in one city; the one rich, and the other poor. The rich man had exceeding many flocks and herds: But the poor man had nothing, save one little ewe lamb, which he had bought and nourished up: and it grew up together with him, and with his children; it did eat of his own meat,

and drank of his own cup, and lay in his bosom, and was unto him as a daughter. And there came a traveller unto the rich man, and he spared to take of his own flock and of his own herd, to dress for the wayfaring man that was come unto him; but took the poor man's lamb, and dressed it for the man that was come to him. And David's anger was greatly kindled against the man; and he said to Nathan, As the Lord liveth, the man that hath done this thing shall surely die: And he shall restore the lamb fourfold, because he did this thing, and because he had no pity.

And Nathan said to David, Thou art the man. Thus saith the Lord God of Israel, I anointed thee king over Israel, and I delivered thee out of the hand of Saul; And I gave thee thy master's house, and thy master's wives into thy bosom, and gave thee the house of Israel and of Judah; and if that had been too little, I would moreover have given unto thee such and such things. Wherefore hast thou despised the commandment of the Lord, to do evil in his sight? thou hast killed Uriah the Hittite with the sword, and hast taken his wife to be thy wife. . . . And David said unto Nathan, I have sinned against the Lord (II Samuel 12: 1-9, 13).

"By comparison with the rest of oriental historical writing," says Moscati, "this narrative is striking in more than one respect: in its unusual theme of private life; in its account of the submission of political authority to a superior moral principle; and, finally, in the expression of this principle through the mouth of the characteristic figure, the prophet, who will dominate so much of Israel's later history."

But, more than that, this masterpiece of literature points up the important Biblical theme that the sinner can yet be a saint.

Unlike so many contemporary political figures, David made no attempt to whitewash his terrible crime. He promptly confessed his transgression when confronted by the evidence. "And Nathan said unto David, The Lord also hath put away thy sin; thou shalt not die"[2] (verse 13).

To the end, just as Abraham and Moses were reckoned as friends of God, David remained a man after God's own heart. That does not mean that he did not pay a heavy price for his sins.

Apart from a plethora of domestic woes that haunted him into the grave, David only named Solomon as his regal heir when it became apparent that another son, Adonijah, was plotting a *coup d'etat.*

Israel's "Golden Age"

Solomon, for all of his fabled glory, has properly been described as "a great son of a greater father." Under his long and prosperous reign, the frontiers of Israel were pushed back to the Euphrates and down to the borders of Egypt.

In light of recent events in the Middle East, it is interesting to note that Solomon's kingdom extended well beyond Damascus in the north, and as far southward as Elath, then known as Ezion-geber. William Sanford LaSor notes that he was in this ancient port city in 1957, when perhaps the first Israeli ship since Solomon's day tied up at Elath after sailing through the Gulf of Aqabah.

Solomon not only introduced Israel to the possibility of international maritime trade; he also transformed Ezion-geber itself into what archaeologist Nelson Glueck once called "the Pittsburgh of Palestine."

---

2. While the designations of saints and sinners might reflect Christian rather than Jewish thought, Aggadic treatment of David is both copious and virtually always laudatory. He is recognized as "David king of Israel [who] lives forever." At the same time, when it is recognized that the king appointed a *mazkir,* a recorder, to keep account of his daily actions, it is somewhat amazing in light of recent political scandals in the United States that the unsavory Uriah logs were not kept secret in the name of executive privilege and national security.

In Solomon's day, Ezion-geber had the largest blast furnace in the ancient Near East, together with copper refineries and factories which produced tools and other metalware for foreign and domestic markets. It is not at all improbable that the Queen of Sheba made the long trip from southern Arabia to negotiate a commercial treaty with Israel's king, who was cutting into the lucrative caravan trade in her own backyard.

While this successful diplomatic venture led Solomon to give the queen all that she desired, the Bible also indicates that he was a clever horse trader in the most literal sense of the term (I Kings 10: 1-29). Indeed, the Biblical indication that his agents exported horses and chariots to other nations at a handsome profit is supported by the archaeological discovery of 450 stalls from the era.

Yet from the religious perspective all of Solomon's commercial pursuits are overshadowed by the Temple he built for the Lord God of Israel.

While David himself had earlier sought divine approval for such a project, the Lord had rejected the plan, promising instead that *He* would build a "house" for David—a dynasty, that is, whose throne would go on forever (II Samuel 7: 1-13). In the end, it was this pledge that gave comfort to a king advanced in years and nearing the close of an illustrious career:

Yes, my House stands firm with God:
   He has made an everlasting covenant with me,
All in order, well assured;
   Does He not bring to flower all that saves me,
All I desire?

Between the lines of these "last words of David" rests a quiet confidence in the grace of God which could only be known by a man who had risen to the exalted office of king only after he had experienced the rigors of life as a shepherd and warrior.

However, when Solomon succeeded his father on the throne, he did so as one who had been "born to the purple." So it is not surprising that he should revive the idea of building the Lord's Temple in the seat of the nation's religious and political life.

Suave internationalist that he was, Solomon enlisted the aid of Hiram the King of Tyre, knowing that Phoenician artisans were more skilled than the Israelites in working bronze, stone, and wood. Said Solomon to David's old friend:

> Thou knowest how that David my father could not build an house unto the name of the Lord his God for the wars which were about him on every side, until the Lord put them under the soles of his feet. But now the Lord my God hath given me rest on every side, so that there is neither adversary nor evil occurrent. And, behold, I purpose to build an house unto the name of the Lord my God, as the Lord spake unto David my father, saying, Thy son, whom I will set upon thy throne in thy room, he shall build an house unto my name (I Kings 5: 3-5).

Although the size of the Temple was rather modest when compared to contemporary structures, skilled Phoenician craftsmen assisted the Israelites in building one of the most impressive sanctuaries of the ancient Near East.[3]

Two bronze pillars were cast to stand at the entrance of the Temple. There was also an elaborate bronze water vessel and several smaller ones, presumably for ablutions. The furnishings—such as the table of shewbread, the candlesticks, and the censers—were of pure gold.

While much of the stone may have been quarried from the rock on which Jerusalem stands, the copper castings

---

3. The Temple was about 90 x 30 x 45 feet in size. It is interesting, however, to note William Foxwell Albright's observation that modern metallurgists remain mystified as to the method used by Solomon for the reduction of copper.

undoubtedly were fashioned from ore drawn out of Solomon's own famous mines.

When this magnificent edifice was finally completed, the Ark of the Covenant was brought from Mount Zion, in David's old city, to its new resting place within the Temple.

In a move to demonstrate solidarity with his past, Solomon himself presided at the spectacular dedicatory rites for the Temple. His lengthy prayer of consecration noted that the God of the fathers had delivered Israel out of the land of bondage that He might claim Israel as His own "inheritance." Declared the king:

> 'O Lord God of Israel, there is no god like thee in heaven above or on earth beneath, keeping covenant with thy servants and showing them constant love while they continue faithful to thee in heart and soul. . . . Now therefore, O Lord God of Israel, keep this promise of thine to thy servant David my father . . . . But can God indeed dwell on earth? Heaven itself, the highest heaven, cannot contain thee; how much less this house that I have built!' (I Kings 8: 23, 25-27, NEB.)

The Lord whom the heavens could not contain responded to this moving demonstration of man's humility by flooding the Tabernacle with His own glory. The *Shekhinah,* the very Presence of God, still resided in the midst of Israel!

However, while the cloud of Presence testified to God's own inviolable covenant, the Bible indicates that Solomon's sense of commitment was far more ambiguous. For no sooner do we read that he spent seven years building the Temple than we also learn that it took 13 years to complete his own palace. "In other words," says Dr. LaSor, "it was about two for Solomon to one for God."

While this represents a pretty good illustration of the king's sense of values, the Temple itself could not help but offend the sensitivities of many Israelites. For its supposedly Phoenician design would be tantamount to an invasion of Canaanite culture right into the center of the nation's life and worship.

"Any conservative Israelite who cherished the faith of his fathers must have been shocked by Solomon's bold imitation of foreign ways," claims Dr. Anderson. "It took some years for the Temple, which was essentially a state sanctuary, to become the focus of Israelite affection."

If this was not enough, broadmindedness proved to be the fatal flaw in Solomon's fascinating personality. None other than the Bible itself condemns the king for his assimilationist policies:

> For it came to pass, when Solomon was old, that his wives turned away his heart after other gods: and his heart was not perfect with the Lord his God, as was the heart of David his father. For Solomon went after Ashtoreth the goddess of the Zidonians, and after Milcom the abomination of the Ammonites. And Solomon did evil in the sight of the Lord . . .
>
> Wherefore the Lord said unto Solomon, Forasmuch as this is done of thee, and thou hast not kept my covenant and my statutes, which I have commanded thee, I will surely rend the kingdom from thee, and will give it to thy servant (I Kings 11: 4-6, 11).

God's censure found expression in Israel's political life. At home, Solomon had alienated many of his constituents by pressing his massive public works program through a combination of taxation, forced labor, and downright nepotism. Abroad, a resurgence of nationalism led to new political intrigues inspired by Assyria and

Egypt. The days of a strong united monarchy were numbered.[4]

With Solomon's death, smoldering rivalries burst into flame, causing a rupture in national unity. On the surface, the break could be attributed to ancient tribal jealousies. But underneath there was evidence of the long-held Biblical principle that moral guilt and political decadence go hand-in-glove.

Two Kingdoms

The actual rift in the covenant community raised havoc on both the political and religious fronts. In the South, the Kingdom of Judah lost much of its former political power, even though it retained control of Jerusalem, the center of the nation's spiritual life. In the North, the Kingdom of Israel, while deprived of so powerful a symbol, nevertheless overshadowed Judah in size and strength.

However, in spite of certain political advantages, Israel very foolishly attempted to adapt to the loss of the Temple by establishing its own sanctuaries. It also maintained, indeed promoted, Solomon's tolerant policy toward foreign cults.

This expediency, supported by both the court and the priesthood, inspired the emergence of the prophets, whose politically independent preachments warned of impending doom in the face of callous apostasy.

Typical of these fearless champions of Israel's God was Elijah the Tishbite, who holds a revered place in Jewish tradition. A rugged individualist if there ever was one, Elijah was divinely empowered to stand against the 450 prophets of Baal and the 400 prophets of Asherah who ate at Jezebel's table (I Kings 18: 19).

4. Solomon hoped to destroy the last remnants of tribal independence by establishing 12 administrative districts controlled by the central authority. Two of these district administrators were sons-in-law of the king.

Unlike those false prophets, Elijah demanded that the Israelites return to the Mosaic tradition. "How long will you go limping with two different opinions?" he chided. "If the Lord is God, follow him; but if Baal, then follow him" (I Kings 18: 21, RSV).

While God's power was subsequently demonstrated in a dramatic way at Mount Carmel, an ingrained syncretism continued to plague the spiritual life of Israel. And with this spiritual decline there was a corresponding diminution of social morality characterized by an effete affluence which could only exist at the expense of the grinding poverty of the deprived.

In the face of this injustice, Amos was commissioned by God to leave his herds in Tekoa and prophesy against the economic tyrants and corrupt jurists who, he declared, "sell the righteous for silver, and the needy for a pair of shoes" (Amos 2: 6, RSV).

Hosea also denounced this moral decadence in the name of a God who had established a binding covenant with wayward Israel. Accusing his countrymen of spiritual harlotry, Hosea reminded them that God's holy love involved both judgment and mercy. This God who had taught Israel to walk, he said, could also discipline a rebellious child. Yet behind any discipline rested the love of the waiting Father:

> *When Israel was a child, I loved him,*
> *and out of Egypt I called my son.*

Meanwhile, external pressures mounted even as the northern kingdom was racked by internal moral decay. At one point, King Jehu attempted to maintain an uneasy peace by paying tribute to Shalmaneser III, an action still preserved on the celebrated black obelisk of the pompous Assyrian monarch. "In those days," says the Bible, "the Lord began to cut off parts of Israel" (II Kings 10: 32, RSV).

Although a brief period of prosperity coincided with the reign of Jeroboam II, crisis followed crisis and, in 723/722, Israel's capital at Samaria fell into Assyrian hands. In equating defeat with decadence, Isaiah had shown little sympathy for the Ephraimites in Samaria:

> Woe to the proud crown of the drunkards of Ephraim, and to the fading flower of its glorious beauty . . . . Behold, the Lord has one who is mighty and strong; like a storm of hail, a destroying tempest, like a storm of mighty, overflowing waters, he will cast down to the earth with violence. The proud crown of the drunkards of Ephraim will be trodden under foot (Isaiah 28: 1-3, RSV).

The sober prophecy was translated into historical reality when the Assyrian king Sargon II deported 27,290 Israelites into the region of Persia, and repopulated Israel itself with colonists from Elam, Syria, and Babylonia.

Through all of this the southern kingdom, Judah, was able to maintain relatively stable government under the Davidic dynasty, which retained control of the throne in Jerusalem.

There had been that period of spectacular progress under King Uzziah, who expanded commerce, developed agriculture, and saw victory on the Philistine plain, thanks to a modernized army.

It was during this period that Isaiah, an urbane intellectual, was called to be a prophet, embarking on a career that was to last for 40 years. Together with this divine commission, Isaiah had the good fortune of serving as a royal scribe in the court of Uzziah, thereby being privy to the most delicate affairs of state (II Chronicles 26: 22).

As Israel wilted under mounting Assyrian pressures, Isaiah warned Judah that any alliance against this rising superpower would involve "a covenant with death."

A similar warning was sounded by Micah, a rural prophet like Amos, and possibly a disciple of the more sophisticated Isaiah. Convinced that Israel's sin had infected Judah, Micah delivered a message that was sure to lose friends and alienate people:

Zion shall be plowed as a field;
 Jerusalem shall become a heap of ruins,
And the mountain of the house [the Temple complex]
 A wooded height.

While people generally may have dismissed this "prophet of doom," Judah's shifting political fortunes had to make sober men pause and wonder.

There had been that heartstopping confrontation with the Assyrian forces of Sennacherib, who boasted that he had Judah "shut up like a bird in a cage." However, he did not know that Judah's able and righteous King Hezekiah had taken precautions against such an eventuality by building a conduit to supply Jerusalem with water in time of siege. Finally, just as Isaiah predicted, the Holy City was temporarily spared as the Assyrians retreated in the wake of a plague and pressing problems at home.[5]

However, Judah itself was about to suffer a plague of a different sort. For Hezekiah's benevolent reign was followed by those of Manasseh and his son Amon, who were scorned by righteous Jews as worse than the heathen.

By the time Josiah ascended the throne, the God of Israel had been reduced to a Canaanite Baal, and his sanctuaries had been turned into brothels. Black magic and every imaginable type of superstition had replaced the religion of the prophets.

5. II Kings 19: 32-37 records Isaiah's prediction and Sennacherib's hasty retreat. The Assyrians' premature announcement of victory is preserved on Sennacherib's clay prism. Arab women and children still bathe and wash laundry in Hezekiah's conduit. This aqueduct, discovered in 1880 by a boy who fell into the Pool of Siloam, is 1700 feet long and is still considered a remarkable engineering feat.

As Josiah battled against these obscene corruptions, a remarkable discovery was made in the Temple. For it was there that the forgotten and forsaken Law of Moses was recovered, and its timeless message was restored as the vehicle for national revival. That recovered Law today includes the Book of Deuteronomy.[6]

As the words of Torah gripped the hearts of Judah, its wayward people realized at long last that they were faced with the eternal choice between light or darkness, victory or defeat:

> The Lord our God made a covenant with us in Horeb. Not with our fathers did the Lord make this covenant, but *with us,* who are all of us here alive this day (Deuteronomy 5: 2, 3, RSV).

> I call heaven and earth to witness against you this day, that I have set before you life and death, blessing and curse; therefore choose life . . . that you may dwell in the land which the Lord swore to your fathers, to Abraham, to Isaac, and to Jacob, to give them (Deuteronomy 30: 19, 20, RSV).

"The reform of Josiah . . . was borne on a wave of nationalism that swept through Judah during the last days of the Assyrian empire," says Bernhard Anderson. "For a while it seemed as though the people were standing on the threshold of a Golden Age like the glorious era of David's empire.

"But the patriots were awakened from their daydream by the shock of a swift succession of events, beginning with the untimely death of Josiah and culminating in the fall of the nation," he writes. "Nationalism died hard during those crowded years, for many prophets flourished by preaching a comfortable message of peace when

---

6. Deuteronomy comes from two Greek words which together mean the Second Law. The Hebrew title is simply "These are the words," the opening phrase of the book. Scholars differ widely regarding the date and composition of Deuteronomy. The author has elected to take the Biblical account of its recovery at face value.

there was no peace, by promising that affairs would soon return to the good old days of national glory."

In the providence of God, Judah's days were actually numbered, even though it had managed to escape a fate similar to that of the northern kingdom for 135 years.

Judah's enemy was no longer Assyria, which had been overthrown by the Medes, but Babylonia, in its last brief period of renewed prosperity. In 586, Nebuchadnezzar conquered and destroyed Jerusalem, burned down the Temple, and transported a large segment of the population into slavery in Babylon.

Although Jeremiah had been maligned and imprisoned as a quisling, he had correctly insisted that resistance was futile, that Judah's defeat was in keeping with the inscrutable will of God:

> Declare ye in Judah, and publish in Jerusalem; and say, Blow ye the trumpet in the land: cry, gather together, and say, Assemble yourselves, and let us go into the defenced cities. Set up the standard toward Zion: retire, stay not: for I will bring evil from the north, and a great destruction. The lion is come up from his thicket, and the destroyer of [nations] is on his way; he is gone forth from his place to make thy land desolate; and thy cities shall be laid waste, without an inhabitant. For this gird you with sackcloth, lament and howl: for the fierce anger of the Lord is not turned back from us (Jeremiah 4: 5-8).

The Exile and its lessons

As brutal as the lesson might be, Jeremiah was convinced that exile alone would cure Judah of its reliance upon the external trappings of civil religion. At the same time, he cherished the hope that his people would one day return to their land and establish a new commonwealth under a Davidic king.

So strong was this element of hope that the prophet bought a plot of land in his native village of Anathoth even as Jerusalem was under siege. After ordering his secretary to place the deeds "in an earthenware vessel, that they may last for a long time," Jeremiah declared from prison: "Thus says the Lord of hosts, the God of Israel: Houses and fields and vineyards shall again be bought in this land" (Jeremiah 32: 14, 15, RSV).

Ezekiel, the great prophet of the Exile, shared this same conviction, an optimism born out of his vision of the valley of dry bones. In the midst of this vision, the Lord declared to His spokesman:

> Son of man, these bones are the whole house of Israel: behold, they say, Our bones are dried, and our hope is lost: we are cut off for our parts. Therefore prophesy and say unto them, Thus saith the Lord God; Behold, O my people, I will open your graves, and [raise you from] your graves, and bring you [home] into the land of Israel. And ye shall know that I am the Lord . . . . And [I] shall put my spirit in you, and ye shall live, and I shall place you in your own land (Ezekiel 37: 11-14).

This prophetic vision of Israel's ultimate return was matched by a strong sense of national and spiritual cohesion among the exiles themselves. Even in their absence from *eretz Yisroel*, most of them retained fond and unfaded memories of their beloved homeland:

> *By the rivers of Babylon,*
> *There we sat down, yea, we wept,*
> *When we remembered Zion. . . .*
> *How shall we sing the Lord's song*
> *In a strange land?*
> *If I forget thee, O Jerusalem,*
> *Let my right hand forget her cunning.*

If I do not remember thee,
Let my tongue cleave to the roof of my mouth;
If I prefer not Jerusalem
Above my chief joy. (Psalm 137: 1-6.)

It is true that there were some defectors among the exiles, who were assimilated into Babylonian life and culture. This group, the size of which is uncertain, established their own communities at Tel-abib on the Chebar Canal near Nippur. There they intermarried, purchased homes, and engaged in normal business pursuits. Some even abandoned the God of Israel for the gods of the Babylonians.

However, most Jews were profoundly affected by their experience in exile. For it was there "by the rivers of Babylon" that the first seeds were sown for the compilation of the *Talmud* and establishment of the synagogue.

But, more than that, any vestiges of paganism were firmly and finally purged from the religion of Israel. Ironically, it took the exile to make the monotheistic ideal of Moses normative in the daily walk of a chastened people.

"It was in exile, deprived of the outward and visible tokens of God's presence—the Holy City and the sacred Temple—that they learned that God meant more to them in adversity than in prosperity," says William Neil.

"It became clear that the disaster which had overtaken Israel was no accident of history, far less the superior power of the gods of the Babylonians," he says, "but the Lord's judgment upon His wayward people from whom more had been demanded because so much more had been given."

Renewal in Judah

Now that this harsh lesson had been learned, an amazing event took place in the classroom of history. In 539

B.C.E., Cyrus of Persia defeated Babylonia just as Babylonia had trounced Assyria short years before. Commencement day dawned for the Children of Israel!

Whereas earlier conquerors had adopted a policy of shifting the conquered to other lands, Cyrus directed his administrators to restore displaced minorities to their native countries. Moreover, the Persian emperor issued a written edict on behalf of Israel:[7]

> Thus says Cyrus king of Persia: The Lord, the God of heaven, has given me all the kingdoms of the earth, and he has charged me to build him a house at Jerusalem, which is in Judah. Whoever is among you of all his people, may his God be with him, and let him go up to Jerusalem, which is in Judah, and rebuild the house of the Lord, the God of Israel—he is the God who is in Jerusalem; and let each survivor, in whatever place he sojourns, be assisted by the men of his place with silver and gold, with goods and with beasts, besides freewill offerings for the house of God which is in Jerusalem (Ezra 1: 2-4, RSV).

If God could use the Assyrians as "the rod" of his anger against a rebellious people, then it was just as possible for Him to ordain a pagan king as the instrument for the restoration of a chastened Israel. In fact, the Lord said of Cyrus through the prophet, "He is my shepherd, and shall perform all my pleasure" (Isaiah 44: 28).[8]

In his royal decree, the benevolent Persian directed

7. The famous Cyrus Cylinder containing the royal edict regarding conquered peoples is now deposited in the British Museum. This edict is preserved in two versions, Hebrew and Aramaic — the latter being the *lingua franca* in international relations at that time. While the Cyrus Cylinder ascribes the Persians' triumph to Marduk, Cyrus regarded himself as the patron of the gods of all of his subjects.

8. In addition to being called a shepherd of Israel, God also refers to Cyrus as His anointed (Isaiah 45: 1). This is an instance when two messianic titles are conferred upon a Gentile leader.

93

the return of "the golden and silver vessels of the house of God, which Nebuchadnezzar took forth out of the temple which is at Jerusalem" (Ezra 6: 5). Moreover, since the Israelites had no idols like the other nations, tradition has it that Cyrus provided the furnishings for the new Temple, when, in 538, 50,000 expatriates returned to Jerusalem under Sheshbazzar (Ezra 5: 14), regarded as a prince of the Davidic line.

But that was only the beginning. This first wave of returnees was followed at a much later date by two other contingents, one led by Ezra (457), the last by Nehemiah (445). With their return, Judaism was faced with new problems and the challenges of a new age.

While the task of rebuilding the Temple was given top priority, repeated delays were caused by the pressing personal needs of the expatriates themselves. Before they could embark on any large-scale building project, they first had to reestablish themselves in a shattered city and its surrounding countryside.

The execution of construction plans was made all the more difficult because of a growing and bitter rift between the Jewish and Samaritan communities. The trouble began when the Jews rejected a Samaritan offer to help in the building program. "So the hand of friendship," says Anderson, "curled into a fist."

Behind the bitterness lay two opposing contentions. The Samaritans, on the one hand, insisted that they had remained faithful to the Mosaic tradition during the Exile. But the Jews denied that claim by arguing that their neighbors had been corrupted through intermarriage with foreigners who had settled in the land during the period of Assyrian occupation.

As the rift widened, the Samaritans sent a letter to Persian authorities accusing the Jews of seditious sentiments and demanding that the building program be halted. In turn, the Samaritans decided to build their own temple on Mount Gerizim. By the time of Jesus, therefore, it was common knowledge that "the Jews have no dealings with the Samaritans" (John 4: 9).

However, despite all of these frustrations, work was eventually resumed on the Temple in Jerusalem. It took four years of hard work under the enthusiastic prompting of Haggai and Zechariah to complete the project; but, in 515, the house of the Lord stood once more on a hill overlooking the Holy City.

Old men who remembered Solomon's Temple wept at the sight of this more modest design (Ezra 3: 12, 13). In time, however, this second Temple won the hearts of a people who still believed that the Lord was enthroned in the midst of Israel.

Buried deep within the Jewish soul was the firm conviction that only the inward solidarity of the religious community could challenge the vicissitudes of an uncertain political future. For no one held any illusions that "the good old days" of David's rule would return in the foreseeable future.

Moreover, the day was not far off when the voice of prophecy no longer would be heard in the land. In this new setting, the priest was to assume increasing authority and responsibility for the spiritual care of the Children of Israel.

One of the most influential figures in the immediate post-exilic period was Ezra, who was not a prophet but a priest and a scribe. As the traditional founder of the Great Assembly, he is credited with laying the foundation for the normative form of Judaism for future generations.

After returning from exile with Persian authority to impose the law of the Torah upon his people, Ezra personally instituted several reforms aimed at uplifting Jewish life. Among these were a stiff ban on intermarriage, a vigorous program for observing the Sabbath and the

Sabbatical Year, and a revival of the Feast of Tabernacles (Nehemiah 8: 13-18).

While the *Talmud* ascribes to him the final decision on the text of the Pentateuch, Ezra is further credited with initiating a drive to make the Bible intelligible to his own and future generations.

To appreciate the breadth of his commitment and scholarship, it must be remembered that Moses and even David did not write in the Hebrew we know today. It is probable, for example, that Moses wrote either in the cuneiform of the Amarna letters or in the hieroglyphs of the Egyptian court in which he was raised. Moreover, David's scribe most likely used an old Phoenician script similar to that found on the Moabite Stone.

It was therefore left to Ezra and the Sages of the Great Assembly (*Knesseth Ha-Gedolah*) to update the ancient Biblical text by recasting it in the square Hebrew letters still familiar to contemporary students of the Bible.

But the Great Assembly did even more than that. It also served as the spiritual and legislative institution of the post-prophetic era, laying the foundations of the *Halakhah,* the *Midrash,* and the *Aggadah.* Above all, these Sages were ultimately responsible for transferring religious authority from the hereditary priesthood to the scholars (*hakhamim*). Ever since then, the scholar has been accorded a singular place of honor in the Commonwealth of Israel.

This recognition of the authority of scholarship found expression in the so-called triple maxim of the Great Assembly:

"Be slow in giving judgment" represented a commitment to judicial decisions based on precedents, due process, and the rule of law.

"Establish many disciples" recognized the need to train numerous experts who were neither priests nor levites.

These *Sopherim* established forever the authority of learning in Judaism.

"And make a barrier about the Law" upheld the sacredness of the secular and raised "a halo of sanctity" above Jewish personal and public life.

The Feast of Purim (Lots)

Meanwhile, it was also in this period of Persian rule that the Jews initiated one of their most joyous festivals, the Feast of *Purim.* Ironically, this happy celebration grew out of a near tragedy. It all came about in this way:

King Ahasuerus (Xerxes), so the story goes, fell in love with a Jewish beauty named Esther and made her his queen. Unknown to the Persian monarch, Esther was the cousin of Mordecai: a member of the court and, according to Talmudic *Aggadah,* none other than the prophet Malachi!

Whatever the case, Ahasuerus had appointed an inflated buffoon named Haman as his prime minister. In turn, Haman sought to exercise his newly acquired power by demanding that people bow down before him, something that Mordecai refused to do.

Therefore, when Haman discovered that his recalcitrant subordinate was a Jew, he responded to the affront by requesting the king's consent to liquidate all of the Israelites within the empire. When permission was granted, Haman cast lots to choose the day on which to carry out his murderous plot. The date decreed by a frivolous throw of the dice was the thirteenth of Adar.

However, Mordecai learned of Haman's scheme in time, and urged Esther to appeal to the king on behalf of her people. Unhappily, the queen wavered because Ahasuerus was not then aware of her own Jewish origin.

But Haman still never got the chance to carry out his evil design. For, in the meantime, Mordecai saved the king's life by reporting a plot against him. Moreover,

Esther ultimately summoned enough courage to inform Ahasuerus about the true nature of Haman's lethal hatred against her people. In the end, Haman was hanged and Mordecai was appointed chief vizier.

Meanwhile, the king also issued a proclamation permitting the Jews to defend themselves on the day slated for the intended massacre. So successful was the battle on the thirteenth of Adar that most Jews were able to celebrate their victory the following day. However, the fighting was so intense in the capital city of Shushan that the festivities could not begin there until the fifteenth of the month. In the Book of Esther, we are told:

> Mordecai wrote these events down and sent letters to all the Jews that were in all the provinces of the king Ahasuerus, both high and low, to enjoin them to keep the fourteenth day of the month Adar, and the fifteenth day of the same, yearly . . . and they should make them days of feasting and gladness, and of sending portions to one another and gifts to the poor. And the Jews took upon them to do as they had begun and as Mordecai had written to them.

"Ever since then Jews all over the world have celebrated *Purim* each year," says Edidin. "The Rabbis of the *Talmud* are quoted as saying that *Purim* will not be eliminated even when Messiah comes."

Observed in February or March, *Purim* means the "casting of lots," and is therefore also known as the Feast of Lots. The name comes, of course, from Haman's method of selecting a date for the liquidation of the Jews, a plan that backfired on this ancient anti-Semite!

As Haman failed, so have others who have attempted to carry out similar plots. The Jews of Egypt, for example, once observed *Cairo Purim* to celebrate their own miraculous delivery on Adar 27, 1524, when Turkish authorities beheaded the Egyptian governor following a scheme directed against both Turkey and the Jews. Still another *Purim* was instituted in Germany a century later when a baker, who declared himself a "new Haman," ended up with a noose around his own neck instead.

Yet this struggle against hatred and injustice should be as much a concern of the Christian as the Jew. For, as James Russell Lowell so aptly wrote:

> *Though the cause of evil prosper,*
> *Yet 'tis truth alone is strong;*
> *Truth forever on the scaffold,*
> *Wrong forever on the throne.*
> *Yet that scaffold sways the future,*
> *And, behind the dim unknown,*
> *Standeth God within the shadow*
> *Keeping watch above His own.*

In that confidence born of long experience, Jews still gather in their synagogues each year to read the *Megillah* (the Scroll of Esther) on the eve and morning of *Purim*. And there, as they contemplate the mischief wrought against their people by all of the Hamans of history, they will recite the customary benediction: "Blessed art Thou, O Lord our God, King of the Universe, who has kept us in life and preserved us and enabled us to reach this season."

But *Purim* is above all a time for rejoicing. In fact, it is the nearest thing that Jews have to a carnival. Youngsters boo, stamp their feet, and wave noisemakers every time the name of Haman is uttered. And, in some communities, Haman's name is even written upon the soles of shoes, so that it might be blotted out underfoot.

Chanukah (Lights)

Meanwhile, there is yct one other Jewish festival that witnesses to the age-long struggle for religious freedom and toleration. It is known as *Chanukah,* the Feast of Dedication, or popularly, the Feast of Lights.

Although *Chanukah* sometimes coincides with Christmas, the Feast of Lights was instituted almost two centuries before the birth of Him whom Christians hail as the Light of the World.

The first *Chanukah* occurred on the twenty-fifth day of Kislev, in 165 B.C.E., when Judas the Maccabee solemnly rededicated the Temple, which had been desecrated three years earlier by the Seleucid monarch Antiochus IV, who called himself *Epiphanes,* or "God Manifest."

Unlike other Jewish festivals, *Chanukah* is not mentioned in the Bible, although its origin may be found in the apocryphal *Books of the Maccabees,* which provide invaluable information regarding the so-called Intertestamental Period.

With the defeat of the Persians in the decisive battles of Marathon and Salamis, the Greek Empire was established under Alexander the Great. And with Greek military power came Greek culture. In a very real sense, the latter represented a far graver threat to the Jews than all of the chariots of war.

However, the struggle between Hebraic and Hellenistic thought did not reach a crescendo until after Alexander's death, when Judea became a bone of contention between Syria and Egypt.

"So Alexander . . . died," says I Maccabees 1: 7. "And his servants bore rule every one in his place. And after his death they all put crowns upon themselves: so did their sons after them many years: and evils were multiplied in the earth."

In a struggle for power not unknown in the 20th century, Alexander's empire was divided into three kingdoms—the Macedonian kingdom of northern Greece, the Seleucid kingdom of Syria and Asia Minor, and the Ptolemaic kingdom of the Nile.

While he was still a general, Ptolemy I entered Jerusalem in 320 B.C.E., thereby establishing Egyptian sovereignty over the land of Judah, a political reality in Middle Eastern affairs that was not to be challenged for more than a century.

During this period of Ptolemaic rule, Hellenistic culture spread even beyond the borders of the kingdom, and Greek became the international language of learning and commerce.

With young Jews no longer able to speak in the mother tongue, the Jews of Egypt decided to take the momentous step of translating the Hebrew Scriptures into Greek. The result was the *Septuagint,* which, according to apocryphal legend, was translated by seventy elders in seventy days.

But the truth is even more compelling than the legend. For, as Werner Keller aptly observes: "What had previously been made known only in the sanctuary, only in the old tongue, and only to the one nation, was now all at once available and intelligible for people of other tongues and other races. The hitherto carefully guarded door into the 'tents of Shem' was thrown wide open."

However, in spite of so great a contribution to the world, Judah herself suffered a staggering blow in 195 B.C.E., when Antiochus III defeated Ptolemy V at the sources of the Jordan and established Seleucid control over Israel. That victory was only a portend of the troubled days that lay ahead.

With the active support of some apostate Jewish priests, Antiochus Epiphanes extended Hellenism in the land of Judah. Moreover, in 168, he plundered the Temple in Jerusalem and initiated the worship of Olympian Zeus within its sacred precincts. To make matters worse, Antiochus decreed that death awaited those who continued to practice the traditional sacrifices, the Sabbath, circumcision, and other Jewish rites.

As thousands of Jews valiantly resisted this assault upon their ancient faith, armed rebellion finally broke out against the hated Seleucids under the leadership of Mattathias, a priest of the Hasmonean family, and his illustrious son, Judah the Maccabee ("The Hammer").

In spite of seemingly overwhelming odds, the Jewish guerrilla forces defeated the enemy at Emmaus, then went on to regain the sacked and gutted Temple at Jerusalem. In all, the skirmishes lasted for three years before Judah was freed from the blight of paganism.

Therefore, when *Chanukah* comes each year, Jews around the world remember that historic fight for religious freedom. They also recall the reputed miracle that occurred when the Maccabees cleansed the Temple so that true worship could be resumed.

Unfortunately, the victors found only enough pure oil to keep the Temple lamps burning for one day. But miraculously, so the story goes, the oil lasted for eight days, until a fresh supply could be prepared by the priests. This, then, is the significance symbolized by the eight-branched *Menorah* used at *Chanukah* to this day.

The fact that one candle is lit each day for eight days has led to *Chanukah* being called the Feast of Lights. But it is more properly understood as a festival of dedication. Moreover, as Theodor Gaster observes, *Chanukah* teaches that "the God whom a man is required to serve is the God revealed to him in the history and experience of his people, not the idol imposed from without.

"The condition of independence is consecration," says Gaster. "And its hallmark is devotion."

Meanwhile, *Chanukah* is the only Jewish holiday that commemorates an act of war, an aspect of the human condition which the prophets deplored. Consequently, it is quite significant that Jews still pay tribute to this ancient victory by including the words of Zechariah in their observance of this joyous festival: "Not by might, nor by power, but by my spirit, saith the Lord of hosts" (Zechariah 4: 6).

4

The Times of the Gentiles

"DON'T TRY TO TELL ME about the love of Jesus," the
old Jewish woman said scornfully. "I have seen it demonstrated!"

Anger flashed through those ancient eyes as the woman
recalled that black day in Eastern Europe when three
priests led a hate-filled mob from the church and into the
ghetto.

Illiterate peasants held the burnished brass crucifix
against the late afternoon sun, as the equally unlettered
priests themselves raised hoarse voices in the age-old cry:
"Get the dirty Jews! Get the Christ-killers!"

Long years had failed to dim the old woman's bitter
memories of that infamous day when the irrational mob
killed, raped, and plundered in the name of Him who
once was hailed by mocking Roman soldiers as "the King
of the Jews."

And the old woman's contempt for "the love of Jesus"
is shared by countless Jews the world over. For through

the centuries they have been maligned, maimed, and murdered by so-called followers of the Galilean.

Origins of anti-Semitism

Edward H. Flannery, an able Roman Catholic scholar and the author of *The Anguish of the Jews,* was led to write his important study of anti-Semitism after he had accompanied a young Jewish couple on a walk through midtown Manhattan one holiday season.

During the course of their walk, Flannery recalls, the young woman winced as she observed the cross on top of the Grand Central Building. "That cross makes me shudder," she said painfully. "It is like an evil presence."

Knowing that his friend was generally well disposed toward Christians, her reaction raised several questions for Flannery himself. The most pressing one was this: How did the cross, the supreme symbol of universal love, become a sign of fear, of evil, for this young Jewess?

"It soon became clear," says Flannery, "that her fearful reaction to it was the fruit of a knowledge which she, but not I, had—a knowledge of the immense suffering undergone by her people at the hands of Christians for many centuries.

"It was," he adds, "my first introduction to the problem of anti-Semitism."

Jules Isaac, the noted Jewish historian who was himself a victim of the Nazi terror, summarily dismisses the notion that anti-Semitism has always existed because of Israel's separatism, "religious intransigence," and "persistent non-assimilation" in the midst of other peoples and cultures.

"That a pagan anti-Semitism existed in antiquity is incontestable," Isaac concedes. "But it turns out to have been much more localized in time and space than is generally believed."

The fact is, says Isaac, that Judaism prospered in Babylonia for centuries following the Exile in the sixth century B.C.E. Similarly, the Jews who migrated to China eventually disappeared into the mass of the Chinese population.

"It could even be maintained that Israel has a natural gift for assimilation," he contends. "Throughout history there have always been assimilable and assimilated elements in Jewish culture, depending upon the reception the Jews have encountered, the environment in which they have found themselves."

Were it not for Jewish "religious intransigence," he writes, the Jews could not have given Mohammedan and Christian "the torch of monotheism, the belief in One All-powerful and Eternal God." In fact, he notes, Jesus Himself agreed that the first commandment was this: "Hear, O Israel: The Lord our God, the Lord is one" (Mark 12: 29, RSV).

Of course, Christians might argue that Hebrew Scripture itself is replete with accounts of pagan anti-Semitism. They have only to point to Exodus, Esther, and the apocryphal Books of the Maccabees to prove a dubious point. To be sure, Pharaoh preceded Pilate, Haman preceded Hitler, and Nebuchadnezzar antedated Nasser by more than 2,500 years.

But all of this only substantiates the point that Isaac is attempting to prove: Were it not for Jewish "religious intransigence," a pagan world would have remained in spiritual darkness. For Babylonian, Egyptian, Greek, and Roman antagonism against the Jews was largely directed against a stubborn people who showed contempt for carnal gods and displayed what Seneca interpreted to be a reprehensible sign of laziness in observing the Sabbath.

Jewish intransigence on these points so inflamed Roman authorities that Tacitus declared: "Roman tempers flared because *only the Jews* refused to yield."[1] As Christians, we can only applaud such courage in the face of overwhelming odds.

Jules Isaac also debunks the myth that anti-Semitism erupted (even in ancient times) because the Jews allegedly had "that gift for making money which earned them such renown." Isaac rather notes that the knowledgeable Marcel Simon has written: "When one considers the [Roman] Empire as a whole, the Jewish population included a large majority of poor people. . . . The complaint most often made against the Jews is not that they were rolling in wealth, but that they were ragged and dirty."

Since then, anti-Semitism has been attributed to phenomena outside the Jewish community itself. Among the most noteworthy psychological interpretations are those which link the virus to a projected form of self-hatred or to the need to find a handy scapegoat when personal or national problems seem insurmountable.

However, it remains one of the supreme ironies of history that anti-Semitism found a formidable ally in a theologically unsophisticated Church. Indeed, this cancer only became more inflamed as many who claimed to follow the Prince of Peace cursed his ancient people with a misplaced text.

In analyzing this anomaly, Jules Isaac came to the conclusion that "the teaching of contempt" rested upon three "erroneous" Christian themes:

> . . . Judaism at the time of Jesus was in a state of moral and spiritual decline.

> . . . The dispersion of the Jews represented a form of providential punishment for the crucifixion.

---

1. *Augebat iras quod soli Judaei non cessissent.*

> . . . The Jews, and the Jews alone, are guilty of
> the monstrous crime of "deicide"—that is,
> killing the Christ.

Before considering each of these themes in detail, it is
worth noting that the Yale Intergroup Study on Faith and
Prejudice found no present relationship between Christian Scripture and favorable or unfavorable images of the
Jews. Reporting on that study, which he directed personally, Bernhard E. Olson has written:

> The image of the Jew 'is created more or less independently of Scripture and is apparently influenced by extra-Biblical factors.' The influence
> of unreconstructed *traditions* of teachings about
> Jews ('bad history' combined with 'bad exegesis
> and theology') is discernible in modern anti-Jewish polemic.

The theory of moral decline

However, it must be admitted that the untutored reader of the New Testament can easily draw the conclusion
that Judaism at the time of Christ had sunk into the abyss
of moral and spiritual decline.

For example, a cursory reading of the Gospels would
indicate that the Pharisees were a brood of hidebound
legalists and bluenosed enemies of the Galilean. It takes
a somewhat deeper understanding of the historical context to appreciate an eternal truth—that one argues best
with his friends!

While the Pharisees shared the frailties of all mortals,
they were the men with whom the Master was most closely identified. He had nothing to do whatever with the
Herodians. And little is said about His relationship with
the Sadducees.

This fact tells us as much about Jesus' devotion to Israel as it does about the turbulent age in which He lived.

Time and again, He made it indelibly clear that He counted Himself a Jew among Jews.

It would therefore appear that Jesus scrupulously avoided any contact with members of the Herodian party. To do otherwise would have meant an identification, no matter how tenuous, with the highly unpopular house of Herod and the despised Roman oppressors.

If Jesus avoided any real contact with the Sadducees, it was undoubtedly by mutual agreement. For so much of the Master's time was spent among the *am ha-aretz,* the common people of the land, who would almost be anathema to this priestly aristocracy which counted among its adherents many ruling families under Herod.

At the same time, Jesus rejected the ascetic life of the Essenes, even though John the Baptist himself may once have been a member of this monastic sect made famous by the Dead Sea Scrolls.

Jesus conceived His mission to be within the world rather than apart from it. As He was a Jew among Jews, so too was He a Man among men. This is one of the crucial points of the Christian doctrine of the Incarnation.

But Jesus also made it indelibly clear that His Kingdom "is not of this world" (John 18: 36). Therefore, He could not accept the radical policies and dark plots of the Zealots who were bent on the overthrow of Rome.

Yet it is possible that two erstwhile revolutionaries were numbered among His disciples. For Luke records that one follower was Simon the Zealot (Luke 6: 15). And some scholars believe that the word Iscariot is a derivation of *sicarii,* which means "dagger bearer."

If this is true, it might suggest that Judas betrayed his Master because He had failed to take drastic political measures against the hated Roman army of occupation. But the irony is that the betrayal was sealed with a kiss, a symbol of peace!

Whatever the case, there was a groundswell of feeling among the freedom-loving Jews of Jesus' day for a new era of national independence, and a yearning for a messianic king like unto David.

"Messianic agitation was not considered a crime by the Jews—far from it," says Jules Isaac, "even though it was feared by the high priests because they were anxious to maintain the established order from which they were profiting.

"It was a crime only in the eyes of the Romans," he says, "for whom any messianic agitation was tantamount to the crime of rebellion against Rome, and was punished as such.

"To be sure," he adds, "Jesus was not a Zealot, but Pilate could easily have mistaken Him for one. It was perhaps as a Zealot, but in any case as a rebel, that Jesus was arrested by the Romans, tried by them, convicted, and crucified."

While there were some self-seeking Jews *of that age* who did wish His destruction, the fact remains that Jesus of Nazareth was apprehended by Roman soldiers, scourged by Roman cruelty, condemned by Roman law, and at last crucified in the Roman fashion.

However, before considering this matter further, it is first important to recognize that Jesus delivered His strongest appeals and most scathing criticisms not to Israel's quislings and enemies but rather to the nation's most stalwart and noble men. And those men were the Pharisees. Says Bernhard Olson:

> The Pharisees play a role in Judaism comparable to that of the saints in Christianity. The Christian would be offended if the Jews were to vilify the disciples, the Apostle Paul, and the Church Fathers. It is equally painful to the Jew to hear his Christian neighbor attribute all manner of

evil to the Tannaitic rabbis and, particularly, to read the many strictures against Pharisees found in Christian instructional material.

Another well-known scholar suggests that the Pharisees shared all of the virtues and the faults of the later Puritans.

"Of all the parties in Israel Jesus was closest to them," he says. "If He visited special censure on them it was because in them He saw the best hope of His people, and to their reform dedicated His attention.

"What He said in rebuke of the Pharisees," this scholar adds, "orthodox Jewish literature also said."

However, we note that the Gospels never speak of Jesus breaking bread with Sadducees, Essenes, or Herodians. That kind of intimacy is rather reserved for the Pharisees alone.

"Jesus' dinner-table argument with a Pharisee (Luke 11: 37-44)," says Gerald S. Strober, "seems to describe a legitimate, if heated, difference of opinion between Him and certain more traditionalist interpreters of basic Jewish teaching.

"There is no reason to assume that every question directed by a Pharisee to Jesus was malicious in intent," says Strober. "Nor is there any Scriptural basis for implying . . . that Jesus condemned the Pharisaic movement as a whole.

"He apparently realized that the Pharisees were a quite human group," Strober feels, "with the same faults and virtues as the rest of mankind."

Although some individual Pharisees openly opposed Jesus, others were equally sympathetic to His cause.

For example, it was the Pharisees who warned Jesus to flee the officers of Herod (Luke 13: 31). It was a Pharisee named Nicodemus who demanded that Jesus be granted a hearing on the charges made against Him (John 7: 50, 51).

"After the crucifixion," Strober notes, "Nicodemus and Joseph, also a Pharisee, retrieve Jesus' body and attend to it (John 19: 38, 39). In later years, Pharisees repeatedly come to the defense of the apostles (Acts 5: 34-39; 23: 6-9)."

Indeed, the basic spiritual integrity of the Pharisees is reflected in Gamaliel's appeal on behalf of the disciples. "Men of Israel," he declared, "take care what you do with these men. . . . For if this plan or this undertaking is of men, it will fail; but if it is of God, you will not be able to overthrow them. You might even be found opposing God" (Acts 5: 35, 38, 39, RSV).

Moreover, if Judaism was the decadent religion of Christian theory, then it may be difficult to understand why hundreds of Jews willingly went to their deaths during the terror-filled reigns of Titus and Hadrian.[2]

In contrast to the thousands of German Christians who shamefully compromised their faith during the Nazi outrage, post-Biblical Judaism stood firm in the face of Hadrian's decrees outlawing circumcision, Sabbath observance, and *Torah* instruction.

One extant tradition surviving from this period relates the typical line of interrogation in Roman courts. "Why are you to be crucified?" the prosecutor would demand of a condemned Jew. "Because," would be the reply, "I ate unleavened bread on the Passover."

There is also the account of two men who were hailed before imperial authorities to answer indictments against themselves. Asked the Roman official: "Why have you been condemned to the pyre and you to the sword?" Again, the reply: "Because we read the *Torah* and permitted our children to be circumcised."

---

2. Hadrian's reign lasted from 117 B.C. to 38 C.E. Titus, of course, was the commander who destroyed Jerusalem in 70 C.E. He later was elevated to emperorship at Rome.

While Christians also suffered during this madness, the severity of their punishment in no way equalled the persecution of the Jews. To this day, there is a *Yom Kippur* lament for the Ten Martyrs—all distinguished teachers of the Law—who perished before imperial power in this period. One was the renowned Rabbi Akiba, who went to his death savoring each precious word of the *Shema*: "Hear, O Israel, the Lord; the Lord is One."

Such sterling integrity left its mark upon the surrounding pagan cultures. Many Greeks and Romans became Jewish proselytes, while others were reckoned among the Jews themselves as "God-fearing" men because of their attachment to the God and *Torah* of Israel.

For example, Luke records the account of a Roman centurion whose beloved servant "was sick, and ready to die." What is particularly pertinent is the fact that this imperial officer did not approach the Great Physician himself. Rather, says Luke, he asked "the elders of the Jews" to implore Jesus to heal his friend.

"And when they came to Jesus," says the gospel, "they besought him earnestly, saying, 'He is worthy to have you do this for him, for he loves *our* nation, and he built us our synagogue' " (Luke 7: 4, 5, RSV).

In addition to demonstrating the wide appeal of Judaism among the pagans, this touching story further illustrates the casual, if not friendly, interaction between Jesus and many Jewish leaders of His day.

Meanwhile, the Dead Sea Scrolls have thrown added light on the once elusive Essenes, who shared many similarities with the first Christians and represented anything but a "carnal" and "worldly" Judaism at the time of Christ.

Members of this sect, drawn from a wide circle of common people, followed strict rules of purity, chastity, and temperance. While they were rigorous in their devotion to the Law, they opposed the sacrificial rites of the Temple.

Their Teacher of Righteousness met a martyr's death for his faith as he identified himself with Isaiah's Man of Sorrows and Servant of God. And although he shared some other similarities with Jesus, says Jules Isaac, "the similarities are outweighed by the differences."

At the same time, the counsel of the Teacher of Righteousness gives lie to the tragic notion that pre-Christian Judaism had degenerated into "a human attempt at reconciliation with God through obedience, good works, and piety." Said this Essene leader:

> For is man master of his way?
> No, men cannot establish their steps,
> For their justification belongs to God,
> And from His hand comes perfection of way . . .
> And without Him nothing is made.
>
> And I, if I stagger,
> God's mercies are my salvation forever;
> And if I stumble because of the sin of the flesh,
> My justification is in the righteousness of God,
> Which exists forever.

While *sola gratia* remained a major theme of the Teacher of Righteousness, says Isaac, the Pharisees themselves had not lost sight of this teaching which would become a cardinal doctrine of the Reformation. For example, he offers, it was a pious Pharisee who counseled his people: "Be not like those servants who serve their master to receive a reward" (*Pirke Avot* I, 3). Isaac therefore writes:

> This Judaism, which was represented on the one hand by masters like Hillel and the Sages of the *Pirke Avot,* [and] on the other by the Teacher of Righteousness, was, though divided, by no means a decadent religion.

115

The theory of Jewish responsibility

Thoughtful Christians should question the degree of Jewish complicity in the "monstrous crime of deicide." Are the Jews alone to blame for the death of Jesus of Nazareth?

It would be a disservice to the Gospels and sound scholarship to absolve any of the figures intimately connected with the crucifixion. It is also true that opposition mounted against the Galilean when He articulated the claim of equality with the Father.

However, if Jesus was to have been condemned for blasphemy, then the prescribed Jewish mode of execution would have been stoning, as in the later case involving Stephen (Acts 7: 54-60). As for crucifixion, the Jews considered it "the curse of God."

The Jews appear to have retained the *ius gladii,* or right to execute, in cases involving capital breaches of their own laws. But the *Mishnah* lists only four sanctioned methods of execution, and crucifixion was not one of them.[3]

It therefore remains one of the ironies of history that the power-crazed Pilate has been depicted in Christian tradition as a well-meaning, although vacillating, pawn of a subjugated race. The mythical "perfidious Jew" of the early Church has wandered over the face of the earth for more than 1900 years as mankind's scapegoat for the crime of Calvary.

What, then, really happened in those fateful hours that brought the hope of salvation to the Gentile world and two millennia of earthly damnation to the Jews themselves?

---

3. Although crucifixion has been traced back to the Phenicians, it was widely used by the Romans to punish slaves, criminals, and foreigners. The fact that Paul was beheaded, not crucified, testifies that crucifixion was not used against Roman citizens. Josephus records *(History of the Jewish War,* Volume II) that 2000 Jews were crucified by Varus (died 9 C.E.).

To begin with, it is sheer nonsense to think that the entire nation of Israel turned against Christ. "If such had been the case," asked *Moody Monthly,* "who would have proclaimed Jesus as Messiah and written the New Testament? (Were not the New Testament writers, all of them with the exception of Luke, of Jewish origin also?)

"The very heritage of the Church—its monotheism, the Old and New Testament Scriptures, the Messiah who came from Jewish lineage—is from the Jewish matrix," the magazine editorialized. "As Christians we are not estranged from the Jewish people, but tied in with them."

Jules Isaac urges us to see that the Gospels themselves indicate Jesus was tried and convicted "without the knowledge of the people, in spite of the people, and through fear of the people." But what people?

"Obviously," says Isaac, "the Jewish people—the common people, that mass of good, simple folk to whom Jesus chose to address Himself and who listened to Him enthralled.

"Why hold all the Jewish people, 'the whole race of Israel,' forever responsible, along with their unworthy leaders—with a man like Caiaphas, or with the high priesthood as a whole?" he asks. "Why dissociate the Jews from those sympathetic multitudes who crowded around Jesus?"

Isaac cites several passages in the Gospels to prove his contention that Jesus remained popular with the masses, even as He incurred the wrath of self-seeking officialdom.

Mark, for example, records that the Master became a marked man when He drove the money changers out of the Temple and accused them of turning His Father's house into "a den of thieves."[4]

---

4. One wonders what Christ would say today about those churches, some of them hotbeds of anti-Semitism, in which bingo has become a secular ritual every week!

"And the scribes and chief priests heard it," says the gospel, "and sought how they might destroy him: for they feared him because *all the people* [were] astonished at his doctrine" (Mark 11: 18).

John also points up the conflict between the people and their leaders when he reports that many Jews had turned to Jesus as their Messiah during the days of His public ministry. "Then gathered the chief priests and the Pharisees a council, and said, What do we? for this man doeth many miracles. If we let him thus alone, all men will believe on him; and *the Romans shall come and take away both our place and nation*" (John 11: 47, 48).[5]

There's the rub!

The incendiary nature of the Master's later triumphal entry into Jerusalem appears to have provided just the spark that was necessary to rid certain self-serving Jewish authorities of this Galilean who was undermining their own authority and threatening to upset the delicate detente with Rome.

There certainly was no possibility that any Jew could misunderstand the messianic implications of that Palm Sunday ride into the Holy City. For, says Matthew, "All this was done, that it might be fulfilled which was spoken by the prophet, saying, Tell ye the daughter of Sion, Behold, thy King cometh unto thee, meek, and sitting upon an ass, and a colt the foal of an ass" (Matthew 21: 4, 5).[6]

However, while this messianic act enraged Caiaphas, the Herodians, and certain other Jewish leaders, their conspiracy against the Galilean was checked by the

---

5. Mark 12: 12; 14: 1, 2; Matthew 21: 45, 46; 26: 3-5; Luke 19: 47, 48; 22: 1-6.

6. Compare Zechariah 9: 9. The reader does not have to agree with the main thesis of Hugh J. Schonfield *(The Passover Plot)* to recognize that Jesus did, as Schonfield recognizes, regard Himself as the fulfillment of the messianic prophecies and acted accordingly, "that the Scripture might be fulfilled."

knowledge that the common people still held Him in deep affection.

In fact, this bond between Jesus and the common man made it all but impossible for the collaborators and the corrupted to take any overt action against the popular prophet even after He continued to offend their sensitivities. While these leaders sought to put Him to death, says Luke, "they feared the people" (Luke 22: 2).

Yet in that week before Passover the missing pieces began to fit into the macabre puzzle.

It is quite likely that the Romans themselves had begun to take notice of the itinerant preacher and His nondescript band of disciples. Apart from the unsavory reputations of some of His followers, Jesus Himself certainly must have aroused official interest when hundreds blocked His way with the cry: "Hosanna! Blessed is He that cometh in the Name of the Lord!"

Now as the Holy City braced itself for the mobs of pilgrims that would arrive for the Feast of Passover, Pilate decided that it would be wise to supervise personally security operations in this hotbed of Jewish nationalism and rebellion. Accordingly, he made a hurried trip to Jerusalem from his official residence in Caesarea to guarantee law and order during the festivities.

Pontius Pilate was anything but a popular administrator as governor of Judea. On two occasions, he was forced to back down on plans to erect standards and shields bearing the names of Roman gods. And, in a third instance, he further enraged the Jews by attempting to finance an otherwise laudable public works program by looting the Temple treasury.

While these crude schemes were recorded by Josephus and Philo, Luke provides further insight into Pilate's warped personality by reporting that the Roman governor once mingled the blood of the Galileans with their own religious sacrifices (Luke 13: 1).

So inept did his administration become that Pilate was ultimately reported to the Emperor Tiberius himself.

Therefore, if the plot to kill Jesus was instigated by corrupt Jewish leaders, Pilate could no longer take lightly their not-too-subtle warning: "If thou let this man go, thou art not Caesar's friend: whosoever maketh himself a king speaketh against Caesar" (John 19: 12).

"The words are nothing less than a threat to report him to Tiberius the Emperor," says William Barclay. "And Pilate could not afford another such report. If it had gone in, dismissal would have been certain."

However, with the arrest of Jesus, John alone among the evangelists mentions the role of the Roman soldiers. "This is so uncharacteristic of him," says Isaac, "that the authenticity of the fact seems thereby assured.

"Who is going to believe that these Roman soldiers and their superior officer were acting on the orders of Judas or Caiaphas?" he asks. "They were acting on orders from Pilate, who had sent them.

"Common sense tells us," Isaac argues, "that in such cases the greatest responsibility lies with those who command the greatest power—in other words, with Pilate."

Of course, there is the possibility that the Roman governor and the high priest were co-conspirators in the plot against Jesus of Nazareth. For John records that the Roman cohort was accompanied to Gethsemane by members of the Temple guard, who were in the service of the Jewish authorities (John 18: 3).[7]

At this point, however, the actual details of the subsequent trial and conviction of Jesus are lost in the dark recesses of history. For the Gospel writers themselves leave crucial questions unanswered.

---

7. The Greek word *speira* denotes a Roman cohort — normally 600 men, but as Everett F. Harrison points out, not necessarily at full strength on this occasion. They were quartered in the Tower of Antonia, at the northern edge of the Temple area (Acts 21: 31ff).

For example, several scholars have noted as many as 27 irregularities in the trial procedures used to convict Jesus. Among these violations of the Sanhedrin code were variances from stipulations that capital cases be tried only during the day and that all court proceedings be adjourned on the Sabbath.

This has led some Jewish scholars to believe that Jesus might have been brought before a minor Sanhedrin composed of low-ranking bureaucrats who functioned as a rubber-stamp judicial body for the Romans.

Others, including Everett F. Harrison, have contended that the part played by the Jewish authorities in Jesus' condemnation is best interpreted as a preliminary investigation similar to the proceedings of a modern grand jury. The actual trial, some claim, was orchestrated by the Romans themselves.[8]

Whatever the case, John records that Pilate sternly directed "the Jews"—the self-serving Jewish leaders, that is—to judge Jesus after their own laws. Then says the evangelist:

> The Jews therefore said unto [Pilate], It is not lawful for us to put any man to death . . . .
>
> Then Pilate entered into the judgment hall again, and called Jesus, and said unto him, Art thou the King of the Jews?
>
> Jesus answered him, Sayest thou this thing of thyself, or did others tell it thee of me? (John 18: 31-34.)

If words ever laid bare the soul, that searching ques-

---

8. Billy Graham and other noted evangelicals have recently decried the unrelieved tendency to condemn the Jewish people for deicide. Two excellent articles dealing with the topic, and written from the evangelical perspective, are: Barbieri, Louis A., Jr., "That Incredible Mistrial," *Moody Monthly* (April, 1973); and Bruce, F. F., "Are the Gospels Anti-Semitic?" *Eternity* (November, 1973).

tion of the Master may well hold the key to what actually transpired between the Roman and Jewish leaders.

It is quite possible, as Dr. Harrison suggests, that Jesus knew that neither the Roman nor the Jewish authorities had entered court with clean hands. However, he adds:

> Pilate, unwilling to be trapped into an admission that he had anything to do with the situation, put the responsibility on the Jews.

To Jesus' question, Pilate replied obliquely: "Am I a Jew? Thine own nation and the chief priests have delivered thee unto me: what hast thou done?" (John 18: 35.)[9]

How typical of the political opportunist in every age! And how typical of Pilate, whom Philo accused of perpetrating "executions without fair trial." He ceremoniously washed his hands of the matter and allowed a small group of corrupt Jewish leaders to hold the bag as they cowered before the power of the Roman *imperium*.

Had Jesus been charged with blasphemy alone, His fate would have rested with the Sanhedrin, which retained jurisdiction in cases involving breaches of Jewish law. But the Jewish leaders in this case confronted Pilate with the claim that they were powerless to carry out the execution of Jesus of Nazareth. The question is, why?

Here was Pilate coming all the way from Caesarea to Jerusalem to make certain that violence did not erupt during the Feast of the Passover. He certainly was not about to be lenient with a Galilean who allegedly numbered Zealots and *sicarii* among His followers. And especially so when the man claimed messianic authority!

When Christ was at length crucified in Roman fashion

9. Ironically, while John has been alleged to be "the most anti-Semitic" of the four Gospels, it alone may hold the key to the puzzle surrounding the condemnation of Christ.

according to Roman law, there certainly was no mention of blasphemy against the God of Israel. Rather the sign, or *titulus,* nailed to the cross charged Him with claiming to be "King of the Jews."

"It was as a king," says Isaac, "or as a pretender to kingship—the kingship of the Messiah—that Jesus was sentenced and crucified."

As for the typical Jew of that turbulent age, Luke records that "a great company of people . . . bewailed and lamented him" as He made His way to Calvary (Luke 23: 27). And when at last He suffered the final agony, these people returned home beating their breasts (Luke 23: 48).

"The trial of Jesus Christ was undoubtedly a mockery of justice," says Louis A. Barbieri, Jr. "The burden of responsibility, however, does not rest upon any one group. 'For of a truth against thy holy child Jesus, whom thou hast anointed, both Herod, and Pontius Pilate, with the Gentiles, and the people of Israel, were gathered together, For to do whatsoever thy hand and thy counsel determined before to be done" (Acts 4: 27, 28).

At the same time, A. Roy Eckardt sagely observes, "the real moral issue" transcends the assignment of blame for the crucifixion. "In the Christian scheme—wrongly, to be sure," he writes, " 'Jewish responsibility for the crucifixion' gets linked to the reputed Jewish refusal in any age to receive Christ as Lord.

"In other words," says Eckardt, " 'Roman responsibility' is a purely historical, superseded matter, while 'Jewish responsibility' is hardly at all a historical matter; it is an existential one.

"What Christian today would ever think of taunting a resident of the City of Rome with the charge or reminder, 'You Romans killed Christ'?" he asks. "That would be like saying, 'You Americans today killed Lincoln.' "

The theory of the Dispersion

Yet "the teaching of contempt" continues to dog the footsteps of the Jewish people after nearly two millennia. As the heirs of an alleged decadent legalism, and as those who opposed and murdered Jesus Christ, their just punishment (it is said) has been their age-long dispersion across the face of the earth. Unhappily, the quest for historical accuracy has never been the hallmark of either blatant or latent anti-Semitism.

For example, in spite of the mythology which has surrounded the Diaspora, the actual dispersion of the Jews among the nations began centuries before Titus and his Roman legions destroyed the Temple and sacked Jerusalem in 70 C.E.

"It is possible that the beginnings (of the Diaspora) go right back to the days of Solomon," says James Parkes. "For he bought horses from the area on the southern shores of the Black Sea, and settled Jewish posts there to secure his supply."

In any event, the Babylonian Exile forced thousands of Jews to become uprooted from their homeland. When Cyrus later permitted their return, untold numbers elected instead to settle in Egypt and elsewhere throughout the vast Persian Empire. Moreover, this process of Jewish migration continued under the sway of Greek rule and culture.

Finally, when Jerusalem became the prize of the Roman general Pompey in 63 B.C.E., many Jews were carried off to the slave markets of Italy, where they subsequently purchased their freedom. Meanwhile, other Jews were brought in chains to Cologne, where they eventually established a well-known Jewish community.

None other than Paul, the "Apostle to the Gentiles," was a child of the Diaspora. He was born at Tarsus in Cilicia as the son of Jewish parents, who had the good fortune of holding Roman citizenship, a fact which was to serve the apostle well during his later imprisonments (Acts 22: 22-29; 23: 23-35).

Apart from his ties with Rome, there is also evidence that Paul was thoroughly exposed to Greek culture. In fact, his knowledge of Hellenistic literature and philosophy, at times so vividly reflected in his letters, gives the impression that he might well have been mistaken for a cultured Greek gentleman.

But the great apostle to the Gentiles was above all else, according to his own testimony, "of the stock of Israel, of the tribe of Benjamin, an Hebrew of the Hebrews; as touching the Law, a Pharisee" (Philippians 3: 5). As such, like the Master whom he sought to serve, Paul was very much at home in that remarkable institution known as the synagogue.

Although its exact origin is unknown, the synagogue appears to have originated during the period of the Babylonian captivity, even though no definite references to its existence are recorded until long after the return from the Exile.

However, we should note that Ezekiel assured the exiles that God Himself would be "a little sanctuary" (a *mikdash me'at*) for them in the midst of their captivity. What is significant about this promise is that it was given when the inhabitants of Jerusalem insisted that the exiles, removed from the presence of the Temple, had lost the protecting favor of God (Ezekiel 11: 15, 16).

Meanwhile, the time came when the synagogue was incorporated into the life of Israel for a three-fold purpose. It became the *Beth Tephila,* the "House of Prayer"; the *Beth Hamidrash,* "the House of Study"; and the *Beth Haknesseth,* the "House of Assembly," a term still used for the legislative body of the Israeli government. Says Max Dimont:

This expansion of the Jewish religious framework to include prayer, learning, and government set the pattern for yet other concepts to come—namely, standard prayer books and liturgy, universal education, freedom of assembly, and self-government in exile, all instituted first by the Jews and later adopted by other nations.

In contrast to the Temple, the synagogue constituted a gathering place for congregational worship—a major innovation in religious history, which profoundly influenced the Christian church, not to mention the worship of Islam.

By the time of Jesus of Nazareth, the synagogue was a well-established institution both in Israel and throughout the Diaspora. It was there that Jesus was to be found on the Sabbath; and it was also there that Paul and the other apostles won many converts to this Gospel that would soon turn the world upside down (Acts 17: 6).

What Christians so often forget is the fact that Jesus was a Jew, who sent forth His own disciples with the firm command: "Go not into the way of the Gentiles, and into any city of the Samaritans enter ye not: But go rather to the lost sheep of the house of Israel. And as ye go, preach, saying, The kingdom of heaven is at hand" (Matthew 10: 5-7). For the Prophet of Nazareth, "salvation is of the Jews" (John 4: 22).

Similarly Paul, burning with the hope "that [Israel] might be saved," was committed to preaching the Gospel "to the Jew first," and only then to the Greeks (Romans 10: 1; 1: 16). Moreover, in this commitment he was joined by Peter, who addressed his first letter to the elect sojourners of the Diaspora "scattered throughout Pontus, Galatia, Cappadocia, Asia, and Bithynia" (I Peter 1: 1, 2).

Therefore the worldwide relationship of the Jewish people to the spiritual heirs of Jesus of Nazareth is, as

Jakob Jocz observed, "the strangest historical phenomenon."

Although the new messianic movement was born on Jewish soil, it soon became apparent that it was not to remain a mere aberration from normative Judaism. This became indelibly clear when the Council of Jerusalem (50 C.E.) decreed that the Gospel was to be shared with all men, both Jews and Greeks (Acts 15: 1-29). It was therefore only a matter of time before Gentile believers were to outnumber those of the House of Israel.

Meanwhile, the breach between church and synagogue was already beginning to take shape during the New Testament period. For example, the charge leveled against Paul before the Roman governor by certain of his erstwhile co-religionists was simply this: "We have found this man a pestilent fellow, and a mover of sedition among all the Jews throughout the world, and a ringleader of the sect of the Nazarenes" (Acts 24: 5).

Behind this charge lay a growing rivalry between church and synagogue. For, in contrast to the commonly held idea that Judaism represented a "dead orthodoxy" at the beginning of the Common Era, Marcel Simon has shown that Jewish missionary zeal continued well into the fifth century. Paul's own evangelistic efforts were therefore not destined to win him many Jewish friends and admirers.

On the other hand, there were Christian Jews who incurred the wrath of a growing church orthodoxy, because they were associated with many of the Christian heresies and contributed to Judaizing tendencies within the early church.

These Judaizers were particularly identified with the Ebionite heresy which, as Edward Flannery comments, "purported to merge faith in Christ and Mosaic monotheism." The Ebionites went so far as to claim that Jesus

Himself was justified (earned salvation) by His perfect obedience to Torah. They dismissed His divinity and virgin birth out-of-hand.

Meanwhile, although the Gnostic heresy wore many masks there was a Jewish variety that dabbled in magic and sorcery, causing the Church Fathers concern that Christians themselves might be led astray by "Jewish superstition."

"If Jews were not the malefic sorcerers that Christian animosity made them out to be," says Joshua Trachtenburg, "they still possessed an ancient and honorable tradition of magic which [would be] solicitously nourished until the Middle Ages, when it reached its highest stage of development."

Whatever the case, Jewish support of the Arians against Christian orthodoxy did nothing to heal the animosity that was growing between church and synagogue. There were occasions when verbal insults flared into violence.

But the crowning insult for the Christian community came when some of its most distinguished leaders reported that the Jews were spreading the word that Jesus Himself was a charlatan and magician, and the illegitimate son of a Roman soldier.

It was within this charged atmosphere that Christian spokesmen responded in kind. For example, Jerome likened the prayers of the Jews to "the inarticulate cries of animals," while John Chrysostom called the Jews themselves "carnal" and "unclean and savage beasts."

As the slander continued on both sides, there emerged what Jules Isaac calls "the recurring theme of murder— of Israel as Cain, as Judas, as a murderous people, a 'deicide' people, an epithet at once indelible and absurd, singled out to be an abomination to the Christian world.

"By one flourish of the magic wand of theology," says

Isaac, "old Israel is transformed from a crucified into a crucifying people. All the insults, all the final torments— the flagellation, the nailing of Jesus to the Cross—become the work of the Jews alone.

"Gone is the Roman Pontius Pilate, the all-powerful Procurator of Judea," he observes. "Gone are the Roman soldiers, the executioners. Gone is all historical reality."

Quite apart from the polemics of the early Christian era, the "historical realities" of which Isaac speaks provided further impetus for the widening breach between Christian and Jew.

Unhappily, the years immediately following the death of Jesus of Nazareth saw only an intensification of Roman cruelty and oppression. Therefore, in 66 C.E. Jewish Zealots decided that the time had come to overthrow the hated foreign yoke.

However, Jewish Christians residing within the Holy Land were caught in a dilemma as to whether they should support the uprising. For, as Roman legionnaires responded to the emergency, these Christians remembered the prophecy of their Messiah:

> And when ye shall see Jerusalem compassed with armies, then know that the desolation thereof is nigh. Then let them which are in Judea flee to the mountains; and let them which are in the midst of it depart out; and let not them that are in the countries enter thereinto (Luke 21: 20, 21).

Although the Christians had no desire to betray their Jewish brethren, they believed they were bound by a higher duty to obey the command of Jesus of Nazareth. Therefore, during a brief lapse in the siege, these believers fled to the mountains in Jordan.

After Titus and his legionnaires completely destroyed the Holy City and burned and looted the Temple in 70

C.E., the Jewish Christians were branded as *meshumodim,* or traitors, by other members of the Jewish community.

However, the resultant hatred must be seen in light of the massive number of crucifixions which Titus ordered to quell the uprising. So barbaric was the conduct of the Romans against the Jews, says Max Dimont, that "the air was redolent with the stench of rotting flesh and rent by the cries of agony of the crucified."

One of the most frightening stories to emerge from this period involves a girl by the name of Maria, daughter of the noble line of Beth-Ezob in Jordan, who had come to Jerusalem to observe the Passover. However, Josephus records, Maria was caught in the city as it continued under heavy siege. Finally, a group of hunger-mad Zealots stormed into her house when they smelled the aroma of roast meat. Threatened with instant death unless she shared her secret prize, the girl turned over to the intruders the body of a half-consumed infant. Maria was eating her own baby.

Jesus' Olivet Discourse did not say that the destruction of Jerusalem was to be accompanied by a total and final dispersion of the Jewish people. What He predicted was that:

> They shall fall by the edge of the sword, and shall be led away captive into all nations: and Jerusalem shall be trodden down of the Gentiles, until the times of the Gentiles be fulfilled (Luke 21: 24).

That is actually what occurred. As Jules Isaac puts it: "Jerusalem and Judea devastated, Jews killed and taken prisoner, the seizure of Jerusalem by the Gentiles: such are Jesus' prophecies, and nothing more."

Messianic movements

As brutal as was the campaign of Titus, the Jews decided some 60 years later to mount a second assault against the Romans, a revolt which turned out to be as bloody and unremitting as the first.

While Jewish Christians may have wished to be identified with this new rebellion, they again withheld their support because of the messianic pretensions of the legendary Simon Bar Kochba, the "Son of the Star" and leader of the Jewish forces. His pretensions took on added weight when no less a religious figure than Rabbi Akiba hailed Simon as the *Mashiach* and a Prince of Israel.

"For a time, Simon made a real fight of it," says Frederick M. Schweitzer. "The Romans were expelled from Jerusalem, for two years sacrifices were renewed on the Temple altar, and an independent state was created that went so far as to issue its own currency."

But the Roman Emperor Hadrian was determined to bring Bar Kochba and his rebels to their knees. In the end he succeeded, but only after three years of bloody fighting, and the loss of 580,000 Jewish men under arms, not to mention women and children.

Soon after Jerusalem fell to the Romans for a second time in the year 135, the Holy City was renamed Aelia Capitolina, and a temple was erected to Jupiter within the sacred precincts. "Jews were forbidden to teach or practice their religion," says Schweitzer, "and were barred from so much as entering what was now a pagan town."

Yet not even the barbarism of Hadrian was able to fully extinguish the light of Palestinian Judaism. Miraculously, the Jews staged a rebellion against Constantine in the fourth century—and another against Justinian some two centuries later. "Each time," says Isaac, "there was a new defeat and a new bloodbath. But the indomitable nation did not yield."

While Isaac resists the term Dispersion because of its association with "the teaching of contempt," he notes that the severest blow against the remnant of Palestinian Jewry occurred during the First Crusade, when so-called Christians set synagogues ablaze, trapping defenseless Jews inside.

However, since the Crusaders did not capture Jerusalem until 1099, Isaac contends that history itself debunks the notion that the final dispersion of Israel occurred in the year 70 as a direct divine punishment for Jewish complicity in the Crucifixion.

"It is not history that must come to terms with theology," he argues. "On the contrary, it is theology that must come to terms with history."

Judaism's disastrous confrontation with both Church and State led to two developments within that community of faith. On the one hand, Jews developed a growing skepticism regarding all messianic claims. On the other, they became determined to build "the Wall of Law" to protect themselves from a growing anti-Semitism, a policy enunciated by the Church and enforced by the State.

While messianic pretenders were to continue to draw converts, the results were always heartbreaking. Palestinian Jewry had placed such high hopes in Bar Kochba, only to drink later the bitter dregs of another defeat. The same was to occur centuries later when David Alroy arose in Mesopotamia. His career was cut short by assassins sometime between 1135 and 1160.

But the most interesting messianic figures by far in later Judaism were David Reuveni and Sabbatai Zvi.

An enigmatic dwarf, Reuveni appeared in Venice about 1524 and announced that he was the brother of the king of one of the Lost Tribes, the Tribe of Reuben, divinely appointed to bring about the redemption of Israel. Reuveni's end was brought about by the Inquisition.

A century later, Sabbatai Zvi appeared on the scene as

Jews were chafing under the repeated and barbaric *pogroms* initiated by the Cossacks. In their search for deliverance, countless Jews rallied around Zvi, even though he married a prostitute raised in a Polish convent. Disenchantment with this pretender only began when he embraced Islam in order to avoid the messy alternative of having his head chopped off by a sultan who was not impressed by his claims to the Holy Land.

Although Christians may be unable to understand why the vast majority of Jews still reject the messianic claims of Jesus of Nazareth, it must be remembered that the Christian Savior represents for them the epitome of the world's barbarity. The Old Rugged Cross, from the Jewish perspective, is not a symbol of redemption but of their *own* "suffering and shame."

The Jewish reaction to the claims of Christ may best have been expressed by a great Jewish theologian, the late Martin Buber, when he was asked if he believed that Messiah had come. In spite of Buber's unusual appreciation of Jesus, he was forced to reply in effect: Of course not. How could He have come when things continue as they are?

Jews and the Church

Ironically, Judaism's initial encounter with Islam was far less explosive than its confrontation with a hostile church. Although the situation was to change dramatically, the Moslems at first expressed their deep indebtedness to the Jews and granted them toleration, thereby making Jewish growth in literature and commerce possible in the opening years of the Islamic advance.

In the West, however, things went from bad to worse, as canon law became the basis of official state policy. In one code, the Jews were defined as a vicious people, while the synagogue was referred to as a brothel.

"By the late fourth century," says Rosemary Reuther,

"this official persecution of the Jews was supplemented by outbreaks of popular violence against the Jews in the form of synagogue burnings, expulsions, and forced baptisms."

However, baptism itself was no assurance of assimilation into and acceptance by the Christian community, as the *Marranos* of Spain and Portugal were to learn to their sorrow hundreds of years later.

Taking their very name from a Spanish word for "swine," the *Marranos* adopted Christianity under extreme pressure, although they continued to practice Jewish rites and customs in private. Ironically, it was this group of crypto-Jews who felt the genocidal fury of the Inquisition of the fifteenth century. It had no jurisdiction over professing Jews because the latter, never having been Christians, could not be accused of heresy.

And when the Nazis ordered every Jew above the age of six to wear the yellow Star of David, they were taking their cue from a 700 years old edict of the Fourth Lateran Council, which forced this same "Badge of Shame" upon Jews of an earlier age.

The Nazis also resurrected almost verbatim another ecclesiastical edict, this one issued by Pope Eugenius IV in 1442: "We decree and order that from now on, and for all time, Christians shall not eat or drink with Jews, nor admit them to feasts, nor cohabit with them, nor bathe with them."

The crowning insult appeared in the *Ordo Romanus* of the Roman Church, which decreed that the Jews were to appear before the Pope with a copy of the *Torah* whenever a new pontiff was elevated. At that point, the Pope would sternly declare: "We praise and honor the Law . . . but we condemn your religion." This formula was later replaced with the shabby quip: "Excellent Law —detestable race!"

It was also the Fourth Lateran Council which decreed

the establishment of prescribed "Jewish Quarters" in every major city. The first *ghetto* was created in Venice, near a cannon foundry (*gheta* in Italian). "But other possible derivations have also been cited by philologists," says M. Hirsh Goldberg, "including the more than appropriate German *gitter,* meaning 'bars,' and the Tuscan *guitto,* meaning 'dirty.'

"And dirty the *ghetto* was," says Goldberg. "For its sponsors saw to that."

Is it any wonder, then, that Jean-Paul Sartre has made the observation that "the true opponent of assimilation is not the Jew but the anti-Semite.

"The Jew has tried to gain acceptance in a society that rejects him," says Sartre. "It is pointless to ask him to hasten this integration, which always recedes before him. So long as there is anti-Semitism, assimilation cannot be realized."

The fact is that the Jews were driven from country after country, the perennial scapegoats of a sick society. In addition to being branded as "the Christ-killers," they were also met with the murderous charges that they killed Christian children and drank their blood at Passover. Tales of sacraments violated and wells poisoned further embellished this "teaching of contempt."

For a while, it looked as though the Jews would find a haven in Russia, Poland, and other countries in Eastern Europe. It was in towns such as Vilna, Lublin, and Cracow, that Talmudic academies and Yiddish culture flourished for many years.

But then came the Chmielnicki massacres of 1648-1656, followed by a wave of *pogroms* that scarcely abated until the rise of the modern Zionist movement. Here is an eyewitness account describing just one of these *pogroms* during the Cossack Rebellion:

> Some of the Jews were flayed alive by the Cossacks, who threw their flesh to the dogs. Some

were severely wounded without being fatally injured, and then were thrown out into the street to prolong their agony. Others were buried alive.

Sucklings were stabbed in the arms of their mothers, others torn to bits like fish. Pregnant women were ripped open and the foetus extracted and thrown in their faces. Other victims had live cats sewn up in their bellies and were fastened up with their arms above their heads so that they could do nothing to help themselves.

Sucklings were hanged from their mothers' breasts; others were impaled on spikes, roasted and offered to their mothers to eat. In some places, Jewish children were thrown in heaps into the rivers.

Whatever hopes the Jews might have held for the Protestant Reformation were soon crushed by the deaf ear of John Calvin and the open hostility of Martin Luther.

While Calvin reportedly demonstrated some sense of solidarity with the people of the "old" covenant, he nonetheless refused them permission to settle in Geneva, believing with other Protestants that the Jews were still being punished for their rejection of the Gospel.

At the outset of his career, Luther roundly condemned his Catholic opponents for treating "the Jews as if they were dogs and not human beings. However much we may boast ourselves," he declared, "we are still pagan born, whereas the Jews are of the blood of Christ." However, when all efforts failed to convert the Jews to Christianity, Luther turned against "this damned, rejected race" with savage fury. He urged his followers to burn their synagogues, homes, and books. He further advised that their rabbis be forbidden to teach and that other Jews be compelled to earn their bread "by the sweat of their noses."

Sadly, when the notorious Nazi Jew-baiter Julius Streicher appeared for judgment at Nuremberg, he was able to appeal with some justification that he had only attempted to carry out the teachings of the great Reformer.

For one can trace the diabolical progression of "the teaching of contempt" from an anti-Semitism blessed with holy water to its ultimate expression in the Holocaust. Raul Hilberg puts the matter in its tragic perspective:

> The missionaries of Christianity had said in effect: You have no right to live among us as Jews. The secular rulers who followed had complained: You have no right to live among us. The German Nazis at last decreed: You have no right to live. [The Nazis] did not discard the past; they built upon it. They did not begin a development; they completed it.

When "the times of the Gentiles are fulfilled," Christians will be confronted by a Jew named Jesus. In the meantime, as Julian Green once remarked, "we cannot raise our hand against a Jew without striking with the same blow Him who is the Man par excellence and at the same time the flower of Israel.

"It is Jesus who suffered at the concentration camps," says Green. "It is always He. His suffering is never ended."

5

He That Keepeth Israel

NAZI Propaganda Minister Josef Goebbels once approached an elderly rabbi with a strange request.

"Jew," demanded the pint-sized Aryan, "I have heard that you Jews employ a special form of reasoning, called Talmudic, which explains your cleverness. I want you to teach it to me."

"Ah, Herr Goebbels," the old rabbi sighed. "I fear you are a little too old for that."

"Nonsense! Why?"

"Well," said the rabbi, "when a Jewish boy wishes to study *Talmud* we first give him an examination. It consists of three questions. Those lads who answer the questions correctly are admitted to the study of the *Talmud*. Those who can't, are not."

"Excellent," said Goebbels. "Give me the exam."

"Very well," the old rabbi shrugged. "The first question: Two men fall down a chimney. One emerges filthy,

139

covered with soot. The other emerges clean. Which one of them washes?"

Goebbels scoffed: "The dirty one, of course!"

"Wrong. The clean one."

"The *clean* one washes?" asked Goebbels incredulously. "Why?"

"Because as soon as the two men emerge from the chimney, they look at each other. No? The dirty one, looking at the clean one, says to himself, 'Remarkable! For us to fall down a chimney and come out clean!'

"But the clean one, looking at the dirty one, says to himself, 'We certainly got filthy coming down that chimney. I'll wash up at once.'

"So it is the clean one who washes, not the dirty one."

"Ah," nodded Goebbels. "Very clever. Let's have the second question."

"The second question," sighed the rabbi, "is this: Two men fall down a chimney. One emerges filthy, covered with soot. The other emerges clean. Which one . . ."

"That's the same question!" cried Goebbels.

"No, no," responded the rabbi. "This is a different question."

"Very well," hissed the proud Aryan. "You won't fool me, Jew. The one who is clean washes."

"Wrong," said the rabbi.

"But you just told me . . ."

"That was an entirely different problem, Herr Goebbels. In this one, the dirty man washes because, as before, the two men look at each other. The one who is clean looks at the dirty one and says, 'My! How dirty I must be!' But he looks at his hands and he sees that he is not dirty. The dirty man, on the other hand, looks at the clean one and says, 'Can it be? To fall down a chimney and emerge so clean? Am I clean?' So he looks at his hands and sees that he is filthy. So he, the dirty one, washes. Naturally."

"Clever, Jew, very clever," nodded Goebbels. "Now the third question."

"Ah," sighed the rabbi. "The third question is the most difficult of all. Two men fall down a chimney. One emerges clean, the other . . ."

"But that's the same question!"

"No, Herr Goebbels. The *words* may be the same. But the *problem* is an entirely new one."

"All right," exclaimed Goebbels. "The dirty one washes."

"Wrong!"

"The clean one!"

"Wrong!"

"Then what *is* the answer?"

"The answer is that this is a silly examination," said the rabbi. *"How* can two men fall down the same chimney and one emerge dirty and the other clean?

"Anyone who can't see that," sighed the rabbi, "will never be able to understand *Talmud."*

While this story may be apocryphal, it reflects that amazing ability of the Jews to find laughter in the valley of tears. In this case, even Nazi wrath is made to praise them!

But beyond the bittersweet humor, there is an authentic Talmudic tone to this story. Indeed, the circuitous logic brims with that engaging type of Jewish *chachma*—or wisdom—which so often baffles Gentile friends.

Unfortunately, too many Christians have approached the wisdom of Israel with about the same deference as the Gentile who demanded of Shammai that he teach him the whole *Torah* while the man stood on one foot.

The Jewish approach to law and grace

In our own day, Rabbi Joseph B. Soloveitchik has claimed that the most open Christians have failed to understand the heart and soul of Judaism.

"They have never tried to penetrate the soul of the Jews," says this Hebrew scholar whose brilliance has been compared to that of Maimonides. "They have read the Bible but neglected the oral tradition by which we interpret it. This makes a different Bible altogether.

"*Halacha* is essentially a method—a way of approaching things and reacting to them," the Rav explains. "However, to equate Judaism with legalism the way Christian theologians are prone to do is like equating mathematics with a compilation of mathematical equations.

"You know the saying about an eye for an eye," he remarks. "The Bible states that this is what a man deserves when he has taken another man's sight. It is the full measure of justice.

"But we also know that no human being can implement such strict justice," says the Rav. "In practical terms, it means you make the man pay compensation."[1]

Rabbi Soloveitchik insists that Judaism is unique in a number of ways. "For one thing," he says, "we are practical. We are more interested in discovering what God wants man to do than we are in describing God's essence.

"As a teacher," he says, "I never try to solve questions because most questions are unsolvable. Judaism is never afraid of contradictions.

"We adore man—we are afraid of men," he explains. "We have never followed Aristotelian logic and the principle of the excluded middle. In many cases, such as the 'eye for an eye' situation, there is a contradiction between

---

1. Those who take pride in man's upward mobility since the days of "an eye for an eye" should ponder the all-too-common warning among belligerents, "You shoot down one of our planes, and we'll shoot down ten of yours."

the demands of love and justice.

"The Medieval man gave truth—or whatever he thought to be truth—precedence over loving kindness and so do the Communists today.

"What is the difference between a Torquemada and Mao Tse-tung?

"Judaism is basically very tolerant and usually comes down on the side of loving kindness," he says. "But it acknowledges that full reconciliation of the two is possible only in God. He is the coincidence of opposites."

This may partially explain why Rabbi Soloveitchik believes that dialogue between Christians and Jews must be limited to social and ethical issues.

"The Jews' relation to God is an intimate one," he says. "It is like a romance, and there is a certain shyness when one speaks of romance.

"The Christian mystic will describe his communion with God in detailed and personal terms," he notes. "With Jewish mystics, you don't find confessionals.

"When I feel the breath of eternity in my face," he says, "I tell you only that it is possible for men to communicate with God. The Jew will translate his personal experience into a concept."

In the course of the long history of Israel, the most enduring of these concepts became codified in the sacred books of the Jews.

"Judaism began in writings and became the most literate, the most book-intoxicated, of the world's great faiths," says Harry Gersh. "Judaism bars worship of any physical thing—animate or inanimate—and so the Jews did not worship their books.

"But," he adds, "study of the sacred books is *a form of worship* and is required of Jews.

Reverence for the Word

"So deeply did the Jews respect their books that

143

they were not destroyed when they became frayed and torn," Gersh observes. "When books of importance ... were too worn for use, they were given honorable burial in a vault beneath the synagogue."

For many years, the most famous *genizah,* or hiding place, was the burial vault discovered in the Synagogue of Fostat, Cairo, built in 882. For it was there that scholars uncovered part of the lost Hebrew version of Ecclesiasticus and other lost Hebrew works, along with extracts from Aquila's Greek translation of the Bible, and the Zadokite Fragments, which portray a *halakhic* system similar both to the Pharisaic tradition and that of the Essene Community of the Judean Desert.

Another type of *genizah* came to light with the monumental discovery of the Dead Sea Scrolls, an archaeological find that ranks above the discovery of even the Epic of Gilgamesh, the Code of Hammurabi, or the literature of Lachish, Amarna, and Ras Shamra of the ancient pagan world.

The first of these scrolls were discovered quite by accident in 1947, when a young Bedouin black marketeer stumbled upon an old Essene *genizah,* located not in the ruins of a synagogue but rather in a cave on the desolate and hilly western shore of the Dead Sea. The actual location is known as Khirbet Qumran, which lies about seven miles south of Jericho.

To their utter amazement and delight, Bible scholars found that these long-lost scrolls threw new light on the monastic Essenes, a sect closely associated with John the Baptist and perhaps even Jesus Himself. Other scrolls provided scholars with the oldest portions of the Hebrew Bible yet uncovered. The remarkable thing about them was the fact that they demonstrated conclusively that the Jews had preserved the text of Scripture with utmost fidelity down through the long centuries. The texts of

Qumran and the text of the contemporary Hebrew Bible were virtually identical![2]

This does not mean that there were not changes in spelling or occasional differences in the text. For prior to the destruction of the Second Temple, an official copy of the canon was kept there and copies had to be made from it. "Despite the fact that, once canonized, the Bible was unchangeable and error was a sin," says Gersh, "errors did creep in, and marginal notes in previous versions were copied as textual parts of the Bible."

However, he says, "about the Sixth Century, schools of scribes grew up in Tiberias, Babylon, and Mesopotamia which established an infallible system of copying.

"These *Masoretes*—from the Hebrew word for tradition—set standards for copying that would eliminate error; they also added the diacritical vowel marks that made reading easier. The Masoretic guides to copying listed the number of letters in a book, listed the chapters by their endings, cited the large and small letters, and gave a hundred other tests for exactness."

As an indication that the Masoretic text is about as close to the original as can be expected of a human agency, one has only to consider this Masoretic reminder at the end of Genesis:

> The total verses of the Book of Genesis is 1534, and half of them is the verse 'and by the sword thou shalt live.' The weekly portions are twelve in number; the sections are forty-three; the chapters, fifty; the paragraphs whose last lines are open to the end of the column are thirty-four, and those which are closed [the next paragraph begins on the same line] number forty-eight.

2. G. Ernest Wright has noted that the text of the Isaiah Scroll and that of portions of Daniel are substantially the same as those of our current Hebrew Bibles (the Masoretic text). "The chief differences," he says, ". . . have to do with the spelling of words."

Apart from this burning desire for accuracy, Jewish love for learning was reflected in the fact that the synagogue itself was to be more a house of study (*Beth Hamidrash*) than a house of assembly (*Beth Haknesseth*).

In fact, the rabbis ruled that it is proper to change a synagogue into a house of study, but it would be improper to change a house of study into a synagogue. In the first instance, they reasoned, it would involve a movement upward; in the second case, the opposite would be true.

"In all these ways," says Gersh, "Jews expressed reverence for the unique capacity of man to give permanent form to his greatest power—to provide through the written word a permanent record of his most exalted thoughts."

The emphasis must be on the words themselves. For thoughts are expressed in words. And words differ according to nations and tongues.

"Hebrew among languages is like Israel among the nations, like the Sabbath among the days of the week," says Rabbi Louis Feinberg. "It lends the Jew a *Neshamah Yeterah,* an over-soul. Strike a note in Hebrew, and rich overtones are set in motion.

"Many nations ascribe holiness to what is dearest to their hearts," he notes. "But Jews are the only ones who, in addition to numerous other holy possessions, have a *loshon ha-kodesh,* a holy tongue."

Rabbi Feinberg observes that even the Jewish story of creation emphasizes the creative force of language. The psalmist, for example, declares, "By the *word* of the Lord were the heavens made." And the Torah itself testifies, "And God *said,* Let there be . . ."

"It is assumed, of course," says Rabbi Feinberg, "that the language employed was Hebrew."

Moreover, he adds, when the Ten Commandments were proclaimed on Sinai, Jewish tradition has it that they were broken up into 70 languages, so that all the world might hear and comprehend.

"But all the nations except Israel received it in translation," he says. "Maybe that is why the world has never grasped all the implications of the *Torah*.

"The sword and the book were offered us from Heaven as defensive weapons," he writes. "We chose the book.

"It was with the Holy Ark that we reduced the walls of Jericho, not with battering rams; and down to this day we march in procession with the *Sefer Torah* on our shoulders, instead of a gun."

If the Middle East crisis has somewhat altered this exalted posture, it must be remembered that Jewish independence itself would never have been achieved in 1948 without the dedication of men like ben-Yehudah who brought new life into the ancient Hebrew tongue.

The indisputable fact is that Gentiles can never hope to understand their Jewish brethren unless they first begin to appreciate the abiding love a Jew has for his *loshon ha-kodesh* and for the sacred books of his ancient people.

Were it not for these guardians of the Law and the Prophets, Christians would know nothing of the moral imperative of God's Commandments, the lyrical majesty of the Psalms, or the messianic hope of Isaiah, Jeremiah, and Ezekiel.

It is of particular interest to contemporary Americans to learn that the very word *"watergate"* had a far different meaning for ancient Israel than it does for a nation disillusioned and divided by official misconduct in the highest echelons of government. You will find that story in the Book of Nehemiah:

And when the seventh month was come, and the children of Israel were in their cities, all the people gathered themselves together as one man into the broad place that was before the water gate; and they spoke unto Ezra the scribe to bring the book of the Law of Moses, which the Lord had commanded to Israel. And Ezra the priest brought the Law before the congregation, both men and women. . . . And he read therein . . . from early morning until midday. . . . And [the Levites] read in the book, the Law of God, distinctly; and they gave the sense, and caused [the people] to understand the reading. . . .

Now in the twenty and fourth day . . . the children of Israel were assembled . . . and [they] cried with a loud voice unto the Lord their God. . . . And yet for all this we make a sure covenant, and subscribe it; and our princes, our Levites, and our priests, set their seal unto it.

It was on this solemn occasion at the water gate that Ezra is credited with establishing and clarifying the text of the *Torah* in the language of his own age. And it was also there that the erstwhile exiles received that Law as the canonical Word of God.

Not long afterward, the Sages of the Great Assembly are reported to have received the books of Ezekiel, Esther, Daniel, and the twelve minor prophets into the canon of Hebrew Scripture.

According to Jewish tradition, it was not until a group of scholars met at Jabneh in 90 C.E.—two decades after the destruction of the Second Temple—that the canon was finally closed. At that time, these scholars argued that, since prophecy ended with Ezra, no books written after his death could be considered authoritative works of Scripture.

Meanwhile, the *Talmud* includes information concerning the authorship of various Biblical materials, which is at variance with much of modern Biblical scholarship. *Bava Batra* (14b-15a) has this to say:

> Moses wrote his book [i. e., the *Torah*], the section of Balaam, and Job; Joshua wrote his book and [the concluding] eight verses of the *Torah;* Samuel wrote his book, Judges, and Ruth; David wrote the Psalms, incorporating therein the writings of ten elders. . . . Jeremiah wrote his book, the Book of Kings, and Lamentations. Hezekiah and his council wrote [i.e., edited] Isaiah, Proverbs, Song of Songs, and Ecclesiastes; the men of the Great Assembly wrote [i.e., edited] Ezekiel, the Twelve Prophets, Daniel, and the Scroll of Esther. Ezra wrote his book, and the genealogy of Chronicles down to himself.

While both liberal and conservative scholars raise many questions concerning Talmudic insights on the text and authorship of Scripture, everyone agrees that *Torah* was "the lip of Canaan," and the Israelites were always "the people of the Book."

In their efforts to preserve the purity of Scripture, the rabbis rejected the 14 books of the Apocrypha, all of which were written by Jews, some in Hebrew, some in Greek, some in Aramaic. However, much of this material, particularly I and II Maccabees, throws considerable light on the so-called Intertestamental Period, between Malachi and the birth of Jesus of Nazareth.

The masters and the Master

When Jesus came, He did so as a *ben brith,* a Son of the Covenant. He sat as a boy at the feet of the rabbis (Luke 2: 46, 47). And, in later life, it was His custom to go "into the synagogue on the sabbath day" (Luke 4: 16).

However, Jewish friends sadly lament that, while Christians search for Christ in the Old Testament, they hear so

149

little from their pulpits about Hillel in the New. And yet this great and good rabbi, a contemporary of the Galilean, shared so many of His teachings regarding the Law. In the charged atmosphere of Roman-occupied Jerusalem, for example, Hillel advised his own disciples to shun politics as a solution to Israel's problems. "Love peace," he declared, "and draw . . . men to the Torah" (Avot 1: 12).

On one occasion, so the story goes, a heathen came to the more rigid Shammai and said, "I am prepared to be received as a [Jewish] proselyte on the condition that you teach me the whole Law while I am standing on one leg." Shammai chased away the impudent chap with a ruler.

Hillel, however, was more understanding. He accepted the man as a proselyte; and he also accepted his challenge. "What is hateful to yourself," he declared, "do to no other. That is the whole Law, and the rest is commentary.

"Go," he said, "and learn."

Moreover, as there are rabbinic parallels to the so-called Golden Rule, so too are there parallels to The Lord's Prayer. "The prayer is thoroughly Jewish," says Sherman E. Johnson. "And nearly every phrase is paralleled in the *Kaddish* and the Eighteen Benedictions (*Shemoneh 'esreh*).

"Thus," Dr. Johnson adds, "it is Jesus' inspired and original summary of his own people's piety at its best."

The same holds true concerning Jesus' teaching on the Law. While there were exceptions, the Galilean basically followed the Pharisaic code of His day. In fact, says Rabbi Abba Hillel Silver, the Jews certainly "did not reject Jesus because of his alleged . . . abandonment of the *Torah*.

"On the contrary," says Rabbi Silver, "He made it abundantly clear that he came not to abolish the Law and the Prophets but to fulfill them." This beloved rabbi has observed:

> Jesus taught the Law "as one who had authority" (Mark 1: 22), that is, not as the Rabbis taught it; not, for example, as Hillel taught it, in accordance with a generally accepted technique of *Halachah* employed in the Schools, but as a prophet would have taught it, *mi-pi Ha-Geburah,* on direct authority received from God. . . . Jesus saw his role as that of a prophet announcing the approach of the Millennium. He accordingly did not feel himself restricted to the Pharisaic technique of interpreting the *Torah.*

"Jesus evidently sought to exercise this prophetic privilege, but only in his exposition of the Law," says Rabbi Silver. "For he announced no new laws nor did he attempt to abrogate any existing law, and he never questioned the authority of the *Torah* as such."

The Master's teaching on Sabbath observance represents a case in point. Jesus declared that "the sabbath was made for man, and not man for the sabbath" (Mark 2: 27). In this saying, He is reflecting an attitude that was widely shared in Pharisaic Judaism.

In fact, says Rabbi Silver, "in the Second Century of the Common Era, when Sabbath laws had been elaborated much further by the Rabbis and culminated in the thirty-nine chief categories of prohibited work, Rabbi Jonathan ben Joseph employed the almost identical words of the gospel: 'The Sabbath is committed to your hands, not you to its hands' (*Yoma* 85b)."

"For Jesus there was only one obligation in life—and that was to help," says William Barclay. "There was only one law—and that was love."

With this the greatest rabbis have always agreed. Rabbi Levi Yitzhak of Berdichev, for example, loved to quote the teaching of *Midrash Tankhuma*: "He who sustains God's creatures is rewarded as though he had created them." Moreover, he declared: "Whether a man really loves God can best be determined by the love he bears toward his fellowmen."

Meanwhile, the *Hassidim* struck a note of irony whenever they explained the difference between themselves and their opponents, the legalistic *Mitnagdim*. "The pious *Mitnagdim* are afraid of transgressing against the Code of Laws," they said. "But the *Hassidim* are in fear of transgressing against God."

What this means is that Jesus has far more in common with Rabbi Levi Yitzhak and many of the *Hassadim* than He does with the legalistic and self-righteous Christian or Jew of any age.

It is true that there were scribes and Pharisees in His own day who condemned Jesus for engaging in acts of compassion on the Sabbath. But there are also a lot of contemporary Christians who would probably find fault with the Master for not subscribing to their own sanctified rules and regulations.

Yet these same Christians, Jules Isaac suggests, will malign *all* of the Jews of Jesus' day because they allegedly were more attached to the letter than to the spirit of the Law. Christian apologists have attacked the Jews as "carnal beings, blinded by Satan, incapable of understanding the meaning of their own Scriptures."

Isaac is willing to concede that pre-Christian Judaism was sometimes marked by the legalism and formalism of the scribes, by the false piety of some Pharisees, and by a harsh and arrogant priestly oligarchy represented by Annas and Caiaphas.

But Isaac will *not* concede that formalism, ritualism, hypocrisy, arrogance, and worldliness represented the best of Judaism or Pharisaism at the dawn of the Christian era. False piety is as much denounced in *Talmud-Torah* as it is in the Gospels, he observes. And for every Caiaphas, there was a compassionate Zacharias of the gospel narratives (Luke 1).

Apparently, Isaac's own compassion and desire for rapprochement will not permit him to clinch his argument by pointing out that self-righteousness is not a Jewish but a human frailty.

At any rate, while Jesus interpreted the Law in love, He subscribed to its demands in the spirit of all committed Jews of His own age. In fact, He declared, the Law is so sacred that not the smallest detail of it will ever pass away.

> For truly, I say to you, till heaven and earth pass away, not an iota, not a dot, will pass from the law until all is accomplished. Whoever then relaxes one of the least of these commandments and teaches men so, shall be called least in the kingdom of heaven; but he who does them and teaches them shall be called great in the kingdom of heaven (Matthew 5: 18, 19, RSV).

Since Jesus did not speak Greek, the translators of the Revised Standard Version would have been more in keeping with the spirit of Jesus if they had referred to a *jodh* and a *tittle* rather than to an *iota* and a *dot*. In any case, the inference is clear that the Master considered the Law so sacred that He warned men not to tamper with even a portion of a single letter of this gift from God.

To better understand this matter, the *jodh* in form was nothing more than an apostrophe. And the *tittle* of the Authorized Version was actually a serif, the little projecting part at the foot of some letters.

No wonder, then, that William Barclay has remarked: "Again and again Jesus broke what the Jews called the Law . . . and yet here He seems to speak of the Law with a veneration and a reverence that no Rabbi or Pharisee could exceed."

How can the contradiction be explained?

To begin with, it may well be that Jesus was referring in this instance to more than the Ten Commandments. It would appear that He was rather speaking of what the Jews call the *mitzvoth,* which technically denote the 613 individual injunctions of the Bible which in their totality make up the *Torah.* Indeed, a *Midrash* offered by the rabbis explains that Israel's election as the Chosen People was based upon the acceptance of this body of law:

> Before God gave Israel the Torah, He approached every tribe and nation and offered them the Torah, that they might have no excuse later to say, 'Had the Holy One desired to give us the Torah, we would have accepted it.'

> God went to the children of Esau and said, 'Will you accept the Torah?' They answered Him, saying, 'What is written therein?' He answered them, 'Thou shalt not kill.' Then they said, 'Our father Esau was blessed with the words, By the sword shalt thou live. We do not want to accept the Torah.'

> Thereupon He went to the children of Lot and said to them, 'Will you accept the Torah?' They said, 'What is written therein?' He answered, 'Thou shalt not commit unchastity.' They said, 'From unchastity do we spring. We will not accept your Torah.'

> Then He went to the children of Ishmael and said to them, 'Do you want to accept the Torah?' They said to Him, 'What is written therein?' He answered, 'Thou shalt not steal.' They said, 'Our father was promised that his hand would be against every man. We do not want to accept the Torah.'

Thence God went to all the other nations, who likewise rejected the Torah, saying, 'We cannot give up the law of our fathers. We do not want your Torah.'

Upon hearing this, God came to Israel and spoke to them, 'Will you accept the Torah?' They said to Him, 'What is written therein?' He answered, 'Six hundred and thirteen commandments.' They said, 'All that the Lord has spoken will we obey and do.'

It is unfortunate that so many Christians have turned to these 613 commandments to support the contention that Judaism at the time of Christ was somehow lost in a morass of legal fear and bondage. For, while the *mitzvoth* were meant to regulate every step of daily living, they were not even incorporated into a single code until the eighth century. And long before that the Rabbis of the *Talmud* had reduced them to their moral essence:

"Six hundred and thirteen commandments were given to Moses . . .

Then came David and reduced them to eleven:
'Lord, who shall sojourn in Thy tabernacle?
Who shall dwell upon Thy holy mountain?
He that walketh uprightly, and worketh righteousness,
And speaketh truth in his heart;
That hath no slander upon his tongue,
Nor doeth evil to his fellow,
Nor taketh up a reproach against his neighbor;
In whose eyes a vile person is despised,
But he honoreth them that fear the Lord;
He that sweareth not to his own hurt, and changeth not;
He that putteth not out his money on interest,
Nor taketh a bribe against the innocent.'

Then came Isaiah and reduced them to six:
'He that walketh righteously, and speaketh uprightly;

He that despiseth the gain of oppressions,
That shaketh his hands from holding of bribes,
That stoppeth his ears from hearing of blood,
And shutteth his eyes from looking upon evil.

Then came Micah, and reduced them to three:
'It hath been told to thee, O man, what is good,
And what the Lord doth require of thee:
Only to do justly, to love mercy, and to walk humbly
with thy God.'

Then came Isaiah again, and reduced them to two, as
it is said, 'Keep ye judgment and do righteousness.'
Then came Amos, and reduced them to one, as it is
said, 'Seek ye Me and live.' Or, one may say, then
came Habakkuk, and reduced them to one, as it is said,
'The righteous shall live by his faith.' "

So it is that committed Jews in every age have performed the *mitzvoth* with a spirit of joy and not out of
duty alone. In fact, says one sage, God prefers the joy to
the *mitzva* itself.

The same holds true for the traditional observance of
the Sabbath. Far from being a day of gloom and austeri-
ty, it is rather welcomed as a queen and bride. Indeed,
says Leo Rosten, "mystics believed that the *Shechinah,*
or Divine Presence, descends [to us] each Friday when
the sun sets."[3]

"More than the Jews have kept the Sabbath," remarked
Ahad ha-Am, "the Sabbath has kept the Jews."

Therefore, the psalmist's experience becomes that of
every faithful child of the covenants: "The fear of the
Lord is clean, enduring for ever: the judgments of the
Lord are true and righteous altogether. More to be de-

---

3. The Jews have always considered properly channeled human
sexuality as a gift from God. Consequently, it is not surprising that
the Sabbath meal is meant to be a seductive overture by the wife
toward her husband.

sired are they than gold, yea, than much fine gold: sweeter also than honey and the honeycomb" (Psalm 19: 9, 10).

What Jesus objected to were the innumerable *miztvoth* of rabbinic origin, such as washing the hands before meals. Unhappily, these regulations were often treated as though they rested upon divine authority.

Seen from this perspective, one can better understand what Jesus really meant when He declared: "Except your righteousness shall exceed the righteousness of the scribes and Pharisees, ye shall in no case enter into the kingdom of heaven" (Matthew 5: 20).

The Talmud: Mishnah and Gemara

Jesus entered into the life of His people about the time that the Oral Law was being preserved by a group of rabbis known as the *Tannaim*. It was the concern of these scholars to "make a fence around the *Torah*" by expanding its inner spirit in such a way that no Jew would even be tempted to transgress the Law. One *Tanna,* for example, declared: "He who publicly shames his neighbor is as though he shed blood" (*Baba Mezi'a* 58b).

What is clear in such teaching is the age-old Jewish concern with proper conduct and the desire to obey the will of God. While the *Torah* itself revealed the mind of the Maker, the Jews often found it difficult to know what specific injunction to follow in a given situation. This was particularly true as Israel developed more complex social structures and was faced with such external threats as Greek culture.

At the beginning there appeared (by about 200 B.C.E.) a body of teaching known as *Midrash,* which was nothing other than exposition of Scripture to meet the demands of a particular age or environment. As extensions of the Biblical text, these *Midrashim* can be said to represent the first body of Talmudic lore.

However, rabbinical teaching took a quite different turn in the period 200 B.C.E. to 200 C.E. For it was during those years that the *Mishnah,* or Repetition, appeared as the storehouse of customs which had been handed down by word of mouth from time immemorial. The scholars who produced this body of teaching were the *Tannaim* mentioned above. And among them were such notable figures as Hillel, Rabban Johanan ben Zakkai, and Rabbi Akiba ben Joseph, who died reciting the *Shema* as he was being butchered by the Romans following the defeat of Bar Kochba.

Another interesting fact concerning the *Mishnah* is that it was being produced in the rabbinical schools of Jabneh, Usha, Sepphoris, and Tiberias during the period that Christian mythology might lead people to believe that the "final dispersion" of the Jews occurred. "It is inconceivable," says Jules Isaac, "that the Talmudic project could have been carried on for centuries in a land drained of its Jewish population."

Another body of material was added to the *Talmud* after the year 200. By far the most extensive portion of rabbinic teaching, it was known as *Gemara,* or Completion, and was authored by a succession of scholars called the *Amoraim,* the Interpreters.

The *Gemara* grew out of an academic atmosphere which is still familiar to students today. For example, there would be times when a teacher would attempt to discuss the various implications of a statement from the *Mishnah* and relate it to Scripture or other rabbinical teaching. On other occasions, students would turn to their academic mentors for light regarding what appeared to them as discrepancies in the Oral Law.

"For a long time the discussions grew in number and length, with each succeeding teacher building upon the work of his predecessors," says Lee A. Belford. "Teachers are inclined to wander, even doing so intentionally if their students seem to be losing interest, and they cannot resist repeating humorous anecdotes and stories.

"The rabbinical students were either remarkable memorizers or prolific note-takers," Dr. Belford adds, "because they preserved everything, regardless of whether some things seemed relevant or not."[4]

At any rate, the *Mishnah* and *Gemara* together form what came to be known as the *Talmud,* or Teaching. This instruction is comprised of 63 tractates, divided into six sections. "It comprises the teachings of the *Tannaim* from at least 150 to around 250 [C.E.]" says Dr. Belford, "and the discussions and comments of the *Amoraim* from about 250 until the *Talmud* was finished shortly before 600."

Actually, there are two *Talmuds,* the Jerusalem and the Babylonian. The first was compiled in the rabbinical schools of Palestine, and was completed about the year 425. However, it was the second, dating from about a century later, that became *the Talmud* of Judaism.

"As the *Talmud* gradually came to be conceived of as a single entity," says Frederick Schweitzer, "new terms came into use to identify different aspects of it.

"Thus *Halachah* (law) designates those precepts and injunctions of the *Talmud* which are legally binding on Jews," he explains. "It is sometimes called the 'bread' of the Talmud. The 'wine' is *Aggadah* (tale), a great body of literary materials—stories, legends, parables, proverbs, epigrams in prose and verse—which have a didactic or inspirational value."

The problem for the uninitiated reader is that it is sometimes difficult to separate that which is law from that

---

4. The author cannot avoid the observation that those of us who have had the privilege of sitting in Dr. Belford's classes at New York University must come to the conclusion that he follows the ancient rabbinical model. There is no need to take notes on his anecdotes; they are immediately memorized and passed on with a chuckle.

which is legend. While the *Mishnah* is almost exclusively *Halachah,* the *Gemara* is interspersed with asides that often lead the casual student to forget the original problem!

Yet this vast body of Jewish tradition represents a perennial inspiration to the Jewish people themselves. "The dreams of the prophets may have given the Jews a reason for living," says Lewis Browne. "But it was the little laws of the priest-rabbis that kept the Jews alive."

There is even a Jewish tradition that contends that Moses received two sets of laws on Mount Sinai, the written and the oral. According to the *Talmud* itself, this second code was transmitted in the following way:

> Moses received the [Oral] Law from Sinai and delivered it to Joshua, and Joshua to the elders, and the elders to the Prophets, and the Prophets committed it to the men of the Great Synagogue. . . . Simeon the Just was of the survivors of the Great Synagogue. . . . Antigonus of Socho received it from Simeon the Just. . . . Jose ben Joezer of Zeredah and Jose ben Jochanon of Jerusalem received from them. . . . Joshua ben Perahyah and Nittai the Arbelite received from them. . . . Judah ben Tabbai and Simeon ben Shetah received from them. . . . Shemaiah and Abtalion received from them. . . . Hillel and Shammai received from them. . . . Jochanon ben Zakkai received [the Law] from Hillel and from Shammai (Aboth 1: 1-12; 2: 8).

This genealogy is interesting for two reasons. On the one hand, it traces the transmission of the Oral Law from Sinai to the beginning of the Christian era. On the other hand, it is significant that it passes quickly over the thousand year period between Moses and the men of the Great Synagogue (circa 450-325 B.C.). Harry Gersh suggests the reason for this:

The Oral Law was relatively unimportant during the years of the Judges, the monarchy, the divided kingdoms, and the Babylonian exile—the years of the development of the Torah. As a more or less self-governing nation, the Jews had little need for the collection of adopted customs, interpretations of various decalogues, and common usages that was the Oral Law before 450 B.C.E. But with their return from Babylon as vassals of a foreign king, and the acceptance by the priestly schools of the realistic probability that the Jews would henceforth always be subject to foreign law, the need for defined religious-secular Judaic law became intense.

Reaction to the Talmud

As the Diaspora continued, the Jews turned more and more to the *Talmud* for guidance in the midst of the *galut*. Although boys were exposed to the *Chumash,* or Pentateuch, they were expected to begin Talmudic studies just as soon as age and ability allowed. By the eleventh century, the *Talmud*, rather than the Bible, became the primary preoccupation of European Jewry.

"To Christians," says Gersh, "the *Talmud* became the symbol of all that was alien, all that was exotic, all that was stubbornly Jewish in the Jews.

"Moreover," he writes, "the *Talmud* was believed by the Church to contain mysteries, devilish powers, even orders to kill Christians."

Therefore, Martin Luther reflected the general attitude of Christian Europe when he dismissed this vast body of rabbinic writing as "nothing but godlessness, lies, cursing, and swearing."

What was particularly reprehensible to Christians were reports that the *Talmud* vilified their Savior and Lord as a charlatan and illegitimate son of a German soldier. They were particularly incensed by the blatantly anti-Christian references of the *Toledot Yeshu,* a Medieval fable about the life of Christ, which the competent Edward Flannery believes may have rested on much earlier sources.

"Though its contents enjoyed a certain currency in the oral traditions of the Jewish masses," says Flannery, "it was almost totally ignored by official or scholarly Judaism.

"Anti-Semites," he adds, "have not failed to employ it as an illustration of the blasphemous character of the Synagogue."

But what Flannery fails to mention is the fact that the admittedly shabby *Toledot Yeshu* gained its greatest circulation as actual atrocities were being perpetrated against the Jews by members of a church that claimed to uphold the Good News of Jesus Christ!

In the heated polemics of the age, the church resorted to violence; the Jews used only words.

Meanwhile, the *Talmud* was not without its critics within the Jewish community itself. As early as 762, for example, there arose the learned and influential Anan ben David who declared war against the *Talmud* and attempted to initiate a back-to-the-Bible movement in Judaism.

As shock waves rippled throughout Jewry, hundreds joined Anan ben David in his march to Jerusalem, where he hoped to establish a community governed solely by Biblical Law. But his disciples, later known as *Karaites*, soon discovered that this was easier said than done.

These Karaites quickly found out that they faced the same problem which had confronted the first rabbis who had rebelled against the tyranny of the priests. As the rabbis found that they had to "interpret" the Law for their age, so the Karaites discovered that the same problem faced them. "In time," says Lewis Browne, "the followers of Anan ended by doing just what they had set out to undo."

Although only small pockets of Karaites still exist in Turkey and southern Russia, they inadvertently paved the way for the renewal of Judaism and for one of the most thrilling chapters of Jewish history. It all came about in this way:

As the Karaites were attempting to return to the Biblical foundations of their ancient faith, the Arabs were rediscovering the wisdom of the ancient Greeks. It was a time when the best minds were either engaged in literary pursuits or scientific inquiry.

Then along came Saadia, born in Egypt in 892 and destined to become Gaon of Sura, the foremost rabbinical academy of Babylonia, when he was only 36 years old. It was he above all others who breathed new life into the Judaism of his age.

Saadia, a scholar well versed in Greek, Muslim, and Christian thought, openly embraced many of the new ideas, just as he rejected those of the Karaites. While he readily conceded the ultimate authority of Scripture, he neverthcless maintained that reason should be employed to prove the truths acquired by revelation.

"Normally we would classify Saadia as a rationalist, because he stoutly defended the importance of reason and denied that philosophy leads to skepticism," says Dr. Belford. "But in his conflict with the Biblical literalists he was something considerably more, because he saved the day for the interpretationalists, the Talmudists."

Unhappily, Saadia died at an early age, the victim of impossible scholarly pursuits and his own philosophy of life. "Rest has value only after toil," he once wrote. "Rest without toil is not rest, but indolence. So the sluggard never attains the rest for which he craves."

Meanwhile, Saadia had initiated a new literary output within Judaism, the production of commentaries on the *Talmud,* which were to become known as the *Re-*

sponsa of the Gaonim. Although his own work is lost, it is known by references to it in the commentaries of other scholars.

Moses Maimonides, b.1135

One of the greatest scholars to follow Saadia was Moses Maimonides, born in Spain in 1135. So great was his impact upon Judaism that it was said of him: "From Moses to Moses there was none like Moses."

Here was a physician who made house calls. In fact, as the family doctor of the Sultan Saladin, Maimonides would often spend the entire day caring for his patients in the royal court. He would then return home only to find a waiting room filled with more patients.

"I entreat them to bear with me while I partake of some slight refreshment, the only meal I take in the 24 hours," he once wrote to a man who wanted to discuss *Torah* with him. "Then I go forth to attend my patients . . . and prescribe for them while lying down on my back from sheer fatigue.

"When night falls," he added, "I am so exhausted, I can scarcely speak."

But could this harried M.D. write! In fact, it is not as a physician that the world remembers Maimonides; it is rather because of his outstanding contribution to the storehouse of Jewish knowledge and literature.

Already in the service of Saladin, Maimonides was only 33 when he published the first of his great works, his commentary on the *Mishnah.* Twelve years later, in 1180, he completed his second major contribution, the *Mishneh Torah,* the latter being written in mishnaic Hebrew.

While Philo Judaeus could rival Maimonides as a philosopher and commentator, says Louis Feinberg, he is unknown to the Jewish masses because he wrote in Greek. And were it not for two things, Maimonides himself might have shared a similar fate: first, his Arabic works were quickly translated into Hebrew; and second, his *Mishneh Torah,* popularly known as *Rambam,* was written in Hebrew.

"It was *Rambam,*" says Feinberg, which "rescued Maimonides from oblivion."

However, it must also be acknowledged that Maimonides' *method* also helped to bring him to the attention of Jews who were struggling through the labyrinth of Talmudic tradition. For unlike Rashi, his equally famous predecessor, Maimonides would give a short review of a Talmudic passage, explain individual words, and determine the law, so that the student obtained a clear picture of the entire subject.

Therefore, it is because of his unusual analytical powers that Maimonides is credited with rescuing *Halachah* from the "sea of the *Talmud.*"

But Maimonides is further remembered for his third great work, *The Guide of the Perplexed,* written in 1190. In this philosophical treatise, he attempts to reconcile revelation and reason. Unafraid of truth from whatever source it might spring, he lived by the motto: "Man should never cast his sound reason behind him, for the eyes are in front and not in back."

While he accepted much of Aristotelian logic, Maimonides rejected Aristotle's notion of the eternity of the universe. He rather held to the traditional view that God created the world *ex nihilo,* out of nothing.

To understand God and His relationship to creation, Maimonides argued, one must understand the nature of the universe and its parts. In this belief, he sounds very much like Thomas Aquinas and the Scholastics, who insisted on the value of "natural theology."

But there is also a "Calvinist" streak in Maimonides' thought. It becomes apparent as he argues that some of the decrees of the Divine are beyond human understanding. However, he departs perhaps from Calvin in his insistence that man's free will is not affected by God's omniscience and foreknowledge.

Above all, Maimonides contends the Commandments are not capricious laws but aids to develop man's moral and intellectual growth.

The thinking of Moses Maimonides comes about as close to what can properly be called "theology" as one will find in Jewish thought. His system of doctrine, if it can be called that, is summarized in the Thirteen Articles of Faith. This doctrinal summation, which has been given liturgical expression in the *Yigdal* sung at synagogue services, articulates faith in (1) the existence of God the Creator, (2) the unity of God, (3) the incorporeality of Deity, (4) His eternity, (5) the belief that prayer is for God alone, (6) the integrity of the Prophets, (7) the supremacy of Moses above all other Prophets, (8) Moses' reception of the Pentateuch, (9) the immutability of the Torah, (10) God's omniscience, (11) Divine retribution, (12) the advent of the Messiah, and (13) the resurrection of the dead.

Cabbalism and Orthopraxy

However, the notion that the ultimate concerns of religion are accessible to reason eventually brought about a sharp reaction within the Jewish community. Among those who resisted the allures of rationalism was Moses de Leon, a thirteenth century writer, who is credited with compiling the *Zohar* (Splendor), often known as the Cabbalist Bible. Its critics have uncharitably dismissed it as "brilliant nonsense," but others have accorded it a sanctity second only to the Bible.

While the Cabbalists insist that the *Zohar* contains ancient materials long lost to the masses, modern scholarship has insisted that the major portion of this mystical work came from the hand of Moses de Leon himself.

Echoing some of the thoughts of Aristotle and the Neo-Platonists regarding God's relationship to the world, the *Zohar* has been described as a mixture of theosophic theology, mystical psychology, anthropology, myth, and poetry.

Drawing upon the insights of the *Zohar,* the Cabbalists claim that every word, number, and accent in the Pentateuch has a secret meaning. They further insist that the *Ein Soph,* the Infinite, must be understood in terms of the *Sephirot,* or ten stages of the inner-divine world through which God descends from the innermost recesses of His hiddenness down to His manifestation in the *Shechinah.*

Apart from these decidedly esoteric notions, the *Zohar* contains some of the most beautiful prayers in Jewish literature. It also performs the valuable function of proclaiming the importance of surrender and submission to God. But above all, the mysticism of the Cabbala helped to save Judaism from degenerating into an arid philosophical system.

Meanwhile, the so-called Golden Age of Judaism—an age which produced great scientists, philosophers, poets, and theologians—drew to a close as mounting persecutions against the Jews culminated in their expulsion from Spain the year Columbus set sail for the New World.

In this climate of growing hostility, the Jews responded by manifesting a deepened devotion to their sacred books. "Everything else seemed comparatively unimportant," says Dr. Belford. "Certainly the outside world was not to be trusted. The result was that the Jews erected or heightened an intellectual wall that was as stifling as the physical wall of the *ghetto.*"

It was in this spirit that the Jews abandoned any interest in Talmudic interpretation and turned instead to the *Shulchan Aruch,* or the "Prepared Table," first printed in 1564, and compiled by Joseph Karo, a Spanish

Jew who later became chief rabbi in Safed, in Galilee.

Soon after its publication, this exhaustive four-volume digest of Jewish laws and customs became the highest authority in the legal literature of Israel. "It covered everything, from a ruling as to which shoe should be put on first when dressing, to how love should be made, and how children should be reared," says Lewis Browne. "It clamped the Jew in an iron mold, and forced all his life and thought to become rigid and unchangeable."

Again, the reaction was not long in coming. There were Jews who, even in the midst of disillusionment and despair, rebelled against the ghetto mentality and the rigidity of the *Shulchan Aruch*. Such people yearned for a personal relationship with God which transcended the emphasis on *orthopraxy*, or the stress on correct conduct.

Israel ben Eliezer

Into this spiritual void stepped the remarkable Israel ben Eliezer (1699-1761), known to his devoted followers as the *Besht*, an acronym for *Baal SHem Tov*, "The Good Master of God's Name."

Still a dynamic force in Judaism, the disciples of the *Besht* became known as the *Hassidim*, or Pious Ones. They can still be seen walking the streets of Jerusalem and New York City in the black silk coats and broad-brimmed hats of their forebears of eastern Europe.

But there was nothing somber about the *Besht* and the *Hassidim*. They rather talked about God's love and sought to bring joy into the lives of fellow Jews who had been crushed by false messianic hopes, even as they continued to chafe under terrible persecution.

One of their number was the great Rabbi Levi Yitzkhak of Berdichev, who was not above accusing the Almighty in his defense of his people.

"Whether a man really loves God," Rabbi Levi Yitzkhak often observed, "can best be determined by the love he bears toward his fellow men."

He would reinforce his claim by quoting from the *Midrash Tankhuma*: "He who sustains God's creatures is rewarded as though he had created them."

That was the spirit of the *Hassidim*.

Meanwhile, with the Enlightenment and the rise of the democratic spirit, Jews began to leave the *ghetto* and move into the mainstream of European society. As they did so, men such as Moses Mendelssohn (1729-1786), grandfather of the great composer, sought to update Judaism so that their co-religionists could better adjust to Western culture.

But there were many false starts and bitter disappointments as sporadic *pogroms* continued in Eastern Europe and the Dreyfus case shocked the sensitivities of Jews in the West. At length came the literature of the modern Zionist movement that was to call the Jews back to their ancient land.

Yet throughout the cruel centuries, the Jews have remained the People of the Book. Again and again, they have been driven back to *Torah* and *Talmud* for hope in the valley of despair.

There is yet one other volume that has helped to maintain the indomitable spirit of this indomitable people. It is known as the *Siddur,* the Prayer Book, and its history testifies to the shame of the nations and the glory of His people, Israel.

While the *Siddur* itself began to be compiled in the period of the Second Temple, it contains prayers of much greater antiquity. One of them is known as *Aleynu;* tradition ascribes its authorship to Joshua.

Medieval persecutors used *Aleynu* against the Jews because it testifies to the election of Israel. But its vision of the messianic reign to come witnesses to Judaism's indomitable hope for all mankind, a hope that unites both

Jew and Christian even in the midst of their own division and the cruelties of an unbelieving world:

> Before Thee, Lord our God, may all bow down and worship, and give honor to Thy glorious Name. May they all accept the rule of Thy dominion, and speedily do Thou rule over them forevermore. For the Kingdom is Thine, and to all eternity Thou shalt reign in glory, as it is written in Thy Torah;

> *The Lord shall reign over all the earth.*

Yea, it is said,

> *The Lord shall reign over all the earth;*
> *On that day the Lord shall be One*
> *and His Name One.*

And all God's people say, Amen!

6

Zion in the Wilderness

AMERICAN ARCHAEOLOGISTS showed little interest when the ancient coins were first discovered in widely scattered areas of Kentucky.

The initial lack of professional attention is largely explained by the fact that the unusual artifacts were uncovered by amateurs who themselves lacked a critical appreciation of their independent finds in Louisville, Hopkinsville, and Clay City.

However, when the Clay City coin was sent to a noted scholar at the University of Chicago, he had no trouble reading the inscription. On one side was the name Simon. On the other, "Year Two of the Freedom of Israel."

Simon turned out to be the personal name of the legendary Bar Kokhba, who led the ill-fated Jewish rebellion against Rome in the years 132-135. The Louisville and Hopkinsville coins were also cast in his honor during his brief but stormy career.

Little attention was being given to these discoveries. But the Smithsonian Institution had earlier come into possession of an unusual stone unearthed at Bat Creek, Tennessee. At first, the carved inscription on the stone was thought to be in the Cherokee script.

The confusion was largely because the inscription was being read upside down. After this minor detail was corrected, it became apparent that the writing was not Cherokee, but Canaanite!

This discovery was left to Joseph B. Mahan, Jr., a museum official in Columbus, Georgia, who communicated his findings to the distinguished Brandeis scholar, Cyrus H. Gordon, now at New York University.

Without going into the critical details, it is enough to say that Dr. Gordon concluded that the Bat Creek stone also came from the Bar Kokhba period—and that the inscription roughly read, "Year One of the Messiah of the Jews."

This stone, together with the coins found in adjacent Kentucky, suggests to Dr. Gordon "the migration of Jewish refugees, who sought the Messianic Order in America," after they fled Judea during the First (66-70) or Second (132-135) Jewish Rebellion against Rome.

Dr. Gordon argues that "the Bat Creek inscription inscribed in Roman antiquity is not a souvenir imported from the Old World after 1492 to gratify some Cherokee chief's love of East Mediterranean archaeology.

"Trying to explain away the Bat Creek evidence as anything other than American contact with Palestine around the Second Century," he says, "can only amount to obscurantism that no sensible scholar or layman should elect.

"The Atlantic was crossed long before the Vikings, by different peoples during different centuries," he concludes. "The significance of the excavations at Bat Creek is that they attest inscriptionally and archaeologically to a migration in early Christian times from Judea to our Southeast."

What is particularly noteworthy about the theories of Cyrus H. Gordon is that they are based upson solid archaeological, ethnographic, and linguistic evidence.[1] Quite the reverse is true of the discredited daydreams of the Anglo-Israelites.

The Jews and Christopher Columbus

Commenting on Gordon's labors, Robert Graves made the somewhat tongue-in-cheek observation: "Columbus, of course, did not even rediscover America. He simply used maps." But what Graves did not say is that the fabled Christopher Columbus may himself have been a Jew.

Encyclopedia Britannica concedes the possibility that Cristobal Colon came from a Spanish Jewish family. The relentless Nazi-hunter Simon Wiesenthal has embellished this notion, in a new book that reads like James Bond.

"Many students of the matter have shrunk from the assumption that Columbus . . . might have been—God forbid—a Jew or of Jewish descent," says Wiesenthal. "Were that to be proved, a great deal . . . would have to be thrown onto the rubbish heap."

One historian who believes that such a drastic step will not be necessary is Harvard's Samuel Eliot Morison, *the* American authority on Columbus and author of the Pulitzer Prize winning *Admiral of the Ocean Sea*.

"There is no more reason to doubt that Christopher Columbus was a Genoese-born Catholic Christian, steadfast in his faith and proud of his native city," says Morison, "than to doubt that George Washington was a Virginian-born Anglican of English race, proud of being an American."

But the equally distinguished Don Salvador de Madariaga y Rojo, *the* source regarding the Jewish Columbus

1. Gordon, Cyrus H., *Before Columbus* (Crown, 1971). See also Wiesenthal, Simon, *Sails of Hope* (Macmillan, 1973).

and an honorary Fellow at Oxford, contends just as strongly that the explorer was a Genoese Catholic descended from Catalan Jews who fled from one of the monstrous pogroms of 1391.

The debate partially centers around the cipher which usually followed the signature of Columbus. Morison claims that it should be translated: "Servant I am of the Most High Savior." But Moses Bensabat Amzalak contends that it may well stand for the words: "God of Hosts. God Holy and One."

Madariaga rejects both of these interpretations, because of the dots between the three S's in the cipher. "It so happens," says Don Salvador, "that a Cabbalistic interpretation of the triangular arrangement, and particularly of the dotted S's, translates this signature into the Shield of David: the double triangle or hexagram."

Meanwhile, there are some who claim that the controversial symbol stands for a ritual formula used to this day by traditional Jews in the *Yom Kippur* service.

Whatever the case, Columbus would never have launched his historic expedition had it not been for the interest, generosity, and skill of several influential Spanish Jews. "All the monarchs of Spain and Portugal were skeptical," says Moshe ben Mordechai. "King Faoa would not listen, Ferdinand was not interested, and Isabella was insolvent."

However, two *Marranos,* Luis de Santangel and Gabriel Sanchez, together with Juan Cabrero, also of Jewish descent, saw the value of such an expedition and promised Isabella that they would raise the funds for the proposed voyage. In just a few days, Santangel arranged for an interest-free loan of 17,000 ducats with which to outfit the Nina, the Pinta, and the Santa Maria.

At the same time, another Jew by the name of Abraham Ben Samuel Zacuto, acknowledged to be one of Spain's greatest astronomers, prepared the maps, tables, and nautical instruments needed for the expedition. "Zacuto's skill later did him little good," says ben Mordechai, "because as a Jew during the Inquisition, he was compelled to flee with his son to Turkey, where he died."

As for Columbus himself, Morison suggests that he left the familiar shores of Spain in the spirit of a true Christ-bearer. "In his name [Christ-bearer]," the Harvard historian declares, "Christopher Columbus saw a sign that he was destined to bring Christ across the sea to men who knew Him not."

But others view the evidence from a different perspective.

"Any investigation of the life of Columbus leads by a direct path to the plight of the Jews of Spain at that time," says Wiesenthal. "His story appears to be intertwined with theirs, and this would be the case whether Columbus was himself a Jew, a *Marrano,* or not of Jewish descent at all."

On this point, Morison and the great explorer himself agree with Wiesenthal. In fact, Columbus was later to reminisce: "In that same month in which the Spanish rulers determined to expel the Jews from the entire kingdom, they gave me my commission to undertake my voyage to the Indies."

Moreover, there is still preserved in the archives at Seville a document relating that the newly expelled Jews watched as Columbus made preparations for his voyage on the docks at Palos, while ships carrying the same Jews to Africa sailed down the Rio Tinto.

"On August 2, 1492, all Jews except the *Marranos* had left Spain," says Werner Keller. "The following day, August 3, the three ships under the command of Columbus set out on their audacious voyage to 'the Indies.' "

What is significant about these dates is that August 2 corresponded to the Ninth of Ab, the Jewish fast day that commemorates the destruction of Jerusalem by Nebuchadnezzar and later by Titus. It was on this memorable day that 30,000 unwelcome Jews turned their backs on Spain and set out for Africa, Turkey, Italy, and Portugal.

Since Columbus was prepared and ready to set sail at any time, there is no rational explanation as to why he waited until half an hour before sunrise on the tenth day of the Hebrew month before he began his own momentous voyage. Unless, of course, Cecil Roth of Oxford is correct when he suggests that the expedition was delayed because, "on the former ill-fated day, no Jew would begin an enterprise."

Therefore, in contrast to Morison's claim that Columbus sailed forth as a Christ-bearer to uncharted shores, Wiesenthal suggests that his voyage was financed by wealthy Jewish-born Christians who nurtured hopes of other than a monetary return: if not the discovery of the lost tribes, perhaps at least a new land to which Jews could migrate rather than convert to Christianity.

Meanwhile, although scholars remain passionately divided as to whether Columbus was in fact a crypto-Jew, Bernard J. Bamberger has observed that "it is ironic that Spanish writers, who out of national pride claim Columbus for Spain, must insist on his Jewish origin."

Surely Simon Wiesenthal is not troubled by the fact that Columbus always appears in his writings to be a devout Christian. "I have met Jews who to save their lives . . . wore crucifixes and religious medals and made a great point of their church attendance and general piety," he remarks. "I could not help feeling that [Columbus] was in this respect like the people I met personally during the time of [Nazi] suffering."

Whatever the case, Jews were among the first to flee a hostile Europe for the virgin lands discovered by Christopher Columbus in the New World.

Colonists in America

Unhappily, officers of the Inquisition dogged the footsteps of Jews seeking freedom from persecution in Brazil, Peru, and Mexico. Even the clergy sent there from the homeland were ordered to keep a sharp eye out for any manifestations of Judaism in the new territories.

In a last desperate move to escape new atrocities, 23 courageous Jews arrived at the port of New Amsterdam in September, 1654. There they were met by Peter Stuyvesant, the severe representative of the Dutch West India Company, which held a charter to exploit the resources of the colony. Solomon Grayzel tells of their reception:

A few days after the arrival of the Jews, the governor wrote to his company in Holland, expressing himself in most vigorous terms about Jews in general and these Jews in particular. Confidently he awaited the answer of his employers permitting him to expel these applicants for settlement in the colony. The answer came some four months later, and its contents shocked Governor Stuyvesant. It told him frankly that the Jews in America deserved consideration because a number of Jews in European Amsterdam had become stockholders in the Dutch West India Company and because the people now seeking admittance to New Netherland had fought for Holland in South America.

Although Stuyvesant was dumbfounded by the letter, he again wrote to company officials and renewed his request that the Jews be expelled from the colony. Back came an even sharper reply: He was to follow orders, and the Jews were to stay!

However, this did not mean that those Jews who arrived on American shores were to escape the prejudices which other colonists brought with them from Europe. For example, the Massachusetts Puritans showed the same hostility toward Jewish settlement as they did toward that of other Protestants. At the outset, the only colony that guaranteed universal religious freedom was Rhode Island, where 15 Jewish families settled in 1658 under the beneficent administration of Baptist Roger Williams.

"Though for a time Jews were excluded from some colonies and were subject to legal disabilities in others," says Bamberger, "there was a general and increasing spirit of tolerance and good will, and Jews were never actively persecuted. They held their heads high, participated in the general life of the community, and felt themselves thoroughly at home on the American scene."

So magnetic was the attraction of "the Golden Land" that Jews soon felt confident enough to establish their first synagogues on American soil. The first congregation, *Shearith Israel,* still known as "The Spanish and Portuguese Synagogue," was established well before 1700 in New Amsterdam.

Mikveh Israel was organized in Philadelphia in 1740, although a building was not erected until the time of the War of Independence. Then, about 20 years later, *Beth Elohim* was established in Charleston, South Carolina—roughly at the same time the growing Jewish community was being organized in Newport, Rhode Island.

A tribute to the tolerant spirit of Roger Williams, the Newport (Rhode Island) community consisted of some 1200 persons by 1776. However, the synagogue there was completed 13 years earlier, with the help of *Shearith Israel* in New York City.

Now a national monument, the Newport Synagogue is the oldest synagogue building in North America. However, there is an even more significant point of history behind this structure, which combines New England Congregational style with traditional Jewish elements in architecture.

The cornerstone for this building was laid by Aaron Lopez, the son of Don Diego, head of a respected *Marrano* family. Although he had been baptized a Roman Catholic in infancy, Aaron forsook his Christian name and was circumcised soon after he arrived in America.

However the Newport Synagogue might well have been of more modest design, had not Aaron Lopez, the Jew, struck up a close friendship with Peter Harrison, a pious Protestant and the leading architect of the day.

Harrison not only designed the building but also supervised its construction. When it was completed, Jews and Christians together attended the dedication ceremonies on December 2, 1763.

Harrison's fee? Just the assurance of the continued friendship of Aaron Lopez!

And this spirit of brotherhood was not limited to these two men. During the British occupation of Newport, for example, the Protestants gratefully conducted worship in the synagogue after their own church had been wrecked by the enemy forces.

Moreover, when the Continental Army badly needed resources, Aaron Lopez contributed generously of his own funds. What's more, he did so at a time when his business was almost ruined because of his refusal to deal with the British.

Another Jewish business leader who reacted in similar fashion was Haym Salomon. In fact, the records show that Salomon turned over $650,000 to the colonial cause during the darkest hours of the war. Not one cent was ever asked for nor repaid.

However, the Jewish community gave far more than money. It also provided fighting men. Indeed, it is somewhat amazing to learn that from their relatively minuscule numbers the Jews filled at least 40 important posts in Washington's army, including four lieutenant colonels, three majors, and six captains.

The Jewish community was not without apprehension immediately following the war, when debate arose over the question of whether Christianity should be recognized as the established religion of the United States.

But any fears in this regard were quickly laid to rest when George Washington was inaugurated as the nation's first President. For the course that America would take on the burning issue of religious liberty was tangibly demonstrated as Washington himself took the oath of office before a Protestant minister, a Catholic priest—and Rabbi Gershon Mendez Seixas! If that object lesson was not enough, the man who was to be acknowledged as "Father of the Country" expressed his faith in America in these words:

> The Citizens of the United States of America have a right to applaud themselves for having given to mankind examples of an enlarged and liberal policy: a policy worthy of imitation. All possess alike liberty of conscience and immunities of citizenship. It is now no more that toleration is spoken of as if it was by the indulgence of one class of people, that another enjoyed the exercise of their inherent natural rights. For happily the Government of the United States, which gives to bigotry no sanction, to persecution no assistance, requires only that they who live under its protection, should demean themselves as good citizens, in giving it on all occasions their effectual support.

"This," says Grayzel, "was the real America speaking."

Later American history

Although there had been few Jews who sympathized with the Tories in the Revolutionary War, the Jewish community was no less divided than the rest of the nation at the time of the War Between the States.

On the one hand, slavery was defended by David Yulee, a Florida plantation owner and the first Jew to be elected to the United States Senate. But, on the other hand, Rabbi David Einhorn was forced to leave Baltimore because of his outspoken opposition to human bondage. As a group, the majority of rabbis favored the abolitionist cause.

That this was the case is not surprising when one considers the three primary waves of Jewish emigration to the United States. For these migrations were inspired by prejudice, and made it possible for Jews to identify with the affronts and discrimination suffered by other minority groups.

The first wave of Jewish immigrants consisted almost exclusively of the *Sephardim*—that is, Jews from the Iberian peninsula, who set out to find new homes after their expulsion from Spain and Portugal. This wave continued throughout the colonial period.

The second wave, beginning in the 1820's, brought the *Ashkenazim,* or German speaking Jews, from Central Europe. They had been jolted by the realization that old civil restrictions were being reinstituted against them after a brief period of legal equality under Napoleonic rule.

The third wave was the largest, and it had the greatest impact on American life and culture. It began in force in the 1870's and was comprised almost entirely of Yiddish speaking Jews from eastern Europe, who fled from the cruelty of the *pogroms* and the restrictions of the *shtetls*. This wave continued until Congress ratified the stringent immigration law of 1924.

With this restrictive legislation, Jewish immigration to the United States substantially subsided until additional numbers were permitted entry at the time of Hitler's Satanic "Final Solution of the Jewish Question." Unfortunately, countless additional lives might have been spared, if only America had responded more generously to the words written by the Jewish poetess Emma Lazarus inscribed on the pedestal of the Statue of Liberty:

> Keep, ancient lands, your storied pomp! cries she
> With silent lips. Give me your tired, your poor,
> Your huddled masses yearning to breathe free,
> The wretched refuse of your teeming shore.
> Send these, the homeless, tempest-tos't, to me.
> I lift my lamp beside the golden door!

Those words were etched upon the hearts of the three million Jews who passed through the not-so-golden gates of Ellis Island by 1914.

There are in America today some six million Jews, more than double the number living in Israel itself. While the majority initially settled in the nation's large urban areas, many were among the first settlers in the Southland. Others moved westward with the Forty-Niners, and still others sought their fortune wherever it might be found—beginning the great American adventure with no more than the packs on their backs.

While Jews have distinguished themselves in American arts, science, finance, and commerce, they have given back to their land of opportunity as much or more than they have received.

But there is an ironic twist to a nation's acceptance or rejection of the Jewish people. For example, Hitler expelled Albert Einstein and lost the war; America gratefully received his genius and won the conflict. Similarly, Spain expelled her Jewish population at the height of her prestige, only thereafter to tumble into steady decline—or, as Moshe ben Mordechai put it: "The Jews lost Spain, and Spain lost its future."

Assimilation as a problem

However, the journey toward the American dream has not been without its restless moments for the Jewish community. And this time around, the growing concern is not triggered by overt persecution, but rather by an almost total acceptance of the Jews within the mainstream of our nation's life.

Recently eleven prominent Jewish sociologists, philosophers, and community leaders completed a series of studies which indicate that Jewish survival will depend in large measure on how the Jewish community reacts to the tendency toward integration.

These scholars demonstrate that the assimilation process has been abetted by the following factors:

... The vast majority of American Jews are native-born.

... They are largely college educated.

... Increasingly they have moved away from the heavily populated Jewish centers to areas of sparse Jewish settlement.

... The rate of intermarriage has been rising at an alarming pace.

... Jews remaining in the large cities find it difficult to maintain the institutional facilities essential for continued Jewish identification.

The perils of assimilation were also noted recently by Israel's Chief Rabbi, Shlomo Goren, in an address before the 63rd annual convention of the American Mizrachi Movement, meeting in Jerusalem. In that address, the Chief Rabbi shared the widespread conviction that

Diaspora Jewry now faces the greatest assimilation threat in its history.

However, Max Dimont has reacted to such fears by assuming the role of a voice crying in the wilderness. "We can state categorically," he says, "that if not for the Diaspora, the Jews would have become an extinct people, like other peoples who lived and died within their own states.

"Because of the Diaspora," Dimont insists, "the Jews did not die culturally when a host civilization died. There were always other Jews in other civilizations to give perpetuity to the Jewish heritage.

"For the Jews," he says, "the Diaspora was and is their escape hatch from cultural death.

"Twice in history the Jews were exiled from their homeland—once at the hands of the Babylonians, and again at the hands of the Romans," he observes. "Each time it was the Diaspora Jews who not only preserved Judaism in exile, but also eventually restored the Jewish State."

Attitudes toward Zionism and Reform

While the optimism of Max Dimont is not widely shared, few would dispute the significance of the role played by American Jewry in the restoration of the ancient homeland. Although many Jews had intermarried and abandoned the traditional ways, they responded to the cry of Rachel weeping for her children with the purse, their prayers, and their prestige.

For example, quite apart from the efforts of well-known American Zionists, there is the engaging story of Eddie Jacobson, the onetime business partner of the late President Harry S. Truman.

When Truman left Missouri to carve out a political career in Washington, so the story goes, he invited Jacobson to call on him at any time he could be of help.

Then Harry Truman marched off to the Senate, at length rising to the responsibilities of the Presidency, while Eddie Jacobson continued to operate the modest haberdashery at Thirty-ninth and Main Streets in Kansas City. Although a Jew, his only Zionist sentiments were an occasional expression of concern for "my suffering people across the sea."

As the years passed by, Jacobson never asked for any personal favors, even though he was one of the few men in the world to whom the door of the Oval Office was never closed.

But then came the day when Eddie Jacobson did have some favors to ask of his now-famous old friend. Nothing for himself, mind you, but rather crucial moral support for the Jewish people, who were even then fighting for independence in *Eretz Yisroel*.

President Truman cussed and took note of Eddie's bald pate in less than flattering terms. But he proved to be as good as the word he gave to an old partner, in those less auspicious days in Missouri.

What Eddie was asking would mean a strain on British-American relations and would also dampen Truman's rapport with his Secretary of State. Nevertheless, Truman agreed to see Chaim Weizmann, in a crucial conference that was to solidify American policy in the Middle East. Twelve minutes after the British Mandate expired in Palestine, the United States became the first nation to recognize the new sovereign State of Israel.

Eddie Jacobson, the Diaspora Jew-turned-diplomat, had not forgotten Jerusalem above his chief joy!

Although the American Jewish community today is overwhelmingly committed to the survival of Israel, Jews no less than Protestants have often been divided on matters of faith and life. So heated has the internecine conflict been at times, a synagogue president once remarked to a Gentile friend, "It's like trying to run a church made up of Baptists, Methodists, and Catholics, and conduct a service to please everyone."

When this same man was elected mayor of a Southern city, he immediately laid to rest any notions that he was a political lightweight. "Being president of a congregation with Orthodox, Conservative, and Reform members," he declared, "makes handling a group of 12 city councilmen a cinch."

At its colonial genesis, the American community bore the characteristics of the predominant Sephardic group. Their congregations, says Werner Keller, "were strictly religious organs, both stringently orthodox in ritual and conception of personal conduct, and narrowly unconcerned with the general impact of Judaism upon the lives of their members." He writes:

> Finally, in 1824, a group of members of congregation *Beth Elohim* in Charleston, South Carolina, presented a petition requesting some modifications in the ritual—including the occasional recitation of prayers in English—but it was rejected. This group then broke away from the congregation—the first organized revolt in America against the normally severe discipline of the Sephardic community leaders, who had always opposed the founding of second congregations in any community—and established a Reformed Society of Israelites. This organization, which disintegrated after a few years for want of a leadership well educated in Jewish thought, is generally considered the forebear of Reform Judaism in America.

However, as Bernard Bamberger notes, Reform remained no more than a trend in this country until Rabbi Isaac M. Wise (1819-1900) appeared on the scene. "He had acquired a mystic faith in free America long before he reached its soil," says Bamberger. "To Wise, the United States was not merely a land where Jews were treated fairly: it was a nation whose institutions were the living embodiment of Jewish ideals. The Federal Constitution was 'Mosaism in action.' The men of America, freed from the political oppressions and social prejudices of the Old World, had it in their power to build a Heaven on earth . . . by a free, rational, ethical religion."

If America embodied the ideals of Judaism for Wise, there is a sense in which this towering figure of American Judaism embodied within himself the democratic values, the prophetic spirit, and the pervasive optimism of a movement which often appeared to be an offshoot of liberal Protestantism.

However, while the United States is now the center of Reform Judaism in the world, the origins of Reform can be traced back to men such as Moses Mendelssohn (1729-1786), grandfather of the great composer, who translated the Pentateuch and Psalms into excellent German, sought an accommodation of revelation to reason, and urged his co-religionists to discard what he considered to be obsolete rites and practices.

Shortly after Rabbi Wise arrived in the United States, the distinctive features of the American Reform movement were enunciated in what became known as the Pittsburgh Platform of 1885, which stressed the prophetic ideals of the Bible as against the regulations of the *Talmud*. Says Grayzel:

> It declared some of the Mosaic legislation no longer applicable, among these the dietary laws. It rejected a return to Palestine. It denied the expectation of a Messiah and substituted the hope for a messianic era, that is, an era of peace and perfection which would come to the world

through cultural and scientific progress. It argued that the Jews were a group with a mission of spreading godliness among the peoples of the world . . .

However, with the rise of the Nazi menace, the Pittsburgh Platform was superseded in 1937 by a new statement of Reform principles, known as the Columbus Platform. While still upholding Biblical faith above rabbinic tradition, this new document emphasized the need for Jewish education and culture in America and further expressed the hope that a Jewish State would be established in Palestine. Gone from the Columbus Platform was much of the rationalistic rhetoric of its predecessor.

Meanwhile, there remained in America a strong segment of Orthodox Judaism, which continued to accept the Written and Oral Law as binding and which further followed the *Shulchan Aruk* as a guide. In the midst of distressing social change, these Orthodox Jews retained their belief in a personal Messiah who would one day lead His people back to their ancient land.

At the same time, Conservative Judaism had emerged as a halfway house between Orthodoxy and Reform. This third branch of American Judaism found an eloquent spokesman in Rabbi Solomon Schechter, who became president of Jewish Theological Seminary in New York City in 1902. While Schechter upheld the right to different opinions among Jews, he labored tirelessly for the growth of a catholic Israel, "bound together by unity, tradition, and scholarship."

Conservative Judaism has remained dedicated to the idea of a Jewish culture in which Hebrew is spoken and a knowledge of Jewish history and tradition are cultivated. It has long been identified with the Zionist movement and support of the State of Israel.

But there is yet a fourth segment of American Judaism, known as Reconstructionism and associated with the name of Rabbi Mordecai M. Kaplan, who has emphasized the view that Judaism is "an evolving religious civilization."

While Reconstructionism has tended to stress the need for strongly centralized Jewish communities and support of the Zionist movement, Rabbi Kaplan rejects the divine origin of the *Torah,* the belief in resurrection, and the advent of a personal Messiah. As for the traditions, Kaplan would agree that the dietary laws should be kept in the home to inculcate a sense of Jewish consciousness, but they need not be followed in the marketplace of daily life.

Voices of Revival

Meanwhile, American Judaism is alive and well, as it faces one of the most challenging periods in its relatively short history.

If many Jewish leaders are concerned about survival, there is nonetheless solidarity on the question of the State of Israel. Moreover, it may be argued that Jewish consciousness has never been stronger—this in spite of concern over intermarriage and the Reform/Orthodox split on such matters as women rabbis and women among those included in the makeup of a *minyan,* the traditional minimum number required for the conduct of religious services.

The revival of a Jewish spirit is possibly best demonstrated on the campus, where Jewish students are learning both Hebrew and Yiddish, as well as other subjects relating to Jewish life and culture. Indeed, if the Yiddish press played a prominent role in helping Jewish immigrants to adapt to life in the New Zion, the revival of the *loshen ha-Kodesh* is casting its mystic spell over their grandchildren, as it turns their eyes eastward to Jerusalem.

Moreover, just as there are indications that Reform Judaism is returning to more traditional ways, there has been a remarkable surge of interest in the *Hassidim* in Jewish centers such as New York City. Commitment to the past has made the *Hassidim* persuasive interpreters of Jewish cultural hopes for the future.

There has emerged a highly articulate and strikingly beautiful modern Esther, the charismatic *Rebbetzin* Esther Jungreis, whose mission belies the erroneous notion that women are second-class citizens in Jewish life and worship. This vivacious wife of a rabbi has launched the *Hineni* or "Here Am I" movement, which has called back hundreds of Jewish young people to their ancient faith, through weekend *Shabbatons* and rallies in Madison Square Garden.

Meanwhile, other well-known personalities such as actor Theodore Bikel are appearing on campuses to remind Jewish youth that Judaism involves far more than eating *gefilte* fish and Levy's rye bread or going to a presentation of *Fiddler on the Roof*. "The American Jew must earn his place in the Jewish community," Bikel recently informed a standing-room-only crowd at Queens College in New York City. "It is not a birthright."

So it is that even in the concrete jungles of the Diaspora, there are Jewish leaders who voice the same cautious optimism which David Ben-Gurion expressed during Israel's War of Independence: *Eleh yamduh.* These shall stand!

7

Can These Bones Live?

DAVID BEN-GURION, architect of the modern Jewish State, thought it only proper to wear a suit, shirt, and tie for the assembly. Secretly, perhaps, he wished for his sports shirt, a Ben-Gurion trademark as well-known as the bushy tufts of his snow-white hair.

It was four o'clock on May 14, 1948. Those charged with leadership of a new nation sat around a T-shaped table in the Tel-Aviv Art Museum—once the home of Meir Dizengoff, the city's first mayor.

A framed portrait of the Zionist apologist Theodor Herzl was on the wall behind Ben-Gurion as he began to read. At least one witness, Golda Meir, fought back tears.

"In the Land of Israel the Jewish people came into being," said Ben-Gurion. "In this land was shaped their spiritual, religious, and national character.

"Here they lived in sovereign independence. Here they created a culture of national and universal import and gave to the world the eternal Book of Books.

"Exiled from the Land of Israel," said Ben-Gurion, "the Jewish people remained faithful to it in all the countries of their dispersion, never ceasing to pray and hope for their return and the restoration of their national freedom . . ."

In recent decades, he observed, thousands of Jews made the *aliyah* to *eretz Yisroel* to "reclaim the wilderness, revive their language, [and] build cities and villages . . ."

Hard-nosed realist that he was, David Ben-Gurion had no illusions that peace between Arab and Jew could be attained by the flourish of a pen and a solemn declaration of national independence. Nevertheless, Ben-Gurion now read the key provisions of the document before him:

> By virtue of the natural and historic right of the Jewish people, and the resolution of the General Assembly of the United Nations, we hereby proclaim the establishment of the Jewish State in Palestine, to be called Israel.

As the breath of life began to restore the "dead bones" of Ezekiel's vision, David Ben-Gurion pledged that this new state would be guided by the principles of "liberty, justice, and peace as conceived by the prophets of Israel."

This meant, he said, that there would be full social and political equality for all citizens, regardless of religion, race, or sex (a pledge that would complicate Israeli politics in years to come).

The beloved leader continued his brief but historic declaration by focusing upon the more immediate political concerns of the Old-New Land. "We appeal to the United Nations," he declared, "to assist the Jewish people in the building of its state and to admit Israel into the family of nations.

"Our call goes out to the Jewish people all over the world," he added, ". . . to stand by us in the great struggle for the fulfillment of the dreams of generations, the redemption of Israel.

"With trust in the Almighty," he concluded, "we set our hand to this declaration . . . in the City of Tel-Aviv on the fifth day of Iyar, 5708, the fourteenth day of May, 1948."

The proceedings had taken just 37 minutes. Yet the dreams of two millennia were crowded into that date with destiny. So hectic were the hours immediately preceding independence that the Jewish Agency's representative in Washington did not even know the name of his country when independence was finally declared!

Eliahu Elath had attempted to resolve this problem by referring to "the Jewish State" in his letter requesting U.S. recognition for his country. When word came from Tel-Aviv that the new state was to be called Israel, Elath hastily penciled the name into his recognition request.

Britain's mandate over Palestine expired at six p.m.—two hours after Ben-Gurion's historic appearance at the art museum. At 6:12, President Truman announced American recognition of the State of Israel. Other nations quickly followed suit, though war clouds were even then forming on the Middle East horizon.

The War of Independence

For 1900 years the Jews had wandered over the face of the earth, hapless victims of the often-barbarous *goyim*. Yet somehow they had managed to survive the ghettos, the Pale of Settlement, the pogroms, and even the Holocaust which claimed the lives of the six million.

Now back in their ancient land, they firmly resolved: "Never again!"

Their resolution was reached in the face of overwhelming odds. At the time of independence, there were less than 700,000 Israelis of Jewish birth, living on a narrow strip of land.

"With 50 million Arabs," said King Ibn-Saud of Saudi Arabia, "what does it matter if we lose 10 million people to kill all the Jews? The price is worth it."

The Israeli leadership nursed no illusions that the Arabs were bluffing. "We have our backs against the wall," conceded Golda Meir. "The only friendly neighbor we have is the Mediterranean."

And the Arabs were bent upon pushing the Jews into that sea.

However, the long march to Zion had taught Israelis to innovate. Somehow they had brought illegal immigrants through the blockade during the period of the British mandate. In skirmishes they had challenged both British and Arab weaponry with submachine guns fashioned out of smuggled war-surplus parts, as well as with antique French mountain guns, affectionately nicknamed "Napoleonchiks."

Therefore, when war erupted six hours after independence had been declared, the Israelis made up in *chutzpa* what they lacked in sophisticated military hardware. *"Eleh yamduh,"* wrote Ben-Gurion in his diary. "These shall stand!" Such optimism in the face of massive Arab power can only have sounded foolhardy or naive to military strategists throughout a largely indifferent world.

When the onslaught came, the Israelis found themselves fighting against the well-equipped armies of Egypt, Transjordan, Syria, Lebanon, and Iraq, supported by contingents from Yemen and Saudi Arabia. All of these troops moved forward under the nominal leadership of King Abdullah of Transjordan, although it was no secret that military strategy was actually being plotted by General John Bagot Glubb, honorary *pasha* and self-styled latter-day Lawrence of Arabia.

All that the Israelis could muster in this life-and-death struggle were improvised "Little David" (*Davidkas*) mortars and an "air force" of Piper Cubs, from which Israeli pilots dropped homemade grenades out of open cockpits.

Amazingly, Ben-Gurion's prophecy turned out to be correct. His own tiny army stood firm against the odds. On June 11, a little more then two weeks after the anticipated "slaughter" began, the Arabs gratefully accepted a U.N. ceasefire.

"What was [to be] *jihad* for the Arabs," says Frank Gervasi wryly, "proved to be a War of Independence for the Jews."

Eleh yamduh! Naked power may have crushed the heroes of the Warsaw ghetto. But this time, Little David was able to put the Arab Goliath to flight, nursing his wounds.

One of the many largely unsung heroines in the struggle for the Holy Land was a matronly woman who really preferred caring for her grandchildren to being burdened with the affairs of state. Golda Meir was trying to raise a family and serve as political secretary of the Jewish Agency, a kind of provisional government between the mandate years and independence.

It was in that capacity that Golda was sent to the United States, to raise funds with which to purchase arms to defend against future Arab encroachments. When she arrived in New York, she carried $10 in her pocketbook. She left a month later with $50,000,000!

"The day when history is written," remarked her beloved Ben-Gurion, "it will be recorded that it was thanks to a Jewish woman that the Jewish state was created."

Zionism and Theodor Herzl

While many Jews still reject the Zionist ideal, few would disagree that Palestine might still be a malaria-infested wasteland, had it not been for the spirit that motivated Theodor Herzl, David Ben-Gurion, and Golda Meir.

It certainly was no accident that the handsome, bearded portrait of Herzl looked down upon the ceremonies at the Tel-Aviv Art Museum in May, 1948. For this leader had made the following entry in his *Tagebucher* for September 3, 1897, immediately after the First Zionist Congress in Basle, Switzerland:

> If I were to sum up the Basle Congress in one word—which I shall be careful not to do openly —it would be this: At Basle I founded the Jewish State. If I were to say this today, I would be met by universal laughter. In five years, perhaps, and in any case in fifty, everyone will see it. The State is already founded in essence in the will of the people to have a state.

Discounting the fact that God Himself may have had a hand in Israel's restoration, Theodor Herzl was a man of commanding vision and frenetic missionary zeal. Can anyone say his prophetic capabilities were marred by the fact that he missed his own outside date for the founding of the modern Jewish State by almost a year?

Never was there a more unlikely candidate to bear the heavy mantle and awesome title of founding father. Theodor Herzl's early career has been described aptly by Herman Wouk as that of "a free-thinking Viennese newspaperman—a gray gloved, top hatted boulevardier, at home in Paris and Berlin."

Born in 1860 of a half-assimilated Jewish family in Budapest, Herzl's minimal religious education ended with his *bar mitzvah* at 13 years of age. His cultural ties were to Germany. Just a smidgen of Judaism was added to give flavor to a *bon vivant* life.

Although a member of the Vienna bar, Herzl forsook law to become a journalist-playwright. Almost immediately his work became so popular that, as Max Dimont remarks, "one simply had to read Herzl every morning with one's *croissants* and coffee."

After a ten-year stint as *feuilleton* editor of the *Wiener Allgemeine Zeitung,* Herzl's reputation as a newsman had become so widely respected that the distinguished liberal daily, the *Neue Freie Presse,* offered him the coveted post of Paris correspondent.[1]

However, Theodor Herzl was not a happy man. "Perhaps the most decisive factor in Herzl's deepening melancholy," says Howard Morley Sachar, "was the bitter anti-Semitism he encountered everywhere in Europe.

"A man of almost morbid sensitivity, he had suffered keenly, while a student in Vienna, from the frigid correctness of his non-Jewish classmates," says Sachar. "As a journalist he was obliged to attend political rallies and public conventions at which anti-Jewish epithets and slogans were far from uncommon."

There was a time when Herzl flirted with the idea of submitting to Christian baptism as a means of avoiding anti-Semitic slurs and even more personal assaults on his already-wounded psyche. But the celebrated *L'Affaire Dreyfus* was to put an end to such notions and change the entire course of his life.

Theodor Herzl had been assigned to cover the trial of Captain Alfred Dreyfus, a French artillery officer of Jewish background, who was charged and subsequently convicted of passing military secrets to the Germans. At the outset, Herzl thought Dreyfus guilty as charged.

However, after the disgraced officer had been shipped off to the infamous Devil's Island, Herzl and many other

1. A *feuilleton* is a section of a European newspaper or magazine designed to entertain its readers.

European intellectuals began to have second thoughts about the case. These doubts were increasingly heightened by new evidence which indicated that it was not Alfred Dreyfus but a profligate fellow officer who was the real culprit in this scheme that tore France apart.

Although Dreyfus was eventually exonerated and admitted to the Legion of Honor, Herzl himself was still haunted by the spectacle of a church and state that sought to preserve their own vaunted honor by capitalizing on the inbred anti-Semitism of an entire nation.

So bitter had Jew-hatred become in France during and after the Dreyfus trial that one priest is reported to have expressed dismay that he could not "circumcize the Jews up to the necks." Others openly warned Jewry that they faced "mass extermination."

If such outbursts were meant as a form of evangelism, Theodor Herzl became a convert overnight. He put away all notions of becoming a Christian and returned to the ancient faith of his ancient people!

Gone was the frivolity which dominated his earlier writing. He became a man possessed with a sense of mission even as the irrational cry still seared his soul, "Death to the Jews!"

As the Nazi sacrifice of the Six Million was later to spur the Jews to fight for their land, the blatant anti-Semitism of the Dreyfus era played a crucial role in giving birth to political Zionism itself.

Herzl's own convictions were set down in a slim volume, *Der Judenstaat,* which created immediate sensation and controversy throughout Europe and even in America. For Herzl's goal in *The Jewish State* was nothing less than regeneration of the Jewish nation as a political entity.

"The Jews who wish it," he declared, "will have their own state. We shall live at last as free men on our own soil, die peacefully in our own homes. The world will be freed by our liberty, enriched by our wealth, magnified by our greatness."

Herzl's almost messianic vision grew out of the conviction that the basic problem of his co-religionists was homelessness. And coupled with this condition was the grim reality of anti-Semitism wherever Jews sought a haven in large numbers. With keen but troubled insight, he wrote:

> Everywhere we have sincerely endeavored to merge with the national comunities surrounding us and to preserve only the faith of our fathers. We are not permitted to do so. In vain are we loyal patriots, in some places even extravagantly so; in vain do we make the same sacrifices of life and property as our fellow citizens; in vain do we strive to enhance the fame of our native countries in the arts and sciences, or their wealth through trade and commerce. In our native lands where, after all, we too have lived for centuries, we are decried as aliens, often by people whose ancestors had not yet come to the country when our fathers' sighs were already heard in the land.

Yet it was not the passion of his prose alone which gained Theodor Herzl almost instantaneous recognition in some Jewish circles as *Herzl ha-melech*—Herzl the King—of this still-unborn state. That honorific title was bestowed upon him because he identified with his people in their silent struggle and spoke in their language of *dos Yidishe Folk*.

"Nor was that all," says Joseph Adler. "Not only did Herzl declare the Jews to be a people; he declared them to be *one* people."

Chaim Weizmann, the brilliant Russian Jewish chemist who would one day become Israel's first president, was later to recall that Herzl's literary missile "came like a bolt from the blue."

"Fundamentally," says Weizmann, *"The Jewish State* contained not a single new idea for us. That which so startled the Jewish *bourgeoisie,* and called down the resentment and derision of Western rabbis, had long been the substance of our Zionist tradition . . .

"Not the ideas but the personality which stood behind them appealed to us," Weizmann recalled. "Here was daring, clarity, and energy.

"The very fact that the Westerner came to us unencumbered by our own preconceptions had its appeal," he added. "We were right in our instinctive appreciation that what had emerged from the *Judenstaat* was less a concept than a historic personality."

However, others were not so favorably impressed. For example, the great Jewish philanthropist Baron Maurice de Hirsch just stared incredulously that day in May, 1895, when Herzl showed up at his mansion to argue that a congress of Jewish leaders should be called "to discuss migration to a sovereign Jewish state."

Herein lay part of the problem, if not for de Hirsch, then certainly for some of the most respected elements in religious Jewry.

Many were simply scandalized by Herzl's novel messianic vision that "a sovereign Jewish state" could be established in any country other than Palestine. Some went so far as to dismiss Herzl as nothing more than "the Jewish Jules Verne."

Their criticism was not entirely unfounded. For there was evidence that Herzl lacked any real understanding of the roots and depth of Jewish nationalism. This became clear when he first toyed with the notion of a Jewish homeland in Argentina.

The idea was not Herzl's alone. For Baron de Hirsch had already announced a grandiose scheme of bringing relief to Russian Jewry by relocating 300 Jews a week in Argentina, until a total of 3½ million had been resettled there under the sponsorship of his Jewish Colonization Association.

In arguing the merits of the Argentine, Herzl allowed that the country "extends over a vast area, is sparsely populated, and has a temperate climate." But he also recognized the force of Jewish public opinion and the fact that "the present infiltration of Jews" in Argentina "has produced some ill feeling there."

By the time Herzl showed up on the baron's doorstep, he had lost all interest in establishing a Jewish colony in South America. With characteristic bluntness, he accused de Hirsch of "breeding beggars" and "debasing the character of our people" by shipping them off to so remote a land.

While Herzl then went on to call for a congress to discuss "migration to a *sovereign* Jewish state," Baron de Hirsch died in 1896, brokenhearted and disillusioned over his well-meaning but impractical vision.

However, Herzl's pragmatism continued to dominate his thinking about a homeland for his people, especially after news reached the West of the terrible Kishinev *pogrom*. Therefore, when British Colonial Secretary Joseph Chamberlain suggested the possibility of establishing a Jewish colony in Uganda, Herzl reluctantly decided that such a temporary asylum might spare his coreligionists additional heartache until the road was opened to Palestine.

But that was not meant to be. The proposal created such a furor at the Zionist Congress of 1903 that the delegations from eastern Europe walked out of the convention hall *en bloc* after the Uganda scheme was approved on the first ballot by a narrow margin.

As Herzl watched the *Ostjuden* exit, he remarked:

"These people have a rope around their necks, and still they refuse!"

At the same time, Herzl recognized his own blunder and later joined the opposition in the interests of restoring Zionist unity. He died the following year at the age of 44, physically and emotionally drained by the rigors of walking in the sandals of Moses.

"Zionism was the Sabbath of my life," Herzl wrote two years before his death. "I believe that my influence as a leader is based on the fact that, while as man and writer I had so many faults, and committed so many blunders and mistakes, as a leader in Zionism I have remained pure of heart and quite selfless."

"History," says Howard Morley Sachar, "has not dimmed that judgment."

Opposition to Zionism

However, as in life so in death, Theodor Herzl was unable to reach those Jews to whom the *very idea* of political Zionism was anathema.

There had always been a large bloc of religious Jewry which gloried in Israel's role as the Suffering Servant of God. They believed passionately that their sufferings were meant to redeem the world and hasten the advent of the Messiah. "As the dove atones for sins," declared the *Midrash Hazita*, "so do the Jews atone for the nations." And this these Jews believed firmly.

No less an authority than Maimonides cited this *Midrash* when, in 1172, he sought to bring comfort to the persecuted Jews of Yemen:

> Our nation speaks with pride of the virulent oppression it has suffered, and the sore tribulations it has endured, to quote the words of the Psalmist, "Nay, but for Thy sake are we killed all the

day." Let those persons exult who suffered dire persecutions, lost their riches, were forced into exile, and were deprived of all their belongings. For the bearing of these hardships is a source of glory and a great achievement in the sight of God.

Apart from this deeply moving conviction, many religious Jews were further opposed to political Zionism because the movement had attracted what Dimont describes as a "horrifying group of *apikorsim*—unbelievers." Says this eminent Jewish chronicler:

> There was Moses Hess (1812-1875), a renegade German Jew who, before hitting the Zionist road, turned to communism and married a French whore to show his contempt for Judaism. There was Russian-born Peretz Smolenskin (1842-1885), a truant from *Talmud* who, at age twelve, tossed his phylacteries out the window and, after living as a bum for a decade, showed up in Vienna for a secular education. There was Judah Pinsker (1821-1891), an over-intellectualized Russian-Jewish army officer who preached integration, until he ran into anti-Semites who confused Judaism with original sin. And there was Theodor Herzl (1860-1904), the rich, handsome, black-bearded, superbly tailored Viennese "Moses" who, while on a fantasy trip to a baptismal font, found Judaism instead.

"Yet it was these four refugees from Judaism who mapped the first section of the road back to Zion," says Dimont. "Each wrote a slender work whose searing words drove home the necessity for a homeland in Palestine."

Moses Hess, 1812-1875

A forerunner of the later Zionists, Moses Hess abandoned Jewish Orthodoxy to lead a rather bohemian life.

Apart from his marriage to an adoring Gentile trollop, Hess threw his entire heart and mind into the socialist movement, only to be taunted by Karl Marx as "the communist rabbi."

His break with the political left came on the heels of a burgeoning German nationalism that fed on inherent racist and anti-Semitic sentiments. The mood of the period was captured by Adolf Stoecker, a clergyman and founder of the Christian Socialist Party. "The Israelites are an alien people," he charged in a typical diatribe. "They can become one with us if they convert to Christianity."

However, Hess clearly understood that not even this avenue of escape was open any longer, as the German nationalists willed nothing less than the total annihilation of the Jews.

"Even baptism will not free them from the curse of German hatred," Hess declared. "The Germans do not so much hate the religion of the Jews as their race. . . .

"It is not possible to be simultaneously philo-Teuton and Judaeophile," he observed, "as it is impossible to love German military glory and German popular liberty."

The only answer to the Jewish dilemma, as Hess saw it, was for the Jews to return to Palestine, there to create a haven against persecution, as well as a spiritual center for Judaism itself.

Hess gave expression to his new convictions in a book entitled *Rome and Jerusalem,* which reflects his indebtedness to the Italian patriot Giuseppe Mazzini, whose "Young Italy" movement attracted the sympathy and wealth of thousands of Jews during that country's abortive liberal-nationalist uprisings in the 1830s.

Where Mazzini had argued that the liberation of Rome would be an act of historic justice, Hess in turn contended that the liberation of Jerusalem would prove to be a blessing for the entire world:

> March forward, Jews of all lands! The ancient fatherland of yours is calling you, and we will be proud to open its gates for you. March forward, ye sons of martyrs! The harvest of experience which you have accumulated in your long exile will help to bring again to Israel the splendor of the Davidic days and rewrite that part of history of which the monoliths of Semiramis are the only witness.

It is clear in *Rome and Jerusalem* that Hess often emphasized the racial uniqueness of his people at the expense of their religious heritage. In fact, Louis Jacobs has remarked that Hess sometimes "comes perilously close to racist theories which are today repudiated by most students of the subject on scientific grounds."

However, as Jacobs has remarked, the call to "Jewish patriotism" and racial pride was made by Hess to evoke self-respect and love of race in a people that had been haunted and hounded from one country to another. It is in this light that the following challenge must be interpreted:

> The Jewish race is a primary race which, despite climatic influences, accommodates itself to all conditions and retains its integrity. The Jewish type has always remained indelibly the same throughout the centuries. . . . If Judaism owes its immortality to the splendor of its religious genius, so the latter is indebted to the fruitfulness and indestructibility of the Jewish people. What the Bible said of Jews in Egyptian bondage is also true of them during the Third Exile: "But the more they afflicted them, the more they multiplied and the more they spread abroad. . . . And the land was filled with them. . . ."

The most inspiring thing about the Jewish prayers is that they are really collective prayers for the whole Jewish community. The pious Jew is before all else a Jewish patriot. The "newfangled" Jew who denies Jewish nationalism is not only an apostate, a renegade in the religious sense, but a traitor to his people and to his family.

Peretz Smolenskin, 1842-1885

A similar note was soon to be sounded by that truant from *Talmud,* Peretz Smolenskin, who took the first opportunity to flee boyhood poverty in White Russia by hopping a freight train, first to Odessa and later to Vienna.

Like Moses Hess, Smolenskin insisted that Jewish nationalism went hand in hand with the Jewish faith. But he added a cultural dimension to emerging Zionist thought that transcended the vision of a return to the ancient land.

By the time Smolenskin rode into Vienna in a boxcar, emancipated Jews in the West had created a culture expressed in the languages of their grudging hosts. In the East, however, secular insights and values were creeping into the Pale of Settlement under the influence of the *maskilim,* who rejected the Yiddish of the masses and sought to revive Hebrew as the language of their people.

In their drive to escape what Dimont calls "the *gefilte* fish milieu of the ghetto," these *maskilim* were committed to bringing about a *Haskala*—or awakening—for the Jews within the Pale. One of their first objectives was to turn their people away from *Hasidic* notions of salvation and turn their thoughts to the mundane problems facing them in the here and now. To accomplish this end, they produced a series of escape novels written in Hebrew and dedicated to undermining the ghetto mentality.

A leading figure in this *Haskala,* Peretz Smolenskin

used his time in Vienna to establish a Hebrew-language literary monthly, *Ha-Shahar* (The Dawn), which soon became the most influential forum of the awakening.

However, as much as Smolenskin opposed Jewish obscurantism, he also warned his fellow *maskilim* against assimilation. "The willfully blind bid us to be like all other nations," he wrote. ". . . Yes, let us be like all the other nations, unashamed of the rock whence we have been hewn, like the rest in holding dear our language and the glory of our people."

This call for a revival of Hebrew language and culture found its most trenchant expression in Smolenskin's now famous essay, *Am Olam* (*The Eternal People*), which was originally published in his own literary journal. "Just as other subjugated nations are not ashamed to hope for their national redemption," he declared, "neither is it a disgrace for us to hope for an end to our exile."

"Although Smolenskin did not at first preach or envisage a program of practical reconstruction in Palestine," says Sachar, "he was the 'bridge' between Jewish cultural nationalism and modern Zionism."

Judah Pinsker, 1821-1891

The idea of an unencumbered piece of real estate as a panacea for Jewish despair became the vision of Judah Pinsker, an Odessa physician and the fourth member of Dimont's quartet of *apikorsim*.

Forced to abandon his earlier assimilationist notions in the face of mounting Russian anti-Semitism, Pinsker wrote an anonymous pamphlet in German, called *Auto-Emancipation,* and sub-titled, "An Admonition to His Brethren, by a Russian Jew."

Attempting to study anti-Semitism scientifically, Pinsker concluded that Jew-hatred is a phenomenon which lies buried deep within the Gentile psyche. In his analysis, he observed:

> We do not count as a nation among the other nations, and we have no voice in the council of the peoples, even in affairs that concern ourselves. Our fatherland is an alien country, our unity dispersion, our solidarity the general hostility to us, our weapon humility, our defense flight, our originality adaptability, our future tomorrow. What a contemptible role for a people that once had its Maccabees!

While the Jews remained a "spiritually distinct nation" even in exile, said Pinsker, this very fact contributed to Gentile "hatred for us as a people. . . . Men are always terrified by a disembodied spirit," he wrote, "and terror breeds hatred."

Pinsker's prescription for Jewish alienation was a homeland for the Jewish people. As with Theodor Herzl, the Odessa physician was initially open to any suggestions regarding a suitable territory. In fact, he talked as much about America as Palestine in his early deliberations. But that ancient yearning for Jerusalem ultimately led him to think solely in terms of the Promised Land.

There is little doubt that Pinsker's focus was influenced by the rise of a new movement called *Hibbath Zion,* the "Love of Zion," which quickly spread to many parts of Europe and even to America.

"In a great number of Jewish centers," says Israel Cohen, "societies were formed of *Hoveve Zion,* or 'Lovers of Zion,' who discussed the question of settling in Palestine as an immediate and practical problem and urged the study of Hebrew as a living language."

While these societies were forced to meet in secret because of fear of arrest, they attracted many influential professional men, including Judah Pinsker, who was elected president of the organization in 1884.

At the same time, Smolenskin's Hebrew-language journal, *Ha-Shahar,* had attracted two particularly penetrating writers, Moses Leib Lilienblum (1843-1910), and Eliezer Perlman (1857-1922). These outstanding figures shared Smolenskin's own love for Hebrew, his visceral reaction against assimilation, and his passionate belief that the Jews were not only a religious community but a people. With him, they helped to bring about a shift from *Haskalah* to Jewish nationalism.

While Lilienblum wrote on "The Rebirth of the Jewish People in the Land of Its Ancestors," Perlman argued for both a return to *eretz Yisroel* and a revival of Hebrew as a living language. Adopting the name of ben-Yehudah, he put his preaching into practice and settled in Jerusalem, where he began work on his monumental dictionary of Hebrew as a vernacular tongue.

However, as much as ben-Yehudah loved the ancient language, his primary concern was for "a national center to serve as the heart feeding the blood arteries of the nation. . . . If I did not believe in the possibility of Israel's redemption," he declared, "I would discard the Hebrew language as a worthless thing."

Although it is impossible to fully comprehend the relationship between the revival of Hebrew and national rebirth, Chaim Weizmann himself hints how the language influenced his own development as a Zionist leader. "I . . . never corresponded with my father in any other language [except Hebrew]," he says, "although to mother I wrote in Yiddish. I sent my father one Yiddish letter; he returned it without an answer."

Back to Israel

Meanwhile, another future Zionist leader, equally distinguished, left his home in Poland at 19 to resettle in Palestine. A year after his arrival there, he made a 2½ day hike from Jaffa to Jerusalem. There he found a virtual Tower of Babel—Jews "speaking to each other in 40 different languages, half of them unable to communicate with the other half."

In an effort to rectify this chaos in communication, the young man returned to Jerusalem shortly thereafter to edit a trade union newspaper committed to the revival of Hebrew. As he was about to sign his first editorial with his Polish name, he thought for a moment, and decided against it. Hurriedly, he scratched out David Green, and wrote instead, David Ben-Gurion—"son of a lion cub."

Ben-Gurion arrived in Palestine in 1906 as a member of the second *Aliyah* inspired by the growing spirit of Jewish nationalism. Many in this wave of pioneers were committed to socialism and to redeeming the land. They shared a passionate dislike for urban life within the Pale, and were determined to "return to the soil."

Although these sturdy settlers were dogged by hunger, disease, and grueling labor, Ben-Gurion himself wrote later of his first night in the Land of Promise:

> . . . I did not sleep. I was among the rich smell of corn. I heard the braying of donkeys and the rustle of leaves in the orchards. Above were massed clusters of stars clear against the deep blue firmament. My heart overflowed with happiness, as if I had entered the realm of legend. My dream had become a reality!

By this time, there were about 70,000 Jews living in Palestine. They represented not only recent settlers but those small pockets of Jews who had fled the Diaspora over the years and had taken up a new life in Jerusalem, Hebron, Safed, and Tiberias, which were called the four Holy Cities. "From the end of the 16th Century," says Israel Cohen, "funds were regularly collected and transmitted to them, and, as they were distributed among them, these funds were called *Halukah,* which means distribution."

It is historically inaccurate to imagine that Palestine was ever completely without a Jewish remnant. Even after the Roman conquest, there were many Jews who maintained a foothold in the country. "At no time," says Gervasi, "not even during the worst period of famine and massacre, did they totally abandon the land." In a tightly woven brief against contemporary Arab claims, he writes:

> . . . The Bible is not the only proof of the Jews' claim to Palestine. It exists in recorded deeds demonstrating Jewish ownership in fee simple of great tracts of land bought from various owners, and converted from marsh and desert into orchards and gardens. And it also exists in a massive body of international law envisioning and sanctioning the creation in Palestine of a Jewish national homeland.

Moreover, the eternal Jewish mystique never separated the people from the land. This mystique somehow was strong enough to survive the bitterest disappointments regarding national restoration.

For example, in the middle of the fourth century, Julian the Apostate met death at the hands of the Persians shortly after he had promised to restore Israel in the land. Then, less than three centuries later, the Persians themselves made a similar pledge, only to honor it with anti-Jewish measures and banishment.

Through it all, the exiles remained resolute. "If I forget thee, O Jerusalem," they prayed, "let my right hand forget her cunning. If I do not remember thee, let my tongue cleave to the roof of my mouth; if I prefer not Jerusalem above my chief joy" (Psalm 137: 5, 6).

The Jews were not alone in their insistence that someday they would be restored in their land. For example, the noted Puritan divine Increase Mather wrote in 1669 that it cannot "justly be denied or questioned" that Scripture affirms that someday the Jews will "again possess the land of their fathers." Similarly, Lord Shaftesbury, the self-described "Evangelical of Evangelicals," issued a personal plea in 1838 for a Jewish settlement in Palestine under the protection of the Great Powers.

Commenting upon Shaftesbury's "remarkable" display of interest, Israel Cohen notes that the great British statesman and social reformer actually moved *The Times* of London to editorialize that "the proposition to plant the Jewish people in the land of their fathers [was] no longer a mere matter of speculation, but a serious political consideration."

While the British Foreign Secretary was not averse to Shaftesbury's proposal, says Cohen, "there was no Jewish organization capable of dealing with so stupendous a problem." Even then, the British Consul in Jerusalem was instructed to accord official protection to the Jews living in Palestine, an overture which Cohen regards as "the forerunner of the Balfour Declaration of 1917."

By the end of the 19th Century, the Zionist ideal had reached full bloom. Philanthropists such as Sir Moses Montefiore and Baron de Rothschild had demonstrated a willingness to back Jewish national aspirations with hard cash. And the long-dormant hopes of countless Jews were revived by the timely evangel of Jewish spokesmen, both past and present, who held forth the vision of "Next Year in Jerusalem." Indeed, the electrifying effect of a Hess or a Herzl can only be fully understood in light of the earlier efforts of men like Jehuda Halevi and Rabbi Zevi Hirsch Kalischer.

Nor was the Zionist vision limited to Europe alone. On this side of the Atlantic, Mordecai Manuel Noah (1795-

1851) appealed to American Christians to support Israel's return to the land. So successful were his efforts that President John Adams was among those who gave moral encouragement to Noah's idea of re-establishing "an independent nation" for the Jews in Palestine.

Another advocate for such a scheme was the gifted poetess Emma Lazarus (1849-1887), who was deeply stirred by the sight of thousands of her co-religionists finding a haven from the Russian *pogroms* in that New Zion called America. Her words of welcome to these and other homeless refugees will forever remain inscribed on the Statue of Liberty in New York Harbor.

But home for the Jews still remained that ancient land of Abraham, Isaac, and Jacob!

So it was that finally, in 1882, a small group of 20 young men initiated the first *aliyah* to *eretz Yisroel,* braving Turkish and Russian immigration restrictions and the harsh realities of life in their ancestral homeland. These idealistic youngsters, fired by the preachments of *Hibbath Zion,* became known as the *Biluim,* a name adopted from the first letters of their motto: *Beth Jacob lechu ve-nelcha* —O house of Jacob, come ye, and let us [go forth]" (Isaiah 2: 5).

The *Biluim* represented an entirely different type of Jew from those who had preceded them. "They went there not to pray and die," says Cohen, "but to live and work and rebuild the country."

The formidable obstacles facing these early pioneers defy description. They knew nothing of agriculture and back breaking physical labor. They were totally unprepared to meet the challenge of the hot climate and disease carrying water. And they were constantly exposed to attack by marauding Bedouin.

Moreover, had it not been for the *largesse* of rich European Jews like Baron de Rothschild, they would have been forced to abandon their magnificent obsession as an exercise in futility. As it was, they had only a few hundred rubles among them when they left for Palestine. And much of that was stolen along the way.

However, these young *Biluim* had something that money could not buy. They were fired by fresh memories of the *pogroms* and the Pale—bitter memories that guaranteed their devotion to the Land of Promise.

If Marxist zeal molded their political outlook, a very un-Marxian type of religious piety energized them in the face of overwhelming odds. Their trust was in the *Shema*: "Hear, O Israel, the Lord our God, the Lord is One." And their hope was in "our land, Zion."

So it was that ten young pioneers ultimately settled not far from Jaffa. They named their new colony *Rishon le-Zion,* the First in Zion. Then came other settlements— *Petah Tikvah* (Gate of Hope) in the same district; *Rosh Pinah* (Head Corner Stone) near Safed; and *Yesod Hamaalah* (Foundation of Ascent) near Lake Huleh.

As dawn broke on the twentieth century, the migration of European Jews had already begun to flow in two directions—to America, the new land of promise, and back to Palestine, the ancient Promised Land. While Jewish immigration to the vast urban centers of the New World is widely known, Israel Cohen has documented the more veiled movement in the Middle East:

First *Aliyah* (1882-1903)	25,000
Second *Aliyah* (1904-1914)	40,000
Third *Aliyah* (1919-1923)	36,183
Fourth *Aliyah* (1924-1931)	84,113
Fifth *Aliyah* (1932-1939)	264,585
W.W. II to Independence (1940-48)	112,512
1948 (to September 30)	70,000
Grand Total	632,393

Allowing for the deduction of some 30,000 Jews who abandoned Palestine between 1920 and 1938, the population of Israel had swelled well past the million mark by the end of 1950. Today that population stands at about three million, including Moslems, Christians, and Druze. And, despite periodic wars, Israel still lives and grows.

Frontier institutions

Much of the credit for the spectacular growth in the Old-New Land must go to three distinctively Israeli institutions—the *kibbutzim,* the *Histadrut,* and the absorption centers.

The *kibbutz,* a term derived from the Hebrew word meaning group, is a communal or collective settlement governed by the general assembly of its workers. Members of the 225 *kibbutzim* throughout the country receive no salaries, but, in return for their labors, they are provided with housing, food, clothing, medical services, and education for their children. While *kibbutzim* are primarily agricultural, many have gone into other enterprises, including food processing and plywood manufacture.[2]

The *Histadrut* represents both a vast workers' collective bargaining agency and a principal Israeli investment institution. Often called the world's only capitalistic union, the *Histadrut* set up its own chain of *kibbutzim,* established its own daily newspaper, and began to provide its members with social services "from womb to tomb." Both David Ben-Gurion and Golda Meir had a hand in shaping this remarkable institution.

Yet even more amazing in many respects are the absorption centers which play so crucial a role in helping new immigrants to adjust to Israeli life. No nation ever faced a more demanding task. As Golda Meir observed,

2. In addition to the *kibbutzim,* there are also various forms of *moshavot.* These are also based on collective economy and ownership; but in many such settlements each family owns its own house and accepts responsibility for cooking, laundry, child care, and other personal matters.

often these immigrants are destitute, "many of them broken in body and spirit.

"They have to be fed, clothed, given a physical examination, their sanitation needs attended to, their sick cared for," she said. "They must be given food, shelter, a roof over their heads. All in one day. The *first* day!"

Integration into Israeli life involves far more than bread and a new address. The waves of immigrants following independence brought Jews from 72 countries. There were Chinese Jews from Kai-Fung-Foo; dignified Indian men in white *dhotis* and their *sari*-clad wives; nomadic *Hadhramautic* Jews whose women paint their faces blue and yellow; dark-skinned Jews from Afghanistan, Abyssinia, and Libya; even Kurdish Jews who spoke Aramaic, the language of Jesus.

To Peggy Mann, some of the most interesting of the new arrivals were the gentle, pious Yemenite Jews who had come straight out of the twelfth century. They boarded sleek new airliners without trepidation, knowing that Isaiah had said, "They that wait upon the Lord shall . . . mount up with wings as eagles" (Isaiah 40: 31). Their only disappointment came when they landed at Lydda airport and discovered that Messiah was not on hand to greet them!

"Never before in history," says Ms. Mann, "had so many, and so many different types of people, descended in so short a space of time onto so small a section of the globe."

The integration of this polyglot people was the herculean task of the absorption centers. But the job remains unfinished as Soviet Jewry and others of the Diaspora continue the long march home.

> I will restore the fortunes of my people Israel, and they shall rebuild the ruined cities and inhabit them; they shall plant vineyards and drink their wine, and they shall make gardens and eat

their fruit. I will plant them upon their land, and they shall never again be plucked up out of the land which I have given them (Amos 9: 14, 15, RSV).

The wilderness and the solitary place shall be glad for them; and the desert shall rejoice, and blossom as the rose (Isaiah 35: 1).

The vision becomes more of a reality each passing day, as hardy Israelis reclaim the desert and dig for mineral wealth deep in the Negev. But as impressive as these gains may be, all is not well in Zion.

Taxes continue to bite deeply into every Israeli paycheck as the nation remains on constant alert against attack. The resolution of the Arab refugee problem appears impossible. Crime is on the upswing as critical housing shortages and technological advances contribute to urban blight. Tel Aviv alone has burgeoned from a population of 40,000 in 1914 to 600,000 today.

Other problems vex the leaders of Israel. On the one hand, the Israeli-born *Sabras* often have little patience with newcomers who betray the *shtetl* mentality of Eastern Europe. And on the other hand, there are still many Jews who oppose Zionism itself on both political and religious grounds.

Yet the very existence of Israel remains one of the real miracles of history. And with it, the supreme touch of irony.

For example, it is quite likely that Zionist aspirations would have remained dormant in the minds of so-called assimilated Jews had it not been for the fact that anti-Semites would not let them forget the rock from which they had been hewn. It took the Dreyfus affair to ignite the burning zeal of Herzl. And it took the Holocaust to inflame the masses of world Jewry, in the conviction that none could rest secure until a national homeland existed for the Jewish people.

"One wonders what would have become of the remnant of European Jewry had there been no Israel," muses Brandeis scholar Michael J. Rosenberg. ". . . There was no alternative to the creation of a state for the European Jewish refugees.

"Israel's struggle," he says, "is for survival."

World events prior to independence

World War I began history's conspiracy to lead the exiles home. It all came about in this way:

Chaim Weizmann, the Russian-born biochemist, had left his native Pinsk to carve out a career and uphold the Zionist ideal in England. There he taught at the University of Manchester, and later became director of the Admiralty Laboratories in London.

When hostilities erupted among the Great Powers, the British found themselves in urgent need of acetone for war production. Without it, all naval guns would have to be rebuilt. But Jewish genius saved the day. Chaim Weizmann discovered a process whereby the critical substance could be produced from horse chestnuts!

In appreciation for Weizmann's contribution to the war effort, Prime Minister Lloyd George asked the celebrated scientist to name his reward. "I want nothing for myself," replied Weizmann in effect. "All I ask is a homeland for my people."

That request was honored on November 2, 1917, when British Foreign Secretary Arthur Balfour wrote a 117-word note to Lord Lionel Walter Rothschild, head of the British branch of the great Jewish banking family. Known henceforth as the Balfour Declaration, the historic document said in part:

> His Majesty's Government view with favor the establishment in Palestine of a national home for the Jewish people, and will use their best endeavors to facilitate the achievement of this object, it being clearly understood that nothing shall be done which may prejudice the civil and religious rights of the existing non-Jewish communities in Palestine, or the rights and political status enjoyed by Jews in any other country.

The only problem with the declaration was that Palestine had been under the control of the Ottoman Turks for four centuries. But even this obstacle was removed a month later, when British troops under General Edmund (The Bull) Allenby staged a brilliant campaign against the forces of the Turks, a German ally.

With America's entry into the war, some 2700 Jewish volunteers joined Allenby's Royal Fusiliers in the historic march on Jerusalem, including Izhak Ben-Zvi and David Ben-Gurion, destined later to become president and prime minister of the reborn State of Israel. Supported by a battalion of Jews recruited in Palestine itself, Allenby's victorious troops entered the Holy City on Chanukah, the Feast of Lights—one of the most joyous and holy days of the Jewish year.

While his fellow soldiers were ecstatic over the victory, David Ben-Gurion's sentiments had been expressed at the time the Balfour Declaration had been made public:

> Britain has not given Palestine back to us. Even if the whole country were conquered by the British, it would not become ours through Great Britain giving her consent and other countries agreeing. . . .

> Britain has made a magnificent gesture; she has recognized our existence as a nation and has acknowledged our right to the country. But only the Hebrew people can transform this right into

tangible fact; only they, with body and soul, with their strength and capital, must build their national home and bring about their national redemption.

Apart from the secular thrust of Ben-Gurion's messianic vision, later events were to prove him eminently correct. For initial Arab hospitality toward the Jews quickly degenerated into blind fury. In April, 1920, riots broke out in the Jewish quarter of Jerusalem, where the survivors of the earlier *pogroms* became the fresh victims of murder, rape and pillage.

A prime figure behind this Arab violence was the sinister Haj Amin el-Husseini whom the British had appointed as *mufti* of Jerusalem, making him the religious head of the Moslem community in Palestine.

The fanaticism of Husseini and his extremist clique soon made it clear to the Jewish settlers that they would have to rebuild their ancient land with a hoe in one hand and a gun in the other.

Moreover, as the Jews continued to face fresh outbreaks of Arab hostility, they were suddenly confronted by an even greater threat—the Nazi "Final Solution of the Jewish Question."

With the outbreak of World War II, Husseini realized that he might be able to solve his own "Jewish question." "To that end," says Gervasi, "the *mufti* entered into a secret alliance with the Nazis: he promised Hitler Arab support in the Middle East in the event of war with England [his own political patron], in exchange for German money and weapons."

Great Britain emerged victorious from the ensuing war. But the Jews still were not free of their struggle for survival. For those who did escape Hitler's gas chambers were now denied access to the ancient homeland by a British government that seemed incapable of administering a country which, as Mix Dimont suggests, resembled "a schizophrenic patient."

As early as 1936, the British had attempted to solve the problem of Arab intransigence and Jewish despair by appointing the Peel Commission to come up with corrective therapy. In due course, that commission recommended that the country be partitioned along ethnic lines, a suggestion that led some Christians to believe that the confrontation of Joel 3: 2 was about to be fulfilled. But then, says Dimont:

> The Jews reluctantly accepted this recommendation, the Arabs vehemently rejected it, and the British diplomatically ignored it, preferring a schizoid patient to none at all. To tranquilize the Arabs, the British gave the Jews a shock treatment, the White Paper of 1939, which would reduce Jewish immigration to 15,000 a year for five years and then stop it altogether, aiming at freezing the Jews into a permanent minority in the Arab majority. The Jews vehemently rejected this, the Arabs reluctantly accepted it, and the British enthusiastically enforced it.

Ironically, however, the Jews continued to support the British in the war effort, just as their Arab neighbors left little doubt that their own sympathies rested with the Axis. "We will make war as though there were no White Paper," declared Ben-Gurion, "and we will fight the White Paper as though there were no war."

That politics sometimes make strange bedfellows is illustrated by the fact that, at the end of hostilities, the British rewarded the Arabs by continuing to control Jewish immigration rigidly. The burned-out hulks that did manage to sail through the British blockade were impounded, their human cargo interned in new concentration camps on the island of Cyprus.

221

This was the volatile situation which existed when the British did ultimately relinquish political control in Palestine on the eve of Israel's independence.

The remarkable growth of the Jewish State has not dampened Arab determination to push the Jews into the sea, even though the Arab nations were beaten decisively in the War of Independence (1948), the Sinai Campaign (1956), and the Six-Day War (1967). The sacrilege of the latest confrontation—the *"Yom Kippur War"*—has only strengthened Israel's resolve.

Meanwhile the God of both Jew and Arab weeps as He witnesses the senseless destruction of the seed of Isaac and Ishmael. His promise remains sure:

> In that day shall Israel be the third with Egypt and with Assyria, even a blessing in the midst of the land: Whom the Lord of hosts shall bless, saying, Blessed be Egypt, my people, and Assyria the work of my hands, and Israel mine inheritance (Isaiah 19: 24, 25).

How long, O Lord, how long!

8

The Myth of the Judeo-Christian Tradition

> Then I came to them of the captivity of Tel-abib, that dwelt by the river of Chebar, and I sat where they sat, and remained there [overwhelmed] among them seven days (Ezekiel 3: 15).

THE MOMENT OF TRUTH came as the stifling noonday sun beat down upon the customs shed at the Syrian-Jordanian border.

There I was, a typical American WASP, awaiting Arab clearance to cross over into The Promised Land.

I had left Beirut, Lebanon, the night before to begin the longest taxi ride of my life. The Lebanese Christian travel agent had arranged for me to share a battered old Chevy with four Arabs headed for Damascus. There I stayed overnight at the New Semiramis Hotel, before continuing my first pilgrimage to Jerusalem early in the morning, in the company of three more garlic-chewing sons of Ishmael.

As I waited for the unsmiling Jordanian officials to check my passport and visa, I thought of my last week in Lebanon and of the evening in Damascus.

Table conversation in the dining room of my hotel in Beirut breathed heavily of threats to "push the Jews into the sea," and the massive display of military hardware along the streets of Damascus made me reconsider my plans to search out "the street called straight." The armored vehicles outside the New Semiramis told me that discretion called for a cup of thick, sweet coffee, and then to bed!

But today an elusive, if not foolhardy, courage gripped me as I moved through Jordanian customs. I thought of the insanity and inhumanity of the Holocaust unleashed by Nazi madmen against a defenseless and innocent people. I thought, too, of the flourishing bitterness against the Jews throughout the Arab Middle East.

My stomach churned as I handed my U.S. passport to the still-unsmiling customs officer. My heart pounded as I waited for the fatal question: "Religion?"

In my heart of hearts, I was fully prepared to answer, "A Jew."

I had counted the cost. I knew that so hated a word could deprive me of liberty—perhaps even of seeing my wife and sons again. But thoughts of home and loved ones were momentarily lost in my mind, fixed upon man's inhumanity to man. Here I stood; I could do nothing else.

In my moment of truth, I felt transfixed by the words of Pius XI: "Spiritually we are all Semites." While this much-abused cliche has sometimes resulted in theological confusion and condescension, the words for me at that moment meant total identification as a Christian with God's ancient people of Israel.

It never occurred to me for a split second that my passport clearly identified me as a clergyman and as an executive of an international Christian organization. With the wave of a hand, the Jordanian officer beckoned me to move quickly across the border. I was only holding up traffic!

In the Holy Land

The ride south to Jerusalem was interrupted by a change of taxis in the nondescript Jordanian capital of Amman, where I jumped into the front seat of a choking Ford, whose driver seemed out to win the Indianapolis 500.

We breezed across the hot desert, up and over twisting mountainous stretches, along a new two-lane highway built with American aid. I tried dutifully to be impressed by the signs showing the U.S. and Jordanian governments linked by the hands of friendship—even though it meant peering through a blood-ringed hole in the windshield on the passenger side of the rasping car.

When my feet finally rested upon the sacred soil of the Old City, I remembered "Jerusalem above my chief joy!" (Psalm 137: 6).

Middle East Airlines, whose Viscount service assured me of a more relaxed trip back to Beirut, quickly arranged for me to stay at the quaint but comfortable Azzahra Hotel at Herod's Gate. It was good—so good— to at last put body and baggage down in Room 21. I enjoyed the luxury of a cooling breeze blowing in from the balcony window.

The date was November 7, 1961. That is important to remember, because ten years later I would shepherd a group of American Christians through the Holy Land under vastly different circumstances. But that first trip to a then-divided Jerusalem will always linger in my memory as the fulfillment of a dream—or almost!

There was the upwelling emotion of walking along the Via Dolorosa, retracing the steps of the Galilean from Pilate's judgment hall to the place called Golgotha. Even the competing and schismatic claims of ancient Christian sects could not dampen the sense of awe I experienced as I knelt before the traditional site of the tomb of my Lord.

I felt that same flush of quiet joy the next day as I made my way over the torturous old road to Bethlehem, the City of David and birthplace of the Nazarene. But, I must confess, it was difficult to visualize the manger scene amid the Orthodox artifacts so alien to Protestant senses.

Like most tourists, I was more amused than offended by the cacophony and the commercialism of Arab entrepreneurs who hustled "rich" Americans all the way from Jerusalem to Bethlehem. I can well appreciate the feelings of a somewhat cynical newsman who later wrote:

> Things haven't changed much in [Jerusalem] since Jesus, on the eve of His crucifixion, told the hawkers to scat. The Temple is gone. Not many doves are for sale anywhere in the Middle East today. But, if anything, the merchants are more onerous and prolific than ever.

> People sell underpants around the corner from Calvary; lads with shoeboxes pick pockets along the Via Dolorosa; the Holy Land Bazaar is outside the tomb of resurrection. Jesus, no doubt, would be as disgusted as before. . . .

> Everyone . . . myself included, searches for belief, and what better place to find it than in the cradle of civilization. Besides, as the Jewish Talmud advises those who deny the possibility of resurrection: "If what never before existed, exists, why cannot that which once existed, exist again?"

Alas, though, the search is difficult for the rubbish in the way. Television antennas spring like weeds from Old Jerusalem. Light bulbs populate the cross atop the Church of the Nativity. A tout in St. George's Cathedral tries to sell visitors assortments of postcards, then asks in a whisper if they'd like an 'Egyptian woman' instead.

But free enterprise must be expected, I guess, in that land which has been overrun by Babylonians, Macedonians, Seleucids, Romans, Byzantines, Persians, Crusaders, British, Jordanians—and now the Israelis. Somehow stifling poverty—as well as the political exigencies of a given moment—creates in some men a sharp business sense and the will to survive.

What disturbed me far more than the crass commercialism and the competing sects was the then-divided city itself and the burning hatred which the Arabs felt against the Jews who resisted annihilation across the narrow no-man's-land.

The Arabs themselves can be a gentle, generous, outgoing people, hospitable to a fault. I found that so on my first night in Old Jerusalem, as I sipped their heavy black coffee and talked endlessly with a local businessman. But later, in writing home to my wife, I felt constrained to comment: "The hatred against the Jews is so thick here that you can cut it with a knife."

My own sense of frustration was heightened by the fact that I had hoped to cross the DMZ the following day, completing my *aliyah* to Zion, the City of our God. But that was not meant to be.

It was rather with a heavy heart that I walked from Herod's Gate, down King David Street beyond the tower-topped YMCA building. Somewhere out there, I knew, lay the Mandelbaum Gate. But, like Moses, I was at that time only to be given a glimpse of the Promised Land.

It shall come to pass in the latter days . . .
  out of Zion shall go forth the law,
and the word of the Lord from Jerusalem.
  He shall judge between the nations,
and shall decide for many peoples . . .
  nation shall not lift up sword against nation,
neither shall they learn war any more.

  (Isaiah 2: 2-4, RSV)

These words lingered in my mind as I brushed past squatting Arabs and an assortment of poultry and livestock on my way to the MEA ticket counter at the old Jerusalem Airport. It was then that I felt the first hard jab in the pit of my stomach.

I was taking with me to India an unsolicited souvenir. At first, I thought it was "Delhi belly." But, recalling the proffered lemonade at the souvenir shop in Bethlehem, I finally diagnosed my problem as a case of the Jerusalem jumps.

Ten years later, bitter memories of that ordeal still haunted me as I watched a member of our tour drink tap water in our Old City hotel. But there was no longer any need to worry. The resourceful Israelis had laid a 20-inch pipeline from the Sea of Galilee in the North to Jerusalem in the South. Sharon once more was beginning to blossom like the rose. And the water was now safe to drink.

Evangelicals and the Jews

Evangelical Christians look with awe and wonder at the drama unfolding in the Holy Land. They remember the hand of God guiding British Foreign Secretary Arthur James Balfour as he penned the momentous words on November 2, 1917: "His Majesty's Government view with favor the establishment in Palestine of a national home for the Jewish people . . ."

228

Surely my own father was thrilled many times over as the very lilt of these words carried the assurance that the day was not far off when "the salvation of Israel [will] come out of Zion! when the Lord bringeth back the captivity of his people, Jacob shall rejoice, and Israel shall be glad" (Psalm 14: 7).

Meanwhile, the Jewish community may point to the still-unchecked virus of Christian anti-Semitism, a disease which seems to incubate for a season before breaking out once again in pandemic proportions. But our own home was never so infected. For my father was both a devout Christian and an ardent Zionist, who prayed without ceasing for the peace of Jerusalem.

Dad and I could argue long and loud over some moot point of Christian theology. But when he talked of Israel, his voice would become soft, his eyes would light up, and this tragically shy father of mine would speak in the power and spirit of the ancient prophets whom he loved so well.

His admonition to his sons was this: "Never forget God's promises to Abraham: 'I will make of thee a great nation, and I will bless thee, and make thy name great; and thou shalt be a blessing: And I will bless them that bless thee, and curse him that curseth thee: and in thee shall all families of the earth be blessed' " (Genesis 12: 2, 3).

No matter that Palestine was then a malarial swampland, first under Turkish and later under British control Dad looked toward that day when the "dry bones" of Ezekiel's vision would take on flesh and live again (Ezekiel 37: 1-14).

His joy knew no bounds that day in 1948 when Israel achieved a shaky independence, and Dad's thoughts and prayers shifted to the prophecy of Zechariah:

> Thus saith the Lord of hosts; In those days it
> shall come to pass, that ten men shall take hold
> out of all languages of the nations . . . of the
> skirt of him that is a Jew, saying, We will go
> with you: for we have heard that God is with
> you (Zechariah 8: 23).

One of my own earliest recollections was of a dear
rabbi friend offering prayers for "our Christian brother"
when that frail father of mine was seriously ill.

The stories of later encounters by my family with
Jews and Judaism are endless and deeply moving. Yet,
as I recently visited a nationally known Jewish leader
with my teenage son, the thought occurred to me that
my own children represent a third generation within a
single Christian family who have come to love the Jewish people for who and what they are.

While all of this may trigger various emotions among
Jews and Christians, the need for such open-hearted
dialogue between elder and younger brothers is imperative in the turbulent world of our age. Martin Buber met
this issue squarely:

> That peoples can no longer carry on authentic
> dialogue with one another is not only the most
> acute symptom of the pathology of our time, it
> is also that which most urgently makes a de-
> mand of us. . . .
>
> To the task of initiating this conversation those
> are inevitably called who carry on today within
> each people the battle against the anti-human. . . .
> In opposition to them stands the element that
> profits from the divisions between the peoples,
> the contra-human in men, the subhuman, the
> enemy of man's will to become a true humanity.

"In a genuine dialogue," says Buber, "each of the part-
ners, even when he stands in opposition to the other,

230

heeds, affirms, and confirms his opponent as an existing other. . . . Those who build the great unknown front across mankind shall make it known by speaking unreservedly with one another, not overlooking what divides them but determined to bear this division in common.

"The name *Satan* means in Hebrew *the hinderer*," Buber observes. "That is the correct designation for the anti-human in individuals, and in the human race.

"Let us not allow this Satanic element in men to hinder us from realizing man!" he declares. "Let us release speech from its ban! Let us dare, despite all, to trust!"

All of this was written by the towering figure of a devout Jew who has left an indelible imprint upon Christian theology. A man who could carry on a dialogue with a chaplain in Hitler's *Wehrmacht,* a man who incurred the biting criticism of his own people by pressing tirelessly for *Ichud*—unity—and reconciliation between Arab and Jew.

Surely the prophetic words of Martin Buber hold special significance for evangelicals in an age when disaster threatens to engulf the globe on the heels of a world-wide energy crisis. It is an age when committed Christians may be called upon to stand firm in love if tiny Israel is made to shoulder the blame for the ills of mankind.

The Jewish community itself has become aware that a correlation exists between anti-Israel sentiment and the more blatant forms of anti-Semitism. Christian self-interest demands that the last vestiges of anti-Semitism be eradicated from the household of faith.

Like it or not, Jew and Christian belong to one another, and the anti-Semite represents a common enemy, bent upon destroying the church no less than the synagogue. For, as Sigmund Freud recognized, "the hatred of Judaism is at bottom hatred for Christianity."

"Anti-Semitism must finally turn against Christianity,"

says Roy Eckardt. "For there is no Christianity apart from Jesus the Jew."

That both Freud and Eckardt stand on solid ground is amply demonstrated by the German experience. For, while many German Christians initially shared the anti-Semitism of the Nazis, they awoke one day to discover that their own faith had been dealt a death blow by these mad anti-messiahs.

Moreover, the unremitted persecution of all Soviet believers, Jewish and Christian, further testifies to the fact that those who reject the Jewish God also reject the Christian Savior!

All of this means, of course, that Jew and Christian must come to a deeper understanding of their *Akeida*—or binding—to one another. For the survival of the one is eternally linked to the survival of the other.

While each human being must come to terms with his own prejudice, the Jewish-Christian encounter can be immeasurably strengthened by mature dialogue that accepts the partner's differences as well as areas of mutual agreement.

But dialogue at this level is not easy to initiate or achieve. For painful historical precedents have created within the Jewish soul what can be described as the what-good-can-come-out-of-Nazareth complex. (And these suspicions have only been deepened by recent Christian attempts to turn Passover into a Christian TV spectacular.)

"In the past," says Rabbi Arthur Gilbert, "Jewish-Christian confrontation was fraught with danger and physical violence. Both the New Testament and testimonies of Jewish history record a tragic tale of man's oppression of his brother because of religious difference.

"The truth is, we have never really spoken words to each other," he laments. "We persecuted, flogged, burnt

232

at the stake, humiliated, mocked, murdered, feared, and hated the other.

"Now guilt and suspicion," he says, "have made it difficult to converse even when we wish it."

This book represents an honest attempt to understand Judaism through Christian eyes but free of Christian bias. For no one can understand another unless both share the same language of the heart.

The author's personal inadequacies for so massive a task have no doubt meant failure at many points. But even in his ignorance, his own Christian faith has been deepened and his love for Judaism immeasurably strengthened.

The myth of a superseded faith

At the same time, it has become quite clear to the author that Rabbi Arthur A. Cohen has provided a valuable corrective for so much that parades as encounter by debunking what he calls "the myth of the Judeo-Christian tradition."

"It was only in the late Nineteenth Century in Germany that the Judeo-Christian tradition, as such, was first defined," says Rabbi Cohen. "It was introduced by German Protestant scholarship to account for the findings developed by the Higher Criticism of the Old Testament, and achieved considerable currency as a polemical term in that period. Cohen writes:

> The negative significance of the expression became primary. The emphasis fell not to the communality of the word 'tradition' but to the accented stress of the hyphen. The Jewish was latinized and abbreviated into 'Judeo' to indicate a dimension, albeit a pivotal dimension, of the explicit Christian experience. It was rather more a coming to terms on the part of Christian scholarship with the Jewish factor in Christian

civilization. It was no less, for all its efforts to be scholarly, an exhibition of what Solomon Schechter called 'Higher Anti-Semitism,' for the Jewish in the Jewish experience was all but obliterated, being retained, rather like a prehensile tail, in the larger, more sophisticated economy of Christian truth.

Arthur Cohen and the distinguished Solomon Schechter are not the only ones who have dared to link Biblical Higher Criticism with "Higher Anti-Semitism." The first to point to this subtle danger was none other than Samson Raphael Hirsch who, as early as 1841, warned that this "pseudo-science" was anti-Semitic in origin and character.

"From mocking irreverence," says Grunfeld, "the language of the German Bible critics changed into one of burning hatred of Israel and its sacred tradition. . . .

"Two generations later," he adds, "Europe was engulfed by a flood of barbarism of unspeakable cruelty, when human values, and especially the value attached to human life, sank lower than ever before in the annals of man.

"Future historians," he continues, "will have to investigate how far the undermining by the Bible critics of the respect for Israel's *Torah* and its eternal values, has prepared the moral climate for the cynical disregard of human freedom and human life, which characterizes the totalitarian paganism and the moral debacle of our epoch."

Whatever the results of such research, J. H. Hertz has sagely observed: "Every attack on the *Torah* is at the same time an assault against Israel as well as a revolt against the spiritual and the divine in history and human life."

It could well be that a common commitment to the integrity of Scripture might provide a common ground for dialogue between the Jewish and evangelical communities.

For example, if earlier conservative scholars had turned to Jewish authorities, they would have found Rabbi Hirsch arguing convincingly against alleged contradictions between the first and second chapters of Genesis.

"Similarly," says Grunfeld, "Hirsch's explanation of the various names of God, and the manner in which these are used in the first chapters of the *Torah,* makes nonsense of the so-called documentary hypothesis of Higher Criticism."

In our own day, the eminent Yehezkel Kaufmann has argued that critical scholars still adhere to the old conclusions even though "the grounds have crumbled away." He particularly labels as "untenable" their basic postulate that "the priestly stratum of the *Torah* was composed in the Babylonian Exile, and that the literature of the *Torah* was still being written and revised in and after the Exile.

"The *Torah* . . . is the literary product of the earliest stage of Israelite religion, the stage prior to literary prophecy," Kaufmann declares. "Although its compilation and canonization took place later, its sources are demonstrably ancient—not in part, not in their general content, but in their entirety, even to their language and formulation."

However, the most colorful account of Jewish disenchantment with Higher Criticism involves Dr. Cyrus H. Gordon, onetime Brandeis Near Eastern expert, now at New York University.

As the story goes, Dr. Gordon argued persuasively against certain critical asumptions in an encounter with a Protestant seminary professor. However, while the professor was convinced by Gordon's breadth of scholarship, he baldly allowed that he would continue teaching the accepted system of Higher Criticism because, he said, "we have standard textbooks."

"What a happy professor!" remarked Gordon in disbelief. "He refuses to forfeit his place in Eden by tasting of the fruit of the Tree of Knowledge!"

At the same time, any dialogue between Jewish and evangelical scholars would soon reach a hopeless deadlock unless the Christian participants recognized the aura of sanctity which Jews place around the oral as well as the written Law.[1]

While Christians may not be able fully to share Judaism's devotion to the oral tradition, they can readily come to appreciate the fact that this "wall of law" time and time again saved the Jewish people from extinction in their dispersion.

Moreover, Rabbi Hirsch has argued that the same fathers who handed down the written Law also passed on the oral tradition. "If our fathers have deceived us with the one," he asks, "how could they be trustworthy with the other?"

Hirsch was not at all surprised that those who stand outside the stream of Jewish tradition should find the written Law full of contradictions. Says the *Gaon*: "The same enemies of Israel's tradition—who now use the argument that tradition is not legitimated in the written Law—would have argued that a clerical error might have crept into Holy Writ!"

However, the equally distinguished Abraham Joshua Heschel has argued just as forcefully that "respect for tradition" becomes "grotesque and self-defeating" when it is made "the supreme article of faith.

"We do not adhere to the specific forms of observance because of their antiquity," says Rabbi Heschel. "Antics of the past are hardly more venerable than vagaries of the present.

---

1. As Christians argue among themselves regarding the integrity and inspiration of Scripture, so the Jewish community is divided regarding the sanctity of the written and oral Law.

"Did not Judaism begin," he asks, "when Abraham broke with tradition and rejected the past?"

But Heschel would not agree for a moment with the erroneous so-called Christian notion that "the Law of Moses commands only right action, and says nothing about purity of heart."

Insisting that Judaism is not another word for legalism, Heschel suggests that the rule of law is translated into the language of love when the committed Jew is seized by the divine admonition: "Circumcise . . . the foreskin of your heart" (Deuteronomy 10: 16).

"The rules of observance are law in form and love in substance," he declares. "Law is what holds the world together; love is what brings the world forward."

Christian anti-Zionism

Sami Hadawi, a noted Arab apologist, recently buttressed his claims against Israel by quoting a well-known New Testament scholar. Here is the quotation which Hadawi used to support his own anti-Zionist stand:

> The evidence is overwhelming that no true Christian, believing in the New Testament, could possibly confuse the modern Israel, brought into being by political machination and military power accompanied by ruthless deprivation of the native inhabitants, with the Israel of God of Christian faith. These two Israels contradict one another completely. . . .

> There is no basis in either Old or New Testament to support the claim of the Zionists that a modern Jewish State in Palestine is justified or demanded by the Bible or by Biblical prophecy. The 'promises' of Biblical prophecy apply to all mankind, and not only to Jews or Zionists; such terms as 'victory' and 'salvation,' in their true Biblical meaning, connote religious and spiritual achievements and not the conquest or degrada-

Unhappily, in my opinion it is just a hop, skip, and a jump from this kind of exegesis to the inflammatory language of Jesuit Daniel Berrigan, who recently justified Arab treachery at the outbreak of the *Yom Kippur* War by excoriating Israel as "a criminal Jewish community . . . the creation of millionaires, generals, and entrepreneurs."

Berrigan's reference to Israel's alleged "imperial misadventure" brought an immediate and angry response from the distinguished Jewish historian Rabbi Arthur Hertzberg. "Underneath the language of the New Left," he wrote, "it is old-fashioned theological anti-Semitism."

What is involved in Berrigan's kind of liberalism is a passionate disdain for the reputed election of both the church and the synagogue. Or, as Bernhard E. Olson puts it: "Students of theological anti-Semitism almost totally ignore the anti-Semitic thrust in theological universalism."

And, he says, "Billy Graham is much nearer the truth when he asserts that the central problem Christians have with Jews is the Christian's mistaken notion that God, in choosing to include the Gentiles in God's promises to Israel, thereby excluded the Jews.

"Christians did not displace the Jews, says Graham; rather Christians are grafted onto the Jewish people," Olson comments. "And that is why Billy Graham, for all his salvific particularity, is a friend of the Jewish people and an enemy of all anti-Semitism."

But this, says Olson, cannot always be said of the liberal Christian. For his very universalism makes him look at the particularity of Israel through jaundiced eyes. "In this universalistic view," Olson writes, "the cosmic God of theological universalism is 'too big' to be concerned with 'a little piece of real estate' [Israel] in the Middle East, or an obscure people, the Jews.

"Thus," says Olson, "the very establishment of the State of Israel is judged by [liberals] to be a reversion to the tribalism and 'tribal religion' of the Old Testament."

Christian Zionists

Against this background stands the alleged "obscurantism" of a sturdy Biblical Christianity that dared to believe that Israel would one day be restored in the ancient land of Abraham, Isaac, and Jacob.

Among those who shared this passionate belief was Increase Mather, the distinguished Puritan divine and one-time Harvard president who, in 1669, wrote a tract entitled, *The Mystery of Israel's Salvation Explained and Applied—A Discourse Concerning the General Conversion of the Israelitish Nation.*

In that discourse, Mather not only predicted Israel's return to its ancient land, but insisted on the basis of Bible prophecy that the Jewish people "shall even fly." (See Isaiah 11: 14.) El Al in prophecy!

Another Christian millenarian was William E. Blackstone, author of *Jesus Is Coming* and a contemporary of Theodor Herzl and other nineteenth century Zionist leaders. In 1891, Blackstone declared: "Israel shall be restored to Palestine. . . . The title deed . . . is recorded, not in the Mohammedan Serai of Jerusalem nor the Serglio of Constantinople, but in [the] Bible."

Based upon this deep conviction, Blackstone presented President Benjamin Harrison with a remarkable memorial signed by many prominent clergymen, other professional men, and Congressional leaders. In this petition, the signatories declared:

> What shall be done for the Russian Jews? It is both unwise and useless to undertake to dictate to Russia concerning her internal affairs. The

Jews have lived as foreigners in her dominions for centuries, and she fully believes that they are a burden upon her resources and prejudicial to the welfare of her peasant population, and will not allow them to remain. She is determined that they must go. Hence, like the Sephardim of Spain, these Ashkenazim must emigrate. But where shall two million of such poor people go? Europe is crowded and has no room for more peasant populations. Shall they come to America? This will be a tremendous expense and require years.

Why not give Palestine back to them again? According to God's distribution of nations it is their home—an inalienable possession from which they were expelled by force. Under their cultivation, it was a remarkably fruitful land, sustaining millions of Israelites, who industriously tilled its hillsides and valleys. They were agriculturists and producers, as well as a nation of great commercial importance—the center of civilization and religion.

Meanwhile, even as American evangelicals were expressing their concern over the tragic plight of Russian Jewry, the stage was being set for the preparation and adoption of an even more remarkable document in Great Britain. It would one day be known to the world as the Balfour Declaration.

British Foreign Secretary Arthur James Balfour acquired his interest in the Jewish people from his mother, Lady Blanche Balfour, the sister of Lord Salisbury. Of his pious upbringing, Norman Maclean has written.

[Lady Blanche Balfour] embodied all that was best in the tradition of Victorian piety. She waited and looked eagerly for the Second Advent [of Christ]. . . . Sitting in the Whittinghame pew in his parish church, young Balfour heard the pure evangelical doctrine of his day

240

with fire: 'The Jew first must return to Zion and then will come the final consummation.' When Balfour met Dr. Chaim Weizmann in Manchester in 1906, he realized that his mother's faith was not a dream, that the New Jerusalem had firm foundations on earth.

However, it was Balfour himself who was to play a major role in turning the age-old dream into a reality when, a little more than a decade later, a document was issued under his signature which expressed the support of the British Government in the establishment in Palestine of a national homeland for the Jewish people.

At the same time, Balfour's own commitment to the Zionist ideal was shared by two other world statesmen whose support was of crucial importance—Prime Minister David Lloyd George and President Woodrow Wilson, both of whom were nurtured on the same doctrine that inspired the British Foreign Secretary himself.

"Zionism claims many noble Jews as its originators," says Maclean, "but few realize that the three men who made the policy possible were Christians—an American Presbyterian, a Scottish Presbyterian, and a Welsh Baptist. These were the men who lifted it up from the oratory of assemblies which had no power, and from the efforts of struggling groups of early settlers, to the council chambers of government which controlled half the world, and which secured for it the sanction of the League of Nations and of all the governments therein represented."

Meanwhile, knowledgeable Jews have not forgotten that a remnant of Christians, including the beloved Corrie ten Boom, risked their lives to protect their Jewish brethren during the dark night of Nazi terror. Indeed, their sacrifice is hallowed at *Yad Vashem,* the Israeli memorial to the martyrs of the Holocaust.

Nor is it forgotten that at least 200 Christians were among the 1,000 Americans and 300 Canadians who fought in Israel's War of Independence in 1948. One of them, the Rev. John Grauel, a New Jersey Methodist, is still known affectionately among his former *Chaverim,* or comrades, as "the Christian rabbi."

But none of this detracts from what Rabbi Arthur Hertzberg has identified as Jewish insistence on "the right of self-definition. I am perfectly prepared to come to terms with a very human Israel that louses things up for a decade or two," the noted Jewish historian recently remarked. "I don't want an Israel cast in the Christian image of the perfect state of the New Zion.

"Nor do I want to live in Israel," Hertzberg added, "on the basis of a renewed Christian theology."

Hertzberg has a staunch supporter in Dr. Franklin H. Littell, a Temple University religion professor and president of Christians Concerned for Israel.

An amiable Methodist, Dr. Littell has insisted that Israel "was born out of Christendom's failure to control its own demonic and lawless elements." Even in the midst of the unprovoked *Yom Kippur* War, he notes, one Protestant board secretary suggested that 'Israel might have to die for the peace of the world.'

"Just how 'Christian' is such objective contemplation of the possible death of others?" he asks. "So far as I know, a Christian takes up his *own* cross."

Jesus and the Jews

Apart from its bearing on Israel's survival, Littell's barb further points up one of the reasons the Jewish community considers it a bit presumptuous for Christians to talk about a "mission to the Jews" or about "Jews for Jesus."

In addition to differences in theological perspective, Jews traditionally have held the Jewish convert to Christianity in utter abhorrence. "Centuries of martyrdom are the price which the Jewish people has paid for survival," says Marshall Sklare, "and the apostate, at one stroke, makes a mockery of Jewish history.

"But if the convert is contemptible in Jewish eyes," he adds, "the missionary—all the more, the missionary of Jewish descent—is seen as pernicious, for he forces the Jew to relive the history of his martyrdom, all the while pressing the claim that in approaching the Jew he does so out of love.

"What kind of love is it, Jews wonder, that would deprive a man of his heritage?" Sklare asks. "Furthermore, given the history of Christian treatment of the Jews, would it not seem time at last to recognize that the Jew has paid his dues and earned the right to be protected from obliteration by Christian love as well as destruction by Christian hate?"

Such a statement from this distinguished Brandeis scholar must cause Christians to ponder our relationship to Israel and the Jewish people, and recognize the widespread resentment of the Jewish community toward all "conversionist efforts" in an age when Israel is once more fighting for survival.

Jews insist that Christian actions speak louder than Christian words. A letter to the orthodox *Jewish Press* recently interjected an eschatological note into the Jewish-Christian encounter:

> In the future all the heathen nations will want to attach themselves to the Jews. They will put *Tfillin* on their heads and arms, *Tzizus* on their clothes, and a *Mezuza* on their doors. But when they see the war of Gog and Magog, they will all throw away these *Mitzvoth* and God will laugh on that day at their behavior (*Gemara Avoda Zara* 3b).

This dismal picture of Gentile duplicity in times of crisis gains credence in the Jewish mind as Jews remember a church which allegedly did little or nothing to aid the Six Million during the Holocaust.

A. Roy Eckardt recalls an occasion in the post-war era when a Christian spokesman informed a Jewish audience that the World Council of Churches had just denounced anti-Semitism as a "sin against God and man."

"They must have recognized much more than the fact that saying something is wrong does not change it," Eckardt observes. ". . . And so the audience laughed. And their laughter sounded like the laughter of judgment."

If this illustration accurately reflects Jewish resentment against a church which allegedly has been interested only in its own comfort and security, it becomes more readily understandable why the Jewish community abhors the Jew for Jesus as a *meshumed,* an apostate, a "destroyed one." As the late Maurice Samuel once remarked:

> The emotional charge in the word did not spring solely from religious intolerance. Mixed with it was the rage of an embattled minority made more of a minority with every defection; but there was an even stronger motivation. One of the characteristics of the *meshumed* has frequently been the zeal with which he becomes the assistant, or even the renewed inspiration, of the oppressor of his people.

Such viewpoints must be borne in mind when Jews appear to overreact to such "innocent" television shows as "Bridget Loves Bernie." For the long history of Jewish-Christian intermarriage testifies to the fact that a spate of such relationships can lead to spiritual genocide. The key word for the Jew is S-U-R-V-I-V-A-L.

How much more odious from the Jewish perspective are television portrayals of such distinctively Jewish festivals as Passover—as object lessons intended to lead the

Jew to the Gospel. It is one thing if *Christians* see Christ in the Passover, say the Jews, but it is quite another to confuse one historical event with another.

But this brings up the crucial question posed by Maurice G. Bowler in a recent issue of *Christianity Today*: Do Jews in fact need Jesus?

One answer to this burning issue has been provided by the Jewish existentialist philosopher Franz Rosenzweig (1886-1929), who propounded the so-called "Two Covenant Theory."

"Go, by all means go into all the world and preach the Gospel," declared Rosenzweig to the Church. "Don't let anybody or anything stop you from going! And your hearers, they should come! There is no other way for them but to come!

"We are wholly agreed as to what Christ and His Church mean to the world," he added. "No one can reach the Father save through Him."

However, Rosenzweig made a distinction between the claims of the Gospel upon Israel and the Gentile world at large. "The situation is quite different for one who does not have to reach the Father because he is already with Him," he argued. "And this is true of the people of Israel."

The author of this book shares the conviction of Maurice Bowler that the world's Messiah is first and foremost the Messiah of His people Israel. He sees, for example, the portrait of Christ in the Suffering Servant of Isaiah and must confess to Jew and Gentile alike: "We have found him, of whom Moses in the law, and the prophets, did write, Jesus of Nazareth, the son of Joseph" (John 1: 45).

As the author has attempted to acquaint evangelicals with the Jewish tradition and perspective, he has been guided in this imperfect exercise by the wisdom of his own beloved professor, Dr. Lee A. Belford of New York University:

In his *Introduction to Judaism,* Dr. Belford writes: "We do not believe that any man should water down his beliefs or compromise his convictions for the sake of others. We believe that every man should be loyal to the highest he knows.

"When a Jew finds his religion meaningful, then in the name of love, he should wish to share his belief with others," says Dr. Belford. "The same applies to the Christian, or to any other person who has found beliefs that give meaning to his life.

"If the desire to share is blended with humility and with the knowledge that 'now we see in a mirror dimly' (I Corinthians 13: 12, RSV)," he adds, "the dialogue between those of different beliefs and practices can lead to creative interaction, to the glory of God and the welfare of man."

Finally, it is the author's deep conviction that authentic witness involves concrete action rather than a plethora of words. For the resentment and hostility of centuries is not likely to be erased by pious verbiage.

Indeed, if the suffering of Christ is instructive for Christian life and action, it demonstrates that love means giving one's life in the service of others. Jew and Christian alike are called not only to respect the integrity of each other but also to respond to the divine imperative:

Teach us, Lord, on earth to show
By our love how much we owe.

Sources Quoted

Bamberger, Bernard J., *The Story of Judaism*. New York: Schocken Books, 1957.

Belford, Lee A., *Introduction to Judaism*. New York: Association Press, 1961.

Bowler, Maurice G., "Do Jews Need Jesus?" in *Christianity Today*, vol. 18, no. 2, October 26, 1973.

Browne, Lewis, *Stranger than Fiction*. New York: Macmillan, 1949.

Cohen, Israel, *A Short History of Zionism*. London: Frederick Muller.

Dimont, Max I., *The Indestructible Jews*. Cleveland: World Publishing Co., 1971.

_____ *Jews, God and History*. New York: Simon and Schuster, 1962.

Eckardt, A. Roy, *Elder and Younger Brothers*. New York: Scribner's, 1967.

Edidin, Ben M., *Jewish Holidays and Festivals*. New York: Hebrew Publishing Co., 1940.

Feinberg, Louis, *The Spiritual Foundations of Judaism*. New York: Jonathan David Co., 1951.

Flannery, Edward H., *The Anguish of the Jews*. New York: Macmillan, 1965.

Gaster, Theodor H., *Festivals of the Jewish Year*. Gloucester, Mass.: Peter Smith, 1962.

Gersh, Harry, *The Sacred Books of the Jews*. New York: Stein and Day, 1968.

Gervasi, Frank, *The Case for Israel*. New York: Viking, 1967.

Grayzel, Solomon, *A History of the Jews*. Philadelphia: Jewish Publication Society of America, 1968.

247

Hirsch, Samson Raphael, *The Pentateuch*. Gateshead, England: Judaica Press, 1963.

Isaac, Jules, *The Teaching of Contempt*. New York: Holt, Rinehart, and Winston, 1964.

Keller, Werner, *Diaspora*. New York: Harcourt, Brace, and World, 1969.

Maclean, Norman, *His Terrible Swift Sword*. New York: Christian Council on Palestine, 1941.

Mann, Peggy, *Golda*. New York: Simon and Schuster, 1973.

Moscati, Sabatino. *The Face of the Ancient Orient*. Garden City: Doubleday, 1960.

Olson, Bernhard E., article on Jewish-Christian relations in *The New Catholic World* for Jan., Feb., 1974.

Reuther, Rosemary Radford, article on Jewish-Christian relations in *The New Catholic World* for Jan., Feb., 1974.

Rosten, Leo, *The Joys of Yiddish*. New York: McGraw-Hill, 1968.

Sachar, Howard Morley, *The Course of Modern Jewish History*. New York: Dell Publishing Co., 1958.

Schweitzer, Frederick M., *A History of the Jews*. New York: Macmillan, 1971.

Silver, Abba Hillel, *Where Judaism Differed*. New York: Macmillan, 1956.

Glossary

aggadah: the non-legal contents of the Talmud and Midrash, complementing the Halakhah, though lacking its binding character. Aggadah often elaborates on Scripture so as to draw out the maximum of moral teaching.

Akeida (or akedah): comes from the Hebrew word for "binding" (Genesis 22:9), and refers to Abraham's supreme act of self-denial in obeying the Divine command to offer up his son Isaac. But it also refers to Israel's obedience even in the face of martyrdom, to sanctify God's name among the nations (see Kiddush ha-Shem).

aliyah: comes from the Hebrew word for "ascent" or "going up," and is used most commonly today in reference to the return or pilgrimage of Jews to the Holy Land, and specifically to Jerusalem.

Aphikoman: is a Greek word of uncertain origin, referring to the piece taken from the middle of the three matzoth on the Passover Seder table, which are eaten by all present at the conclusion of the service.

Bereshit Rabba: a Midrash on the Book of Genesis. Bereshit is the Hebrew title of Genesis and literally means, "In the beginning," the opening words of the book itself.

bris (or brith): means covenant, a term usually associated with the circumcision rite, the Brith Milah.

chutzpa: audacity, incredible nerve; a term to which no English word can do justice.

eretz Yizroel: literally, the land (eretz) of Israel.

galut: the Exile, or dispersion of the Jews among the nations.

Gaon: a genius, or learned rabbi.

Gevalt: an all-purpose word in Yiddish, used, as Leo Rosten says, both as an exclamation and as a noun.

ghetto: section of certain European towns designated by law as the Jewish quarter. While many have suggested that the term originated from an Italian word for cannon foundry, next to which the first ghetto was located in Venice, others have traced the word back to terms for "bars" or "dirty."

goy (goyim, pl.): comes from the Hebrew for "nation," but refers to those who are Gentiles or non-Jews.

Haggadah: from the Hebrew word for tale, but having special reference to the recounting of the Exodus and the legends read aloud at the Passover Seder.

hakafot: processional circuits made by the people during certain ceremonial occasions.

hakhamim: the body of scholars associated with the establishment of normative Judaism after the Exile.

Halakah: refers to the Jewish law, or corpus of Jewish jurisprudence, which, Judah Goldin says, "protected legislation from inflexibility and society from fundamentalism."

halakhic: referring to binding regulations of the Halakah.

Hallel: means "Praise," and refers to Psalms 113—118, recited in the synagogue after the morning services on the three Pilgrim Festivals and at Hanukkah. Some suggest Jesus and His disciples sang the Hallel (a hymn) in the Upper Room.

Hassidim: literally, "the pious ones," but especially referring to a great segment of orthodox Jewry who follow the teachings of the Baal Shem Tov (the Besht).

Hazzan: refers to a cantor, who sings the long passages of the Jewish liturgy at synagogue services.

jihad: is an Arabic word meaning a "Holy war."

Kiddush: means "sanctification" in Hebrew, and refers to the prayer that sanctifies the Sabbath and Jewish holy days.

Kiddush ha-Shem: to sanctify God's name by any generous or noble deed.

maror: from the Hebrew meaning "bitter herbs," referring to the bitterness of bondage in Egypt. Hence, bitter herbs are still served at the Passover Seder.

Mashiach: Hebrew for Messiah, or "the Anointed One."

matzah (pl. matzoth or matzos): the unleavened bread eaten especially during Passover (Exodus 12: 15).

mezuzah: from the Hebrew word for "doorpost," but referring to the oblong case containing a rolled piece of paper or parchment on which is printed the Shema, Israel's confession of faith (Deuteronomy 6: 4-9, 11, 13-21). It is affixed in a slanting position to the right of the front doorjamb of many Jewish homes.

Midrash (pl. midrashim): the exposition and exegesis of Scripture by the rabbis from the fifth century B.C.E. to 70 C.E. The word means "commentary" or "interpretation."

minyan: is the Hebrew word for "counting" or "number," but refers to the ten male Jews required for religious services. Some groups now permit women to be part of a minyan.

Mishnah: or "the repetition," is one of the two basic parts of the Talmud, the other being the Gemara, of much later date. The Mishnah is the codified core of the Oral Law.

mohel: is the Hebrew word for "a circumciser," and therefore the one who circumcises a male Jewish child, eight days after birth in the Brith Milah ritual.

Ne'ilah: from the Hebrew for "closing," i.e., of the gates. It is now used to connote the last five prayers on the Day of Atonement and is recited at nightfall when the fast ends.

Pale of Settlement: represented the newly won provinces, to which the Jews were restricted, with the partition of Poland by Russia in the late 18th century. This partition made Russia the governor of the largest body of Jews in the world.

pogroms: is a Russian word for "devastations," and represents a whole series of violent actions against the Jews of eastern Europe.

Seder: Hebrew for "order," or "order of the service," used particularly in connection with the traditional Passover meal.

Shabbat Shalom: literally, a Sabbath's peace, but more than that, a beautiful Sabbath greeting.

Shabbatons: refers in the text to weekend meetings being held today for young Jews and adults, to reintroduce them to their heritage.

Shema: from the Hebrew word for "Hear," the first word of Deuteronomy 6: 4, "Hear, O Israel, the Lord Our God, the Lord is One." Because of its emphasis on the unity of God, the Shema is considered the Jewish "confession of faith."

shtetl: the small towns or villages in which Jews lived in eastern Europe. Unlike the large city ghettos, Jews moved freely within these communities. But they were not permitted within Mother Russia itself.

sidrah: means "arrangement" in Hebrew, and the sidrot or sedarim represent the weekly portions of the Pentateuch read publicly in the synagogues on Sabbath. There are 54 sidrot, and Simhat Torah (a service of "rejoicing in The Law") is celebrated annually when all have been read for the year.

Sopherim: is the Hebrew plural for "scribes," from whose ranks came the men of the Great Assembly (Knesset ha-Gedolah) in the age of Ezra and Nehemiah.

Tfillin: the phylacteries worn by male Jews of thirteen years and older, on the basis of the Biblical injunctions of Exodus 13: 1; 13: 11; Deuteronomy 6: 4-9; and 11: 13-21.

Torah: first five books of Scripture.

Tzizus (or tzitzit): in Hebrew means "fringes" and refers to the fringe worn on garments to remind the Jews of all of the Commandments, to do them (Numbers 15: 39, 40).

yeshiva bucher: a young man who is a student of Jewish Law and tradition.

Yigdal: from the Hebrew, "magnified and praised be the Living God." The Yigdal is a hymn sung at the conclusion of Sabbath and festival evening services. It is based on Maimonides' Thirteen Articles of Faith, each line dealing with one of these articles.

Index

Y

Yad Vashem memorial, 241.
Yahweh, 13-14, 16-17, 34 (footnote), 73-75.
Yale Intergroup study, 109.
Yiddish language, 181, 189, 199, 206.
Yigdal, hymn, 166.
Yitzhak, Levi, rabbi, 67, 151-152, 169.
Yom Kippur, 65-68, 242.
Yom Kippur War, 53, 242.
Young Italy movement, 204.

Yulee, David, 181.

Z

Zadokite Fragments, 144.
Zacunto, Abraham, astronomer, 174, 175.
Zealots, 110-111, 122, 129.
Zechariah, prophet, 95.
Zionist Congresses, 196, 201.
Zionists, 184-185, 196-218.
Zohar, 166-167.
Zvi, Sabbatai, 132-133.

REACH OUT
with additional copies of this book...

If you've just finished this book, we think you'll agree...

A COOK PAPERBACK IS

REWARDING READING

Try some more!

LOOK AT ME, PLEASE LOOK AT ME by Clark, Dahl and Gonzenbach. Accepting the retarded—with love—as told in the moving struggle of two women who learned how.
72595—$1.25

THE 13TH AMERICAN by Pastor Paul. Every 13th American is an alcoholic, and it could be anyone. A sensitive treatment of alcoholism by a minister who fought his way back.
72629—$1.50

THE EVIDENCE THAT CONVICTED AIDA SKRIPNIKOVA edited by Bourdeaux and Howard-Johnston. Religious persecution in Russia! The story of a young woman's courage.
72652—$1.25

LET'S SUCCEED WITH OUR TEENAGERS by Jay Kesler. Substitutes hope for parental despair—offers new understanding that exposes the roots of parent-child differences.
72660—$1.25

THE PROPHET OF WHEAT STREET by James English. Meet William Borders, a Southern Black educated at Northwestern University, who returned to lead the black church in Atlanta.
72678—$1.25

WHAT A WAY TO GO! by Bob Laurent. Your faith BEYOND church walls. Laurent says, "Christianity is not a religion, it's a relationship." Freedom, new life replace dull routine!
72728—$1.25

THE VIEW FROM A HEARSE (new enlarged edition) by Joseph Bayly. Examines suicide. Death can't be ignored—what is the Christian response? Hope as real as death.
73270—$1.25

WHAT'S SO GREAT ABOUT THE BIBLE (new enlarged edition) by James Hefley. Hefley presents the Bible as a literary miracle, an indestructible influence.
73288—$1.25

(Cont.)

WHAT ABOUT HOROSCOPES? by Joseph Bayly. A topic on everyone's mind! As the author answers the question posed by the title, he also discusses witches, other occult subjects.
51490—95¢

IS THERE HEALING POWER? by Karl Roebling. A keen interest in healing led the author to a quest of facts. A searching look at faith healers: Kathryn Kuhlman, Oral Roberts, others.
68460—95¢

SEX SENSE AND NONSENSE by James Hefley. Just what does the Bible say, and NOT say, about sex? A re-examination of common views—in the light of the Scriptures.
56135—95¢

THE KENNEDY EXPLOSION by E. Russell Chandler. An exciting new method of lay evangelism boosts a tiny Florida church from 17 to 2,450 members. Over 50,000 copies sold.
63610—95¢

STRANGE THINGS ARE HAPPENING by Roger Ellwood. Takes you for a close look at what's happening in the world of Satanism and the occult today . . . and tells what it means.
68478—95¢

You can order these books from your local bookstore, or from the David C. Cook Publishing Co., Elgin, IL 60120 (in Canada: Weston, Ont. M9L 1T4).

------------------Use This Coupon------------------

Name _____

Address _____

City _____ State _____ ZIP Code _____

TITLE	STOCK NO.	PRICE	QTY.	ITEM TOTAL
		$		$

Sub-total $ _____

NOTE: On orders placed with David C. Cook Publishing Co., add handling charge of 25¢ for first dollar, plus 5¢ for each additional dollar.

Handling _____

TOTAL $ _____

MORE REWARDING READING

...from Cook

TELL ME AGAIN, LORD, I FORGET by Ruth Harms Calkin. Joyful poetry and sensitive drawings for sinkside musing, help on a drab winter day . . . with a way of turning gloom to gladness.
77263—$1.25

O CHRISTIAN! O JEW! by Paul Carlson. A Presbyterian pastor pens a book that is at once an odyssey for Christian readers—from Abraham to contemporary Israel—and a helpful guide to the ways, wit and wisdom of their Jewish friends. 272 pages.
75820—$1.95

BEYOND THE EXIT DOOR by Robert J. Vetter. Following his wife's untimely death, a family man draws on Divine strength for readjustment. Help for anyone facing the loss of a spouse.
77586—$1.25

LOVE MY CHILDREN by Dr. Rose B. Browne and James W. English. (Rev. ed.) A brilliant, highly educated black woman—dedicated to better teaching for the underprivileged—tells her story.
81828—$1.95

INVISIBLE HALOS by David C. Cook III. The president of a Sunday School publishing company introduces people who are for him unique, if unlikely, examples of Christianity in action.
77289—$1.25

Order books from your local bookstore . . . or David C. Cook Publishing Co., Elgin, IL 60120—in Canada: Weston, Ont. M9L 1T4. (On orders placed with David C. Cook Publishing Co., please add handling charge of 25¢ for the first dollar, plus 5¢ for each additional dollar.)